T0140049

Energy-Efficient Modular Exponential Techniques
for Public-Key Cryptography

Satyanarayana Vollala ·
N. Ramasubramanian · Utkarsh Tiwari

Energy-Efficient Modular Exponential Techniques for Public-Key Cryptography

Efficient Modular Exponential Techniques

 Springer

Satyanarayana Vollala
Department of Computer
Science and Engineering
IIIT-Naya Raipur
Naya Raipur, Chhattisgarh, India

N. Ramasubramanian
Department of Computer
Science and Engineering
National Institute of Technology
Tiruchirappalli, Tamil Nadu, India

Utkarsh Tiwari
Department of Computer
Science and Engineering
IIIT-Naya Raipur
Naya Raipur, Chhattisgarh, India

ISBN 978-3-030-74526-4   ISBN 978-3-030-74524-0   (eBook)
https://doi.org/10.1007/978-3-030-74524-0

This Springer imprint is published by the registered company Springer Nature Switzerland AG
The registered company address is: Gewerbestrasse 11, 6330 Cham, Switzerland

Foreword

Security is a major concern in data communication. Various cryptographic protocols are used for system security. Both software and hardware implementations of these protocols exist. As compared to software implementations, hardware realization of cryptographic algorithms ensures a higher level of security without a tradeoff in performance. Public-key cryptography is an important tool used for maintaining secrecy and to provide a digital signature. The security of public-key cryptography mainly depends on the complexity of solving the integer factorization problem and the discrete logarithmic problem. The core operations of public-key cryptography are **modular exponentiation** and **modular multiplication**. Hence, the performance of any public-key cryptography is primarily determined by the efficient implementation of these two operations. In order to optimize the time requirements of the public-key cryptographic transformations, it is essential to develop algorithms which minimize the number of modular multiplications. These algorithms also have to reduce the time required for a single modular multiplication in modular exponentiation.

This book discusses the algorithms for optimizing the time requirements of public-key cryptographic transformations. Specifically, it covers various methods to evaluate modular multiplication based on the Montgomery method. It also discusses the energy-efficient modular exponential techniques for public-key cryptography. To enhance the throughput of RSA public-key cryptography further in terms of the number of encryptions/decryptions per unit time, single-core demands for higher frequency results in the consumption of more power and dissipation of more heat. A Dual-core RSA processor with a hardware scheduler has been discussed for performing concurrent cryptographic transformations to attain better throughput without increasing the frequency.

Naya Raipur, India
March 2021

Pradeep K. Sinha
Vice Chancellor & Director
IIIT Naya Raipur

Preface

Phenomenal demands for all kind of real-time e-commerce transactions and internet usage insist security as an essential part for protecting sensitive data. Many organizations use cryptographic techniques for achieving system security. The cryptographic techniques can be classified into two types, symmetric (secret) key cryptography and asymmetric (public) key cryptography. Among these two cryptographic systems, the public-key cryptographic system has been widely employed as it minimizes the need for a secure channel to exchange secret information. These techniques can be realized both in software as well as in hardware. But the hardware implementation will be an optimal choice for its performance and also assures a higher level of security.

This monograph discusses the various ways to implement the modular multiplication and modular exponential techniques. Modular exponentiation is the series of modular multiplications and modular multiplication involves the trial divisions. Hardware realization of modular multiplication is difficult as it involves the trial divisions. The techniques for optimizing the time vital operations of public-key cryptography are discussed in this monograph. It also discusses exploiting the multi-core domain for implementing modular exponentiation in two cores resulting in an enhanced throughput.

Naya Raipur, India
March 2021

Dr. Satyanarayana Vollala
Dr. N. Ramasubramanian
Mr. Utkarsh Tiwari

Acknowledgements

This book would not have been possible without the help and cooperation of many people who helped me directly and indirectly during my work.

First and foremost, we would like to express our sincere and deep gratitude to Dr. P. K. Sinha, Director and Vice-Chancellor, IIIT-Naya Raipur and Dr. Mini Shaji Thomas, Director, NIT, Tiruchirappalli for their enthusiastic and constant support to perform our research activities.

We thank the Department of Science and Technology (A department within the Ministry of Science and Technology in India) for their financial support for the execution of the project entitled "Energy Efficient implementation of Multi-modular Exponential techniques for Public-Key Cryptosystems" under Integrated Cyber Physical Systems.

We would like to thank Dr. A. Raghunathan, Additional General Manager, HRDC, BHEL-Tiruchirappalli and Dr. S. Venkatraman, Scientist H, ISRO, Hyderabad for their encouragement and constructive input at various stages of our research work. I must also thank Dr. R. Mahapatra, Dr. Ruhul Amin, Dr. U. Venkanna, Mr. Varadhan V. V., Dr. Shameedha Begum, and Mr. Amit D. Joshi who have given me worthwhile suggestions and for providing quality technical inputs during the research work.

We would like to express our gratitude to our family members for their constant support and patient understanding. All our fulfillments have been not possible without the support of our family. Finally, we cannot forget to thank the almighty for making me stronger and perseverance in difficult situations and bestowed blessings on us.

Dr. Satyanarayana Vollala
Dr. N. Ramasubramanian
Mr. Utkarsh Tiwari

Scope of the Book

The cryptographic techniques are classified into two types secret-key cryptography and Public-Key Cryptography (PKC). This book focuses on PKC. The robustness of public-key cryptography relies on the intractability of solving the integer factorization problem and the discrete logarithmic problem. In the part I of this book, a few PKC has been discussed in detail and provides a brief introduction of secret-key cryptography. These cryptographic techniques have two kinds of implementations: software based and hardware based. The hardware realization of cryptographic techniques will be the ultimate choice, as it provides the higher level of security without compromising performance.

The core operations of most of the PKC are Modular Exponentiation (ME) and Modular Multiplication (MM). Hence the performance of any PKC is primarily determined by the efficient implementation of ME & MM. In order to optimize the time requirements of the encryption and decryption, the optimized ME and MM are desirable. This book covers the optimized ME and MM algorithms as well as their hardware implementation.

ME is series of MMs. This book has covered different versions MM algorithms. The main focus is on Montgomery multiplication, as it provides a way of hardware implementation. Montgomery multiplication version for radix-2 and high-radix has been covered along with its hardware realizations. Moreover, this book covers various ME techniques including left-to-right binary exponentiation, right-to-left binary exponentiation, sliding-window technique, M-ary technique, and Bit Forwarding (BFW) techniques. The part IV of the book focuses on BFW techniques. Hardware realization of BFW techniques has also been discussed.

To enhance the throughput of RSA in terms of the number of cryptographic transformations per unit time, single-core demands for higher frequency which results in the consumption of more power and dissipation of more heat. Multiple cores can be effectively utilized by designing a scheduler that can function at the software level as well as hardware level. The part *V* of the book covers the description of a Dual-core RSA processor with a hardware scheduler, which can perform concurrent cryptographic transformations. The dual-core implementation of ME is also discussed in this book.

Contents

Acronyms

AHRMM	Adaptable-high-radix-montgomery-multiplication
AMM	Adaptable-montgomery-multiplication
ASIC	Application-specific-integrated-circuits
BFW	Bit-forwarding
BFW-1	Bit-forwarding-1-bit
BFW-2	Bit-forwarding-2-bits
BFW-3	Bit-forwarding-3-bits
BFW-j	Bit-forwarding-j-bits
BRAM	Buffer-random-access-memory
CRT	Chinese-remainder-theorem
CSA	Carry-save-adder
DCHRM	Dual-core-high-radix-multiplication
DCRSAP	Dual-core-rsa-processor
DLP	Discrete-logarithmic-problem
ECC	Elliptic-curve-cryptography
FCS	Full-carry-save
FPGA	Field-programmable-gate-array
HRMM	High-radix-modular-multiplication
HSOS	High-switching-operand-scanning
HSPS	High-switching-product-scanning
IFP	Integer-factorization-problem
IOS	Independent-operand-scanning
LR	Left-to-right
LSB	Least-significant-bit
LSHS	Less-switching-product-scanning
LSOS	Less-switching-operand-scanning
ME	Modular-exponentiation
MM	Modular-multiplication
MMM	Montgomery-multiplication
MSB	Most-significant-bit

MSM	Modified-square-and-multiply
NIST	National-institute-of-standards-and-technology
NZW	Non-zero-window
PE	Processing-element
PKC	Public-key-cryptography
PKDS	Public-key-distribution system
R4MM	Radix-4-modular-multiplication
RL	Right-to-left
RNS	Residue-number-system
RSA	Rivest–shamir–adleman
SCS	Semi-carry-save
TTA	Transport-triggered-architecture
VLSI	Very-large-integrated-circuit
WSN	Wireless-Sensor-Networks
ZW	Zero-window

Part I
Introduction

Chapter 1
Cryptographic Techniques

1.1 Cryptography

From the early 90's the use of LAN (Local Area Network) and WAN (Wide Area Network) especially in the field of the internet is growing rapidly. The property of the internet to reach out to the maximum number of people remotely is most effective. Anyone who has the basic knowledge of using computers can share and learn information easily over the internet. Accessing the information worldwide without any expertise restriction, also raises the requirement of transmitting mechanism in secure manner. **Cryptosystems** were developed to meet the security related demand.

Cryptography is the technique or creativity of confidential writing. The essential goal of cryptography is to help two people (sender and receiver) to exchange private message or information using an insecure communication network in a process that the intruder (Oscar) should not be able to guess what message has been exchanged.

In Fig. 1.1 we can see that Alice(sender) wishes to communicate some message *(Hi Bob! How are you?)* but Oscar(intruder) interrupts and changes the message *(Hi Bob! Can you lend me 1000$)*. Bob(reciever) knows Alice and would want to help him but as an intruder, Oscar snatching the money without the knowledge of two.

Important Terms Used in Cryptography

When two entities are communicating they follow certain protocols. Understanding the complete communication one needs to know important terminologies used in the process.

Plain-Text

It is a set of all possible texts that a sender wishes to communicate with receiver. The possible text can contain private messages or information. This can also be termed as *message 'm'* which needs to be sent.

© The Author(s), under exclusive license to Springer Nature Switzerland AG 2021
S. Vollala et al., *Energy-Efficient Modular Exponential Techniques for Public-Key Cryptography*, https://doi.org/10.1007/978-3-030-74524-0_1

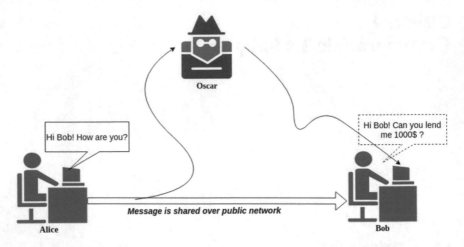

Fig. 1.1 Need of cryptography

Cipher-Text

It is a set of all possible texts that a receiver received after encryption. This can also be termed as *encrypted message 'c'* which needs to be decrypt.

Encryption

The process of converting the plain-text into cipher-text using an encryption algorithm is known as encryption.

Decryption

The process of reverting the cipher-text into its plain-text, using a corresponding decryption algorithm is known as decryption.

For a given scenario a sender encrypt a message (*plain-text*), with the help of a mutually agreed *KEY* and a standard *encryption algorithm* and send the resulting encrypted message (*cipher-text*) to receiver over the insecure public channel.

Cryptology: It is consists of two competitive areas namely cryptography and cryptanalysis.

Cryptography

Cryptography is a process of generating designed or written codes that help message or information to communicate or save secretly (*in encrypted form*). Cryptographer can change the form of data (message or information) into another form that is not understandable for an intruder, making it possible to communicate it without any worries of re-changing it into its original form by an intruder, thus securing the data from intruder (*or unauthorized person*). we can say cryptography is the process of designing the algorithms(codes) for encryption.

In general, cryptography can be understood as a technique of protecting the message or information from intruders and enable the exchange of it. For the development of the protection techniques, software or hardware techniques are used. The software technique is mainly about a secret code (or Key). Which is implemented such that the exchanged message or information can be understood only with whom the sender wants to share them. The word *Cryptography* is made up of a prefix "crypt" means "hidden" or "vault" and the suffix "graphy" stands for "writing."

If we want to discuss and understand the *Cryptography* from the perspective of computer science applications, we can refer to it as protecting the information while communicating it over an insecure channel. One can achieve this from software or hardware means or using both ways. Software means are based on mathematical concepts and algorithms(set of rule-based calculations) are used to convert(cipher) the message or information such that it is very hard for intruders to revert(decipher) it to the original message or information. Whereas for hardware means provide better security as it is infeasible to modify the code burnt into the chip. Moreover, stopping the illegal access is an inherited property of hardware-based technology.

Cryptanalysis

It can be identified as a process of breaking a written or designed code for changing the form of original data. This process is carried out by the cryptanalyst. Here cryptanalyst tries to break the code designed for encryption. This analysis is important for the secure and hack-proof design of the encryption algorithm (Biham and Perle 2018). This task is performed by a trusted authority and the drawback of the designed algorithm is provided as feedback so that it can be used for the betterment of the algorithm (Todo 2017). For example:

1. Differential cryptanalysis
2. Linear cryptanalysis
3. Cipher cryptanalysis
4. Statistical cryptanalysis

The cryptographic algorithms are used for various applications such as verification, digital signing, web browsing on the internet, key generation, confidential communications and to protect data privacy for example, banking transactions and emails.

1.2 Information Security Objectives

A cryptosystem is comprised of all its important features related to the security of data(message or information) for example confidentiality (privacy), data integrity, authentication, and Non-Repudiation. *Cryptography* is the analysis of mathematical methods and applications related to features of cryptosystem security. Cryptography is about providing security to one's data and a set of techniques to achieve it (Santhi et al. 2019; Yan et al. 2019).

Confidentiality

Confidentiality (*privacy*) is a way of keeping information secure(unreadable) from all people in the network but not from those who are authorized to read it. Internally it covers two concepts one is *Data confidentiality* and another is *Privacy*. Data confidentiality is a service provided by cryptographer to keep the contents of message or information secure from intruders i.e., unauthorized users are not allowed to access it. Whereas the privacy (*secrecy*) provide control or influence over the data. There are a large number of techniques of providing confidentiality, it can be either hardware technique or software methods with the purpose of rendering data unintelligible.

Generally, if we want the receiver to understand the secret information which we have already known, the simplest method is to tell the receiver the secret information directly. Information must not be read by an intruder because, it can consist of some private data which by telling directly not only does the receiver know the secret information but also the intruder may know the secret information, and then the secret information is no longer confidential i.e., to achieve the *confidentiality* as an information security objective, no intruder(unauthorized person) can read the data other than the receiver.

Data Integrity

This feature ensures that there must not be an unauthorized modification of messages or information. The main aim of the data integrity is to prevent the alteration of data irrespective of the attacks on the system. This is a feature of establishing faith, that message or information being communicated has been not been tampered. We can say integrity is the process of making certain that if a message has been altered by an intruder then check it and identify it. This feature of information security enables the sender to identify the unauthorized manipulation of data (i.e., message or information).

Authentication

This feature ensures that source or sender of the message or information is genuine, verified and can be trusted. An intruder can play a role of receiver, from the intention of stealing private information. Thus, for secure communication, both entities (sender and receiver) may want to be sure of the identity of each other. This service is applicable to both parties and the information itself. Message or information communicated over a public channel should be authenticated because it contains data, place and time-date of origin and sending timestamp, etc.

From the above discussion, this feature of cryptography is better understood if it can be further sub-divided into two major sub-divisions: *Entity authentication* and *Origin of data authentication*. Origin of data authentication implicitly provides data integrity (if the information is altered, the source has compromised). Moreover, the system ensures the sender's authenticity before accessing the information.

Non-repudiation

This feature of information security ensures prevention from the denial of preceded actions or commitments. This is a service that ensures that any one of the parties(sender or receiver) cannot deny the communicated message which they have committed. This service is necessary to resolve the issue, when anyone of the parties is denying certain actions was taken by them. For a real-world example, a seller may authorize the selling of the property to a buyer and later denies such authorization was granted. This is a procedure which involves a trusted third party to resolve the dispute between two parties.

Two important properties that help to achieve non-repudiation is:

- **Anonymity:** Encrypting the identity of an entity involved in some communication.
- **Revocation:** Reverse engineering of authorization or certification.

From a legal point of view for communication to have a juridic value, let say communication needs to be evidence in a court trial, the sender of the message must not be able to deny the content of the message.

1.3 Techniques of Cryptography

Two main types of cryptography techniques are used in nowadays. *The categorization is done based on the use of KEY.*

1. **Symmetric or Secret Key Cryptography:** In this type of cryptography single *key* is practiced in communication by both sender and receiver. For secret key encryption, a strong encryption algorithm is needed. At a minimum, we would like the algorithm to be such that an intruder who knows the algorithm and has access to one or more cipher-texts would not be able to obtain the plain-text from cipher-text or figure out the key. We can intensify this requirement for a more secure form as the intruder should not be able to obtain the plain-text by decrypting cipher-text or discover the key even if the intruder is in possession of a number of cipher-texts together with the plain-text. The secret key needed to be obtained by the sender and receiver in a secure manner and they must keep the key secure. If an intruder who already knows the algorithm somehow discovers the key then all communication using this key is readable (Stallings 2006). Examples are AES, DES/3DES, RC4, Blowfish, MARS, Twofish (will be discussed in brief in the next Sect. 1.3.1).
   In Fig. 1.2, Alice encrypts the original information with the help of a secret key and encrypted information is sent over a public network(insecure), upon receiving the Bob decrypt the information with the help of same secret key and obtain the original information.
2. **Asymmetric or Public Key Cryptography:** In this type of cryptography double key is used, one is public key which is announced by receiver (Bob) publicly (can be stored in public key repository), which is used to encrypt the Plain Text (by Alice) and another one is private key which is private to Bob and used for decryption.

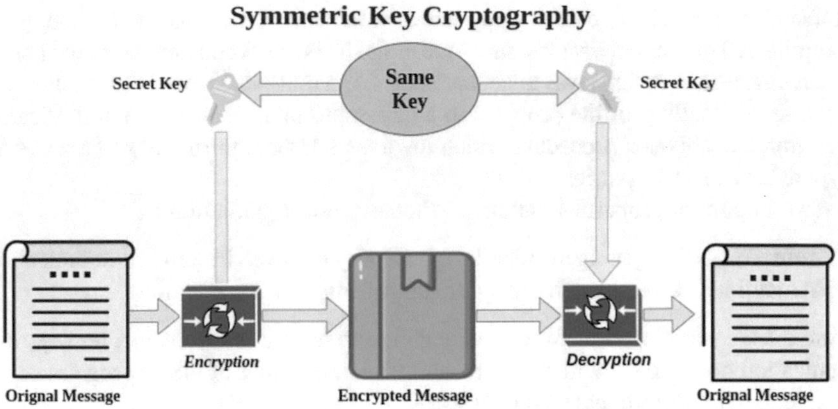

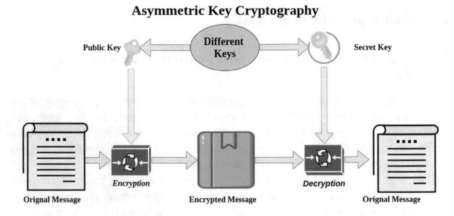

Fig. 1.2 Symmetric key cryptography

Fig. 1.3 Asymmetric key cryptography

In Fig. 1.3, Alice encrypts the original information by using Bob's public key and send the encrypted information over a public network(insecure), upon receiving the encrypted information the Bob decrypt the message using his private key and obtain the original message. Asymmetric key cryptography is a one-way trap i.e., if a sender has encrypted a message using the public key of a recipient then it can only be decrypted by the recipient's private key, even sender itself cannot decrypt the message. For a given scenario suppose Alice wishes to send a message and she encrypted it using Bob's public key, further if she lost the original message, but have the encrypted message she herself cannot decrypt the encrypted message even though she is the owner of the message, it can only be decrypted by Bob using his private key.

1.3.1 Symmetric Key Cryptography

There are various Symmetric-key algorithms also termed as secret key algorithms that includes AES, DES, 3DES, Blowfish, Twofish, etc. Out of these the most commonly used algorithms are DES, 3DES, and AES.

1.3.1.1 AES

Daemen and Rijmen (2013) are the cryptographers behind the development of Advanced Encryption Standard (AES). It is accepted by the National Institute of Standards and Technology (NIST). NIST organized a contest in the year 1997 for which they have developed it and in the year 2000, it was available for world of network security. They named the algorithm as *Rijndael* which is also a well-known term for AES. With 128-bits data block processing, this algorithm is one of the securest in the field of secret-key cryptography. Advanced Encryption Standard(AES) uses a block of the length of 128 bits. This is the well-known block cipher which supports 3 different key lengths:

1. 128 bits AES
2. 192 bits AES
3. 256 bits AES

The AES algorithm works on a principle of substitution permutation network (Thakur and Kumar 2011). This algorithm uses 10, 12, or 14 number of rounds for the key size of 128 bits, 192 bits, or 256 bits depending on the number of rounds. let say for 128 bits We can subdivide the working steps of AES as:

1. **Byte Substitution:** First it will compute the round key's set from cipher keys it using S-Box byte-by-byte substitution is done.
2. **Shift Rows:** Then in the second step it will add the initial round key to the starting address this step is a simple permutation.
3. **Mix Columns:** In the next step it executes state manipulation exactly 9 rounds which are known as the Substitution method where data of each column is multiplied by shift row is of the matrix of given AES technique.
4. **Add Round Key:** At final state it executes the final 10th round, and the current form of information is XOR-ed to get a final output as an encrypted array.

The objective of the first 3 steps is to misguide the intruders, the real intention of encryption is achieved in 4th step (Santhi et al. 2019). The length of the key is long enough to make it difficult even for the computer to guess the correct sequence out of all possibilities. This enables AES attack proof from various possible attacks.

1.3.1.2 DES/3DES

Data Encryption Standard (DES) is one of the secret-key methods for securing the communication information.

Data Encryption Standard

IBM invented and started using it by the year of 1974–1977. First LUCIFER was developed and after some required modifications DES was introduced. For more than 20 years DES was preferred for the encryption process. DES is based on Feistel block cipher. This standard meets the demand of a universal encryption standard to be followed by all over the network. NIST (National Institute of Standards and Technology) declares it as the first standard for encryption. With the help of 2 inputs, first is plain-text itself and second is a 56-bit long secret key. The length of the encryption block is 64-bit i.e., it can encrypt the 64-bit long plain-text at once. Length of the key is independent of the block length. Each byte(*total 8 octets of 8-bit = 64 bit*) in DES is having its LSB(least significant bit) or MSB(most significant bit) to play a role of parity bit or as arbitrary. If the DES is having block size of 64-bits then the plain-text is divided into equal blocks of 64-bits length. If $Length(plain\text{-}text)\%64 \neq 0$ then padding of extra bit is done for the plain-text. The 56-bit long key is the base of performing permutations and substitutions such that breaking it becomes more and more hard task for intruder (Santhi et al. 2019). A total of 16 cycles of permutation and substitution are performed in order to achieve a more secure encryption algorithm.

The length of the key for DES is 56-bit that is not so long which makes DES vulnerable. Cryptanalysts have found lots of methods to challenge the securing capabilities of DES, which proofs it an insecure block cipher (Thakur and Kumar 2011).

Triple DES (3DES)

The idea of using 3 separate keys with DES is known as Triple DES. As IBM noticed the vulnerability of DES they come up with this idea. It is simple and securer than plain DES. Based on the uniqueness of keys Triple-DES is of two types:

1. First approach needs 3 whole unique keys
2. Second approach needs only 2 whole unique keys.

The first approach which runs with the help of 3 unique keys (K1, K2, K3) used sequentially(one after another), as the length of one key is 56-bits therefore in total the key length is very long i.e., $168\text{-}bits(56 \times 3)$ which in the real world practical application takes a long time to run, on the other hand, provide high-class security. To reduce the running time IBM introduces the second approach which runs with the help of 2 unique keys (K1 and K2). The encryption is done in sequence of:

$$M1 \xrightarrow{EncryptUsing\,K1} M2 \xrightarrow{DecryptUsing\,K2} M3 \xrightarrow{EncryptUsing\,K1} C$$

i.e., Encrypt-Decrypt-Encrypt. This approach needs only 2 unique keys, the first M1 is encrypted with the help of key K1. The output of this step 'M2' is then decrypted with key K2. And finally, the decrypted message M3 is encrypted once more with the help of K1 as the key to obtaining the final encrypted message(cipher-text) C. There can be one question that why are we using Encrypt-Decrypt-Encrypt (EDE) why not Encrypt-Encrypt-Encrypt (EEE)? The answer is simple i.e., if we want to preserve compatibility with regular DES, a hardware circuit that implemented 3DES (with EDE) could also be used to implement regular DES. If we use a single key for all three steps then it will be similar to regular DES and its implementation can also decrypt that message. This makes this version of 3DES backward compatible with regular DES. The EEE is also a valid method it can be implemented using three different keys therefore require extra space. It is very essential to use different and strong keys for all the steps, or else this method will be not more than a slower interpretation of DES. However, EDE is usually preferred for the reasons mentioned above.

Despite its high security and complex structure, the cryptanalysts are able to break it and this approach is not that much secure as modern days approaches are. The complexity of the approach also makes it unfit for a large amount of information encryption.

1.3.1.3 Blowfish

To overcome the demerits of the DES, the Blowfish approach is considered. The DES is being outdated and Blowfish is an effective and new approach. This approach uses block which is symmetric in the property for encryption of message or information. Blowfish was designed in 1993 by Schneier (1996, 1993) it has less running time and also available without any cost.

This algorithm can be divided into 2 phases:

1. The encryption phase.
2. The key-expansion phase.

The key-expansion phase performs the transformation of the key into several sub-keys(arrays totaling 4168 bytes). The sub-keys length can vary from 32-bits to 448-bits, This variable key-length makes this encryption scheme more secure. It's property of variable-length key, for example, a 64-bit block-blowfish-cipher can use either a 128-bit or a 64-bit length of blocks, but it is more suitable for applications if the *key* is not changing frequently (Gangireddy et al. 2020). Large microprocessors are used for increasing the efficiency of this approach. The main encryption function is executed 16 times over a Feistel network. The network is termed as 16-Feistel for Blowfish. In this approach, the data is manipulated in large size blocks preferably 32 bits in size (unlikely from DES, where it is in single bit). Cryptanalysis has proved it to be suffering from weak keys problems, but not able to identify a successful attack for it.

1.3.2 Asymmetric Key Cryptography

The notation of Keys are different in Symmetric and Asymmetric key cryptography. In symmetric key cryptography a single K denotes the key used by two parties, but *Asymmetric key encryption*, denotes the keys in another way. Asymmetric key cryptography uses a subscript for denoting the key of the sender or receiver entity according to who generated it. Entities has a key pair, let say for example Bob has a key pair as (K_{B_e}, K_{B_d}).

- K_{B_e} denoting an encryption public key of Bob.
- K_{B_d} denoting a decryption private key of Bob.

   Public key K_{B_e} can be made publicly available as Bob's public key. Private key K_{B_d} kept secretly and should not be shared with anybody. Bob would like to keep a copy of its private key K_{B_d} as a back-up. But it is suggested that he should keep the original copy, or the backup copy in encrypted format in a trusted memory space (van Oorschot 2020). The scenario where Alice wants to send some secret message to Bob, she encrypts original message(M). Initially, Alice needs to obtain Bob's public key K_{B_e}, then with the help of Bob's public key and encryption algorithm E, the original message m is encrypted into an encrypted message C. Then Alice communicate C with Bob over a public channel, as shown in Fig. 1.3. The key K_{B_e} is used as a parameter for algorithm E. After receiving encrypted message C Bob Uses his own private key K_{B_d} as a parameter of a decryption algorithm D and retrieves the original message M from C.

$$C = E_{K_{B_e}}(M) \qquad\qquad M = D_{K_{B_d}}(C) \qquad\qquad (1.1)$$

Here we can see that $K_{B_e} \& M$ are input parameters for encryption algorithm e and $K_{B_d} \& C$ are input parameters for decryption.

   Cryptographers observed that some mathematical operations can be performed in non-polynomial time but the reverse of the operation requires non-polynomial time. Two of the such kind of problems are discussed below:

1. Integer Factorization Problem.
2. Discrete Logarithmic Problem.

1.3.2.1 Integer Factorization Problem

Out of various field of mathematical-science the Number Theory is earliest interest of researchers and of theory of prime numbers is one of the primeval topic in number theory. Integer Factorization Problem (IFP) is primeval out of various areas in Number Theory (Yan et al. 2019).

$$Mathematics \xrightarrow{has\ a\ field} Number - Theory \xrightarrow{has\ a\ field}$$
$$Theory - of - Prime - Numbers \xrightarrow{has\ a\ field} IFP.$$

Fundamental theory of arithmetic claims that, any integer n such that $n > 0$ can be uniquely represented into its prime decomposition form, e.g.

$$2025 = 3^4 \times 5^2 \qquad 12345678987654321 = 3^4 \times 37^2 \times 333667^2$$

Public-key cryptography techniques use IFP to achieve higher security. Nowadays, RSA cryptography and its versions are used by most of the cryptographic applications in the world of internet security.

RSA Cryptography Hypothesis for Using IFP

RSA hypothesis states that it is as hard as IFP to find plain-text M if we are given the public-key pair (e, N) and cipher-text C. That is,

$$IFP(N) \xrightarrow{NonPolynomialTime} RSA(M)$$
$$IFP(N) \xleftarrow{PolynomialTime} RSA(M)$$

Till now, no one has given a solution to solve the IFP in a given polynomial time. On the other-hand it is also not proved that IFP can be determined in polynomial time. The security of RSA depends on hardness of solving IFP. Cryptanalysts has found difficulties in finding N because of the hardness of factoring a large integer N. As if N is large enough and chosen arbitrarily and plain-text(M) and cipher-text(C) are such that $0 < M \& C < N - 1$. Contradictory it can be stated as *"One can find the plain-text M in polynomial time from cipher-text C if we can solve IFP in polynomial time for a sufficiently large integer N."*

With sub-exponential time the most effective and widely practiced factoring approach is *Number Field Sieve* (Lenstra et al. 1993), have asymptotically complexity as:

$$\mathcal{O}(exp(c(\log n)^{\frac{1}{3}}(\log\log n)^{\frac{2}{3}})) \qquad (1.2)$$

Now for a scenario, the task of guessing plain-text M (original message) from cipher-text C for an intruder as well as for cryptanalyst is as hard as factoring N. The *Number Field Sieve* (Lenstra et al. 1993), is well know IFP solving approach which runs in least given time in Eq. 1.2. RSA cryptography is the most foremost cryptographic scheme which is well known in internet security techniques (Yan et al. 2019).

1.3.2.2 Discrete Logarithmic Problem

When logarithms were invented by Napier it certainly makes the computing task easier. With discovery of logarithms the *discrete logarithmic problem(DLP)* was defined. DLP is also a field for number theory. The essential requirement of the cryptography technique is that it should be computationally hard to reverse the encryption process and *DLP* is exactly qualified this property as it is computationally intractable. Currently available supercomputers are also having trouble in computing discrete logarithms. We can define the discrete logarithm problem (DLP) as:

let Z_P is a multiplicative cyclic group and $g \in Z_p$ is a generator of group Z_p, then α is a natural number such that, for every element X in the group Z_p there is:

$g^{\alpha} \cong X \pmod{P}$

In other words, if g is an arbitrary integer relatively prime to P and α is a primitive root of P, then there exists among the numbers $0, 1, 2, \ldots, \phi(P) - 1$, where $\phi(P)$ is the totient function, exactly one number μ such that:

$g \cong \alpha^{\mu} \pmod{P}$

The number μ is then called the discrete logarithm of g with respect to the base α modulo P and is denoted $\mu \cong \alpha^{-1}g \pmod{P}$.

The modulus value P belongs to composite or a prime. The hardness of finding discrete logarithms depends on the groups. Even though DLP is one of the oldest mathematical problems, there is not a well known effective approach that has been found to solve the DLP. Even the complexity of solving DLP is considered to be more complex than the integer factorization problem (IFP). Gordon has used NFS and gave the solving algorithm for DLP which is best to be known till now (Gordon 1993), time taken by this algorithm is:

$$\mathcal{O}(exp(c(\log n)^{\frac{1}{3}}(\log \log n)^{\frac{2}{3}})) \tag{1.3}$$

As we discussed that DLP is intractable and there is no such approach is known which can claim to solve DLP efficiently. Cryptographer has observed and taken this opportunity as before IFP has been used by RSA, in the same way, DLP can also be used for cryptography. The oldest public-key cryptosystem in the field of computer security, the DHM (Diffie–Hellman–Merkle) key-exchange scheme, was proposed in 1976 (Merkle 1978), The hardness of solving DLP is used by them and its security measure is dependent on the intractability of the DLP problem. In the next Sect. 1.3.2.3 we will discuss the DHM key-exchange protocol based cryptographic systems.

1.3.2.3 Diffie–Hellman–Merkle

The public-key-distribution system (PKDS) is proposed by Diffie and Hellman (1976). They are the first to propose the theory and practical implementation of exchanging the key over public channel. They also propose a PKC which was relying on Merkle's seminal work (Merkle 1978). The intractability of Discrete Logarithm Problem(DLP) was the basis of the first public-key system. Their encryption technique was not only to simply encrypt a message and send it to another party but first they exchange a few parameters to get agreement on a common key which is private to both. All this agreement is done over a public channel that is insecure and can be

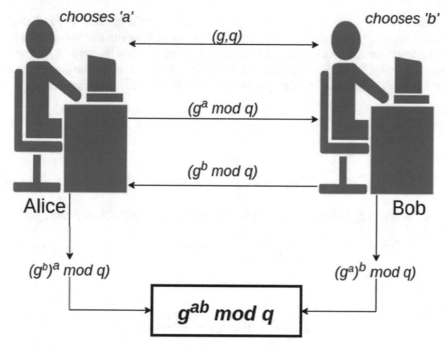

Fig. 1.4 Diffe–Hellman–Markle key exchange

tampered by any intruder like Oscar. After the two parties get to agree on common secret-key they can use that key in any conventional symmetric-key algorithm (e.g. AES, 3DES, BlowFish) to encrypt the message or information. Moreover, the essential feature of the Diffie–Hellman–Merkle key exchange protocol is that, it requires very less amount of time and it is very fast. Even though the encryption process is one of the secret-key approach. This is still public-key cryptography because of its key-exchange protocol. We can understand the working of DHM (Diffie–Hellman–Merkle) key-exchange protocol in the following simple steps given in the Fig. 1.4

- First of all, a prime number q and a generator g is chosen randomly and publicly disclosed (Before that we ask all users to get agreed upon a finite group over a fixed finite field F_q),
- The first party Alice chooses an arbitrary number $a \in F_n \& 0 < a < q - 1$ and communicate $g^a \pmod q$ with Bob,
- Then the second party Bob chooses an arbitrary number $b \in F_q \& 0 < b < n - 1$ and communicate $g^b \pmod q$ with Alice,
- Then both the parties Alice and Bob determine $g^{ab} \pmod q$ and mutually agree to use the value as a secret-key in a further exchange of information.

From the above steps it is obvious that the intruder(e.g. Oscar) can have parameters $g, q, [g^a \pmod q]$ *and* $[g^b \pmod q]$, it is up-to the capability of intruder whether he can calculate [g^{ab} (mod q)] using DLP. If the intruder is capable of recovering integer a and b with the help of the parameters mentioned above, then he can understand the communicated information. It implies that he can simply find a way to counter the Diffie–Hellman–Merkle system. We can say that the presumption for the Diffie–Hellman–Merkle system for information security scheme is:

It is computationally intractable to find g^{ab} (mod q) from $g, q, [g^a$ (mod q)]$and[g^b$ (mod q)].

$$g, q, g^a \quad (\text{mod } q), g^b \quad (\text{mod } q) \xrightarrow{hardtofind} g^{ab} \quad (\text{mod } q) \qquad (1.4)$$

In another way we can represent the Discrete Logarithm Problem presumption:

$$g, q, g^a \quad (\text{mod } q) \xrightarrow{hardtofind} a$$

or

$$g, q, g^b \quad (\text{mod } q) \xrightarrow{hardtofind} b$$

There is no practical approach has been found to use information of g^a (mod q) and g^b (mod q) to find g^{ab} (mod q). Without finding a break-through for DLP no one can find g^{ab} (mod q) from g^a (mod q) and g^b (mod q).

1.3.2.4 Importance of Asymmetric Key Cryptography

Basically we categorise all the cryptography schemes into two categories one is asymmetric another is symmetric. Essential security services like confidentiality, data integrity, authentication, non-repudiation can be achieved by both, but there are some additional importance of asymmetric key cryptography which are discussed here.

Cost-Analysis For any kind of investment in an organization, the analysis of its cost is essential. Here we need to analyze the installation cost of security services and the amount we are saving from it. The cost can be measure in the unit of time, monetary, or quality of service. If the installation cost of a security system is not justifying the saving i.e., not returning the expected output from the investment, then the installation of the security system is not fit from the perspective of cost-analysis. There is another way of analyzing the importance of the security system by the measurement of loss in the absence of it.

Consider a scenario of One Time Password(OTP), where a user was unable to complete the transaction because of missing OTP, then he would have to use help-desk. Using the help desk will cost $5 to the service provider. On the other hand, if the system allows the user to get the OTP three times by using *Resend OTP* option, which will cost $1 per OTP to the service provider. This will decreases the overall cost by saving help-desk costs.

Integrity   In PKC announcing the public key can be done in different ways, consider a scenario of phone-book where contact details of all are publicly available as the secrecy is not required, But its integrity (and authenticity) is questionable, if any intruder (Oscar) who wants to get someone's(Alice) information then he can tamper the public phone-book and could replace Alice's public key by his own, then sender let say Bob will use Oscar's public key instead of Alice's public key and send it over an insecure channel, which is completely undesirable.

Digital Certificates   For Integrity and Authenticity in public-key cryptography (PKC) reliability of the third party is needed. The third-party should be capable of issuing digital certificate and they are termed as certificate authorities(CA). A digital certificate for a user is comprised of name of the user(server or organization), the identity of the certificate-issuing authority, email of user & address and the public key. When two parties need to communicate using PKC then they ask the CA to provide the digital certificate of each other which the CA sends. Then public key can be obtained from the certificate, and the certificate is also an identity of a party in a public network.

1.3.3   Difference between Symmetric and Asymmetric Key Cryptography

Information sharing over a public channel is protected by security services like confidentiality, authentication, integrity etc. The security services are provided by various cryptographic techniques, which can be categorised in to two categories: symmetric key cryptography and asymmetric key cryptography. This subsection acknowledges some differences between these two cryptographic technique based on key distribution, complexity, swiftness of execution, purpose and some existing techniques.

Key Distribution   A vast amount of keys are needed in symmetric key cryptography. Consider a scenario where a group of n users wants to use symmetric key cryptography in pairs to communicate with each other. Each pair needs to have a separate and unique symmetric key. This scenario needs $C_n^2 = n(n-1)/2$ unique keys, $i.e.$, $\mathcal{O}(n^2)$ keys. For a small group of four people keys needed is only six, but in a real-world where the group size can be of more than 100 i.e., $n \geq 100$ the required number of key is more than 4950. As the keys requirement grows with the size of n, keys become inconvenient to manage and exchange securely. Whereas in PKC, each entity requires only one pair of (public, private) keys for communication. Therefore needs n number of key pairs only.

Figures shows Fig. 1.2 Symmetric-key and Fig. 1.3 Asymmetric-key encryption. The identical key is used by both parties in the symmetric-key scenario. The Asymmetric-key (public-key) scenario different keys are used for encryption and decryption one is the public key and another one is the private key. "private key" is also termed as *symmetric-key* in asymmetric systems, similar to *secret key* as in symmetric-key systems.

Complexity Secret-key cryptosystem has less complicated algorithms whereas public-key cryptosystem algorithms are more complicated, as in secret-key cryptosystem only one key is employed to carry out both the operations. Public-key cryptosystem uses two different keys one for encryption and another for decryption which causes the algorithms to be more complicated. Whereas in secret-key the simple execution of the algorithm for both the task (encryption and decryption) is executed fast and with less complexity.

Swiftness of Execution PKC used complex mathematical fundamental techniques like IFP and DLP which causes the task of encryption and decryption to execute with higher complexity. Whereas the secret-key-cryptography has less complex executions, and execute the task of encryption and decryption swiftly.

Purpose PKC is preferred where the requirement of small data is needed like exchanging the key or passwords. Whereas the secret-key-encryption is preferred where the bulk amount of data is needed to transmit.

Example Algorithms Secret-Key-Encryption: AES, DES/3DES, Blowfish, QUAD.
Public Key Cryptography: Diffie–Hellman–Markel, DSA, ElGamal, RSA, ECC. Some of these techniques has been discussed in next chapter (refer Chap. 2).

1.4 Software Versus Hardware Implementation

Implementation of any given cryptographic technique needs careful caution for its software as well as its hardware implementation. One can enhance the security services provided by particular cryptographic technique by it's efficient software and hardware implementation. The basic benefits, which can be achieved in better way by the hardware implementation in comparison to the software implementation is discussed below.

Shared Memory Security

No software applications can have their physical memory. Therefore applications have to use external memory which is governed by the operating system on which they run. Any Operating system cannot guarantee the isolation of memory space provided to your application, i.e., other applications can also have shared access to that memory space at any point of time. Although OS has its algorithm for memory allocation which is random but cannot guarantee beyond the capability of the Operating System's security protocols. Moreover, protection of the secondary memory is a more difficult task. Secondary storage sometimes needs an equal level of confidentiality protection as main storage. *Long-Term Keys* are stored in secondary storage devices and also the data which require to be stored for a longer period. Prevention of the confidentiality of secondary storage materials on a system that uses the application-shared platform is difficult.

Based on the above discussion we can conclude that a high level security system which uses applications that share memory is required for the software-based cryptographic technique.

Hardware-based solutions can have their personal storage space which they can manage internally and solves the problem of memory protection from other software application as this memory is need not to be shared. Furthermore, the hardware method also prevents illegal access of memory which makes it inherently more safe and secure than operating system based prevention methods. *Software-based* cryptographic modules have an inherent weakness in compare to cryptographic solutions that are hardware-based.

Shared usage of memory space can lead to many consequences e.g.:

- **Integrity Assurance:**

  The application code is stored in secondary storage and security of secondary storage is not assured. Therefore the integrity of the application code cannot be assured. Instructions are stored in secondary storage and a set of instructions is known as a program/software. During execution of the application the instructions are fetched upon demand or prior to the instruction-execution. Since the security of secondary storage is not assured, the code-integrity itself cannot be assured either.

An intruder can alter the program-code, either to cause it a malfunction or to steal some critical information. Program-code can be altered manually, or automatically with the help of malfunction. The malfunction can be present in the form of Trojan-horse(virus) executing on the same operating system(OS) or the same platform. The OS or platform already has access privileges to the program code. Whereas, in hardware-based cryptographic solutions the program-code is burnt onto a chip physically, which makes it read-only and more secure.

- **Reverse Engineering:**

  The attacker can reverse engineer the software implementations as it is not immune from this kind of attack. An attacker who wants to reverse engineer the software implementation can find it in memory as it is merely a set of instructions stored in memory. Cryptographic modules are already publicly known so reverse engineering of that is not a problem but other application modules that have classified information are more susceptible, as security of memory is not guaranteed. Access of such high-level secured information can exploit security.

- **Resistance to Side-channel attacks:**

  These types of attacks are motivated by the internal implementation of operations in the computer system instead of the weakness of cryptographic modules or by susceptible memory locations. Here, the attacker is concern about *Timing information, power consumption, electromagnetic leaks or even sound* which has a well-known pattern for a few internal operations that can provide information, which can be exploited.
  By collecting the required details about the execution state of a program the intruder can construct a well-defined process to collect the secret-key that is being used by the program. Hardware-based techniques can use special precautions that can mask the power consumption's fluctuation, to prevent the intruder from obtaining power consumption details which is helpful in finding the secret key.

- **Session Key Storage:**

  Storing the session key needs access to secondary memory which is more prone to security attacks. As it needs to be stored for while we need to store it in a nonvolatile memory location and at the same time we need to secure the key from other external applications. The session key can also be stored in secondary storage, which is made inaccessible to other software by hardware implementations.

- **Dependence on Underlying Program Security:**

When a program is running on top of another lower-layer program (e.g. operating system) the security of upper-layer programs automatically dependent on the security of the underlying programs(OS) in terms of flaws. If any flaw in an underlying application such as Operating system is found, then this flaw can lead to additional breach to the security of application running on a higher level. We can say the cryptographic module which is running on top of any operating system is greatly dependent on the operating system's security level. One way of getting private information from an Operating system is via swap memory's files.
Whereas, hardware implementations are independent of any high-level service provided by the operating system which makes it independent from secure implementations of these services.

- **Use of third party service:**

For faster results, the software implementation of cryptographic modules tends to use the third party add-on which in result cause compromise to the security e.g. use of DSP circuits that are able to achieve more efficient multiplications. The DSP circuit gives efficient multiplication result for large size integers on the other hand it is very less concerned about the security. The only solution to discard the inherent issues with third-party software is by discarding it completely, as done by independent hardware implementations.

1.5 Multi-core Architectures

For the implementation of cryptographic modules targeting differing applications, various design approaches have been used. We can broadly understand these approaches in three ways i.e., General Purpose Processor (GPPs), Application-Specific Integrated Circuits (ASICs) and Flexible Architecture/Hardware.

Where GPPs are flexible and limited in performance the ASICs provide higher performance but they are specific to a set of applications and also costly. As a result, the trade-off between these two approaches is Flexible Architecture, which is used to cover the design space between performance and flexibility. The increasing importance of flexible architectures with high performance caught the attraction of most researchers to work in this field. For better understanding of this vast variety of work done by researchers we can categorize their work broadly in three classes (Rashid et al. 2019): 1 Crypto Processors, 2 Crypto CoProcessors and 3 Multi-core Crypto Processor (refer Fig. 1.5).

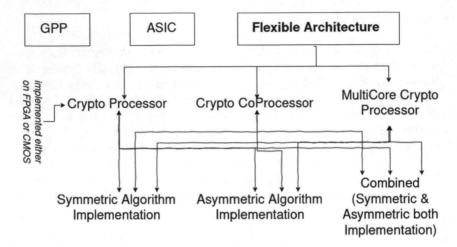

Fig. 1.5 Architectures for cryptogrphic algorithm implementation

- A **crypto processor** has it's own instruction set, and it's hardware is programmable. we can program the hardware with its own dedicated instruction set.
- A **crypto coprocessors** doesn't has it's own processor it is configured and controlled by the host processor with whom it is attached. But it's hardware module is programmable or re-configurable.
- A **multi-core processor** is a simple coupling of multiple cores designed such that it can perform cryptographic tasks efficiently.

The flexible architecture for a multi-core processor can be implemented either on Complementary Metal Oxide Semiconductors (CMOS) or Field Programmable Gate Arrays (FPGA). The performance comparison of the various processor under flexible architecture can be done in the terms of different design constraints.

Design Constraints of Flexible Architectures

While implementing the architecture was categorized into three categories:

1. Symmetric algorithm implementations,
2. Asymmetric algorithm implementations and
3. Combined (symmetric as well as asymmetric) algorithm implementations.

Further, each implementing algorithm based on architecture is classified into three design classes termed as: 1. Crypto Processors, 2. Crypto CoProcessors and 3. Multi-Core Crypto Processors (refer Fig. 1.5).

1. **Crypto Processor** The Crypto processor implemented on programmable hardware, which has a dedicated instruction set and has main memory, arithmetic logical unit (ALU), and a control unit.
   Main memory can be further categorized based on its use in instruction memory and data memory. Instruction memory stores the instruction's opcodes whereas

Data memory stores address of operands of corresponding instructions. For maximization of throughput, multiple ALUs and single ALU can be coupled. As the name implies all-controlling task is managed by the control unit. A better architecture of crypto ALUs provides better efficiency and performance. Examples of crypto processors with a single ALU are Parallel sub-pipelined architecture (Rahimunnisa et al. 2013), point multiplication on Koblitz curves (Azarderakhsh et al. 2014). Whereas to enhance the throughput, multiple crypto ALUs in a single design has proposed point multiplication on binary Edwards and generalized Hessian curves (Azarderakhsh and Reyhani-Masoleh 2011), Elliptic curve cryptography for low power applications (Keller et al. 2009).

2. **Crypto CoProcessor** The host processor is controller here which controls the processing element i.e., crypto coprocessor. Host processor configures and runs crypto coprocessor through a system bus. Moreover, to increase the security the crypto coprocessor has its memory to store key. The host processor is also responsible for computing general-purpose instructions. Single-core or multi-core both can be used for designing the architecture of a crypto coprocessor but each crypto core has its own ALU and local memory. Performance can be limited by the communication speed between the host processor and crypto coprocessor, so architecture designer takes good care of that. An example of a crypto coprocessor: *A coprocessor for ARX-based cryptographic algorithms* (Shahzad et al. 2013).

3. **Multi-core crypto processor** Multi-core crypto processors can be imagined as the parallel architecture for cryptographic computing elements. It achieves better performance by executing more than one operation in parallel (Jain et al. 2015). The inheriting benefits of multi-core processors are simultaneous acceleration, better programming implementation and less power consumption. The multi-core cryptosystem is the collection of items such as scheduler, storage space for data and program and number of cores termed as crypto processor or processing element(PE). Scheduler is a main controller. With the flexibility of having a number of cores multi-core systems are having a variety of hardware architectures and it's supporting storage structures. For example, Very Long Instruction Word (VLIW) architecture has the option of having one, two, four, eight or even more embedded cores that can be configured. In the same way for performing the different operations, heterogeneous cores can have different hardware architecture.

The parallel computing algorithms are designed by keeping in mind that it should overcome the functional dependency issues in the given objective. It should be a configurable and expandable cryptographic algorithm that supports a parallel computing environment. It should provides better information security & performance efficiency. We have various parallel execution supporting language technologies which support execution of threads in priority which execute perfectly for multi-core architectures such as Python, OpenMP, JAVA, OpenCL, S2P, etc. Furthermore, we have many researchers who have done comparison experiments between GPU and parallel computing on multi-core CPU (Jain et al. 2015), where GPU performs much faster because of it's fine grained thread. GPU is suitable for executing a large amount of data in parallel and can bear load of high density(e.g. Big-Data) computing but has simple branching logic in comparison to

CPU, whereas GPU is preferable where the execution of complex logic is needed. There is a non-linear correlation between power supply & frequency of a core. These parallel algorithms exhaust more energy on one processing element because the large computation is executed by them.

As of now, the use of multi-core crypto processors has simple implementation such that it can execute the parallel computing algorithms, concurrently at both client and the server site. The encryption and decryption operation of security algorithms can have compelling benefit from parallel executions that can be implemented on these multi-core crypto processors. Parallelism is an inherited benefit and light-weight architecture can be achieved by multi-core crypto processors. Because of these properties it is gaining more attention. Whereas the parallelism enhance efficiency and saves the energy it also requires more area, which is a trivial task to reduce.

Note: Embedded systems are updating itself to process computing and storage-centric programs with large data sets, dynamic task loads, and dynamic processing aspects. Continuously improving distributed and adaptive heterogeneous embedded systems are crucial in dynamic execution. So apart from the above given three different basic architecture, we will discuss the heterogeneous architecture also (Nam and Lysecky 2018).

1.5.1 Homogeneous Architecture

In homogeneous architecture we have multiple processing elements (PE), performing similar kind of task. Which increases the overall performance. The fabrication cost for the intellectual properties (IP) based on the homogeneous architecture is low. Homogeneous architecture can perform either of one task efficiently i.e., the data computation dominated tasks or control flow dominated tasks. Performing both the task efficiently is not possible by the homogeneous architecture (Han et al. 2015).

There are lots of work performed which implemented the well-known PKC algorithms over a homogeneous architecture. The PKC like RSA has been implemented by Chen and Schaumont (2011). A homogeneous multi-core architecture for computing Montgomery multiplication in parallel is given by Han et al., where the Montgomery multiplication algorithm has been partitioned using the mixed task partitioning method, and implemented over the multi-core platform. Several PE performing same operations are designed to achieve parallelization (Han et al. 2013).

1.5.2 Heterogeneous Architecture

Present scenario lots of providers are providing intellectual property (IP) cores such as systems-on-chip (SoCs) designs, processing elements. As the number of providers are increasing the executable code loses its integrity, as all are running on the same operating system and share resources. This gives an intruder a very easy chance to steal the private information. The consent of today's computing world is that ordinary technique and software-based security schemes are not up to the mark for the required level of security objectives. In the process to obtain a higher level of security a heterogeneous SoC architecture can be a solution. With multiple processing elements(PEs) a hybrid architecture design of secure and non-secure cores into the same chip can be embedded where one can:

1. Provide individual PEs security.
2. Protect data leakage and its integrity.
3. Promote communication between PEs.
4. Allow certain defective PEs which can have faulty purpose.

A trustworthy routing algorithm and a highly secure router are common fundamental elements of the Heterogeneous architecture. Based on the security level of processing elements (PEs), the architecture can cut off them practically in any other access modes of the storage blocks. Even if any PE is being dishonest while accessing the shared resource the overall architecture works smoothly. for e.g. Kinsy & Lake developed a heterogeneous architecture named *Hermes* (Kinsy et al. 2018).

It is obvious to have a little bit of hardware overhead for Heterogeneous architecture, but it is capable of the execution of multi-core systems. Which is also having a key management scheme for multiple keys, where the keys can be distributed over different groups. One of the benefit of heterogeneous architecture is configuration of a secure computing system out of unsecured components. With the help of rules which are defined by the user's concern about security, heterogeneous architecture can act as a hardware-level virtual zones to enforce these security rules.

1.5.3 Software Defined Radio (SDR)

In order to meet the requirement of flexibility, Software Defined Radio (SDR) is one of the solutions. To achieve the objectives of internet security i.e., confidentiality, integrity and authentication (secure-radio) the assimilation of these objectives into SDR devices is required (Kinsy et al. 2018). To achieve more than one objective at once systems tend to embed programmable crypto processors. As a result, we achieve higher flexibility for crypto processors but it also tends to give less throughput than dedicated accelerators. Buchty et al. proposed a crypto processor which is programmable and termed it as *Cryptonite* (Buchty et al. 2004) this crypto processor is capable of supporting security algorithms like AES, DES, MD5 and others. Two clusters are used to build Cryptonite crypto processor. Where each cluster performs a specific task intending to achieve the objective of internet security. Buchty et al. claims to achieve a throughput of 2.25 Gbps at 400 MHz for the AES-ECB algorithm which targets ASIC platform.

Fronte et al. proposed SDR termed as *Celator* (Fronte et al. 2008) having a number of Processing Elements (PEs) as it's component. The PEs forms a matrix the way they are inter-connected to each other which is like a block cipher state variable. PEs are connected and designed in such a way that after each clock cycle cryptographic functions are executed. Asymmetric-Key-Cryptography schemes like AES, DES or SHA are supported be Celator, Fronte et al. claims to achieve a throughput of 46 Mbps at 190 MHz when we compute AES-CBC algorithm.

Software Defined Radio (SDR), also helps in handling the profusion of standards of wireless communication, require internet security objectives such as confidentiality, integrity and authentication. The work is done by Grand et al. (2011) and Wang et al. (2009) integrates internet security objectives into SDR systems by given multi-core crypto processor for multi-standard & multi-channel communication systems. Han et al. also given the implementation of PKC (ECC and RSA) algorithms over a heterogeneous multi-core crypto processor supporting by cloud computing and also achieve the internet security objectives such as confidentiality, integrity and authentication (Han et al. 2015). Schneider et al. designed AES and RSA on a lightweight architecture, termed it as *asynchronous GA144 ultra-low-powered Multi-Core crypto processor* (Schneider et al. 2014). This design was motivated by extensive computing and it was majorly assembled with cost-saving processors offering limited computing power.

System software such as network-servers and cellular-sites need heavy computing, they also need to fulfill the service request of large numbers of customers in a fraction of second. The work by Zhang et al. gives a design of ECC hardware implementing architecture to obtain high-efficiency also gives an option of achieving parallelism as instruction level (Zhang et al. 2010). Whereas, the implementation by Fan et al. (2008), is to execute ECC on a multi-core platform with an objective of adding new programs without any major complexity.

1.6 Scheduler for Multi-core Architectures

In multi-core architecture the number of processors are increased for better performance. Here the primary objective of a *Scheduler* is to keep minimum number of processors in idle state such that the increased number of cores can provide better performance. Designing such kind of a scheduler for multi-core architecture is a challenging task (Kinsy et al. 2018). The scheduler can be designed either in hardware or in software, though hardware design is preferred over software design as a good choice to achieve better performance speed as it can schedule parallel executions.

We can use one of the core as a controller to schedule the task for other cores in multi-core architectures. It will also help in gaining high data rates while remaining flexible. The cores are cryptographic-core and the scheduler core is termed as *task scheduler*. A piece of information can be processed by single-channel or from different channels by individual cores. In this way, high efficiency can be achieved on multi-channel radios irrespective of the execution mode. The multi-core crypto processors has nearly an equal amount of pros and cons as a multi-core general-purpose processor approach (MPSoC issue) e.g. *CryptoManiac* (Kinsy et al. 2018) is a multi-core architecture, Where Kinsy et al. claim to achieve a throughput of 512 Mbps on ASIC platform at 360 MHz.

1.7 Organization of the Book

The main focus of this book is to discuss the various ways to improve the performance of public-key cryptographic transformations. The second chapter deals with various types of Public-key cryptosystems and their applications. The benefits of asymmetric-key cryptography over symmetric-key cryptography is also discussed in this chapter. The pictorial representation of the organization of the book is given in the Fig. 1.6.

The part *II* covers the modular exponentiation in detail. The third chapter deals with the different types of ME techniques along with its mathematical aspects. The fourth chapter focuses on the algorithmic ways of optimizing ME. The fifth chapter elaborates on the hardware techniques for enhancing the performance of ME. In the fifth chapter different hardware techniques like parallelization, path reduction and other hardware optimization techniques are also discussed.

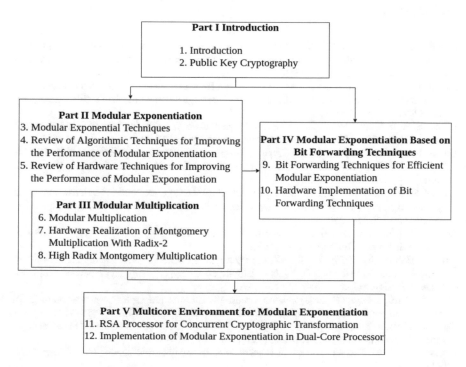

Fig. 1.6 Organization of the book

The part *III* is focusing on MM, where the seventh and eighth chapters are particularly based on Montgomery multiplication (MMM). The basics of MM are covered in the sixth chapter. The variations of MMM algorithms are also given in this chapter. The seventh chapter discusses the various MMM techniques with Radix-2. In this chapter Hardware and software, both areas are explored for efficient implementation of MMM. The eighth chapter deals with the modification of radix-2 algorithms to their corresponding high-radix implementations. Various aspects of upgrading the MMM algorithm in higher radix are also discussed in this chapter.

The part *IV* has two chapters both are on an optimal ME techniques i.e., Bit forwarding techniques given by Satya et al. (Vollala et al. 2014). The ninth chapter discusses the techniques of reducing the number of required MMs by Bit Forwarding (BFW) techniques and how they can be implemented in hardware. Whereas, The tenth chapter illustrates the energy-efficient hardware implementation of the BFW techniques. This chapter also covers the analysis of different parameters like energy, power and throughput.

The part *V* is exploiting the multi-core domain in PKC. It also discusses the DCRSAP given by Satya et al. (Vollala et al. 2017) & the right-to-left ME with two cores (Vollala et al. 2019).

References

Azarderakhsh R, Järvinen KU, Mozaffari-Kermani M (2014) Efficient algorithm and architecture for elliptic curve cryptography for extremely constrained secure applications. IEEE Trans Circ Syst I: Reg Papers 61(4):1144–1155

Azarderakhsh R, Reyhani-Masoleh A (2011) Efficient fpga implementations of point multiplication on binary edwards and generalized hessian curves using gaussian normal basis. IEEE Trans Very Large Scale Integ (VLSI) Syst 20(8):1453–1466

Biham E, Perle S (2018) Conditional linear cryptanalysis–cryptanalysis of des with less than 242 complexity. IACR transactions on symmetric cryptology, pp 215–264

Buchty R, Heintze N, Oliva D (2004) Cryptonite–a programmable crypto processor architecture for high-bandwidth applications. In: International conference on architecture of computing systems, Springer, pp 184–198

Chen Z, Schaumont P (2011) A parallel implementation of montgomery multiplication on multicore systems: algorithm, analysis, and prototype. IEEE Trans Comput 60(12):1692–1703. https://doi.org/10.1109/TC.2010.256

Daemen J, Rijmen V (2013) The design of Rijndael: AES-the advanced encryption standard. Springer Science & Business Media, Berlin

Diffie W, Hellman M (1976) New directions in cryptography. IEEE Trans Inf Theory 22(6):644–654

Fan J, Sakiyama K, Verbauwhede I (2008) Elliptic curve cryptography on embedded multicore systems. Design Autom Embed Syst 12(3):231–242

Fronte D, Perez A, Payrat E (2008) Celator: a multi-algorithm cryptographic co-processor. In: 2008 international conference on reconfigurable computing and FPGAs, IEEE, pp 438–443

Gangireddy VKR, Kannan S, Subburathinam K (2020) Implementation of enhanced blowfish algorithm in cloud environment. J Ambient Intell Hum Comput 1–7

Gordon DM (1993) Discrete logarithms in gf(p) using the number field sieve. SIAM J Discr Math 6(1):124–138

Grand M, Bossuet L, Le Gal B, Gogniat G, Dallet D (2011) Design and implementation of a multi-core crypto-processor for software defined radios. In: International symposium on applied reconfigurable computing, Springer, pp 29–40

Han J, Dou R, Zeng L, Wang S, Yu Z, Zeng X (2015) A heterogeneous multicore crypto-processor with flexible long-word-length computation. IEEE Trans Circ Syst I: Reg Papers 62(5):1372–1381

Han J, Wang S, Huang W, Yu Z, Zeng X (2013) Parallelization of radix-2 montgomery multiplication on multicore platform. IEEE Trans Very Large Scale Integ (VLSI) Syst 21(12):2325–2330

Jain V, Sharma P, Sharma S (2015) Cryptographic algorithm on multicore processor: A review. In: 2015 international conference on advances in computer engineering and applications, IEEE, pp 241–244

Keller M, Byrne A, Marnane WP (2009) Elliptic curve cryptography on fpga for low-power applications. ACM Trans Reconfig Technol Syst (TRETS) 2(1):1–20

Kinsy MA, Bu L, Isakov M, Mark M (2018) Designing secure heterogeneous multicore systems from untrusted components. Cryptography 2(3):12

Lenstra AK, Hendrik Jr W, et al. (1993) The development of the number field sieve, vol 1554. Springer Science & Business Media, Berlin

Merkle RC (1978) Secure communications over insecure channels. Commun ACM 21(4):294–299

Nam H, Lysecky R (2018) Mixed cryptography constrained optimization for heterogeneous, multicore, and distributed embedded systems. Computers 7(2):29

Rahimunnisa K, Karthigaikumar P, Christy N, Kumar S, Jayakumar J (2013) Psp: Parallel sub-pipelined architecture for high throughput aes on fpga and asic. Open Comput Sci 3(4):173–186

Rashid M, Imran M, Jafri AR, Al-Somani TF (2019) Flexible architectures for cryptographic algorithms–a systematic literature review. J Circ Syst Comput 28(03):1930003

Santhi H, Gayathri P, Katiyar S, Gopichand G, Shreevastava S (2019) Study of symmetric-key cryptosystems and implementing a secure cryptosystem with des. In: Information systems design and intelligent applications. Springer, Berlin, pp 299–313

Schneider T, von Maurich I, Güneysu T, Oswald D (2014) Cryptographic algorithms on the ga144 asynchronous multi-core processor. J Signal Proc Syst 77(1–2):151–167

Schneier B (1993) Description of a new variable-length key, 64-bit block cipher (blowfish). In: International workshop on fast software encryption, Springer, pp 191–204

Schneier B (1996) Applied cryptography, 2nd edn. Wiley, New York

Shahzad K, Khalid A, Rákossy ZE, Paul G, Chattopadhyay A (2013) Coarx: a coprocessor for arx-based cryptographic algorithms. In: 2013 50th ACM/EDAC/IEEE Design Automation Conference (DAC), IEEE, pp 1–10

Stallings W (2006) Cryptography and network security, 4/E. Pearson Education India

Thakur J, Kumar N (2011) Des, aes and blowfish: symmetric key cryptography algorithms simulation based performance analysis. Int J Emerg Technol Adv Eng 1(2):6–12

Todo Y (2017) Integral cryptanalysis on full misty1. J Cryptol 30(3):920–959

van Oorschot PC (2020) Computer security and the internet: tools and jewels. Springer Nature, Berlin

Vollala S, Varadhan V, Geetha K, Ramasubramanian N (2017) Design of rsa processor for concurrent cryptographic transformations. Microelectron J 63:112–122

Vollala S, Ramasubramanian N, Begum BS, Joshi AD (2019) Dual-core implementation of right-to-left modular exponentiation. In: Recent findings in intelligent computing techniques, Springer, pp 43–53

Vollala S, Varadhan V, Geetha K, Ramasubramanian N (2014) Efficient modular multiplication algorithms for public key cryptography. In: 2014 IEEE international advance computing conference (IACC), IEEE, pp 74–78

Wang MY, Su CP, Horng CL, Wu CW, Huang CT (2009) Single-and multi-core configurable aes architectures for flexible security. IEEE Trans Very Large Scale Integ (VLSI) Syst 18(4):541–552

Yan SY, Yan SY, Lagerstrom-Fife (2019) Cybercryptography: applicable cryptography for cyberspace security. Springer, Berlin

Zhang Y, Chen D, Choi Y, Chen L, Ko SB (2010) A high performance ecc hardware implementation with instruction-level parallelism over gf (2163). Microproc Microsyst 34(6):228–236

Chapter 2
Public Key Cryptography

2.1 Introduction

2.1.1 Public Key Cryptosystem Domain

We can formally define Cryptosystem by set of these Five tuples:
  Cryptosystem: (P, C, K, E, D)

- P: Set of all possible Plain-Text/Plain-Text space
- C: Set of all possible Cipher-Text/Cipher-Text space
- K: Set of all possible Key/Key space
- E: Set of all possible Encryption Algorithm/Encryption Algorithm space
- D: Set of all possible Decryption Algorithm/Decryption Algorithm space

If $e \in E, m \in P, k \in K, c \in C, d \in D$, then, for a given k belongs to key space K there exist an encryption algorithm e_k belongs to Encryption algorithm space E and there exist d_k from decryption algorithm space D such that:
  $\forall k \in K, \exists e_k \in E \ \& \ d_k \in D$
  $\forall m \in P \ \& \ c \in C$

$$e_k(m) = c \mid d_k(c) = m$$

$$d_k(e_k(m)) = m$$

2.1.2 Euler's Theorem

For understanding Euler's theorem one should have a prior knowledge of an important entity in the field of number theory termed as *Euler's totient* function, represented as $\phi(n)$. This Euler's totient function is described as the integers present in between the range $(0, n)$ i.e., >0 and $<n$ must be relatively prime to n (Stallings 2006).

© The Author(s), under exclusive license to Springer Nature Switzerland AG 2021
S. Vollala et al., *Energy-Efficient Modular Exponential Techniques for Public-Key Cryptography*, https://doi.org/10.1007/978-3-030-74524-0_2

Initialization: Let i be an integer $\in Z$ such that $\dots 0 < i < n$
$\phi = 1$
for $i = 2\, to\, n - 1$ **do**
  if $GCD(i, n) = 1$ **then**
    $\phi = \phi + 1$
  end if
end for
Return ϕ ▷ ϕ is Euler's totient function

By default, $\phi(1) = 1$
Example: Let us find $\phi(53)$ and $\phi(30)$
For $\phi(53)$: as we know 53 is prime itself so all positive numbers less than 53 i.e., from 1 to 52 (total 52) are relatively prime to 51.

$$Thus\ \ \phi(53) = 52.$$

For $\phi(30)$ we check each number greater than zero and lesser than 30 that has *GCD* with 30 equals to 1 i.e., relative prime:

$$1, 7, 11, 13, 17, 19, 23, 29$$

We can count that total 8 numbers are there in list, so $\phi(30) = 8$. From first example it is clear that, for a prime number N,

$$\phi(N) = N - 1 \tag{2.1}$$

Consider a case where two prime numbers are given N & M: $M \neq N$. It can be proved that, for $P = N \cdot M$,

$$\phi(P) = \phi(N \cdot M) = \phi(N) \times \phi(M) = (N - 1) \times (M - 1) \tag{2.2}$$

To prove that $\phi(P) = \phi(N) \times \phi(M)$, Let us suppose that the all positive integers less that P is belongs to set $1, \dots, (N \cdot M) - 1$. Other 2 set of integers that are not relatively prime to P are the set $N, 2N, \dots, (N - 1)M$ and the set $M, 2M, \dots, (M - 1)N$. Subsequently,

$$\begin{aligned}
\phi(P) &= (N \cdot M - 1) - [(M - 1) + (N - 1)] \\
&= N \cdot M - (N + M) + 1 \\
&= (N - 1) \times (M - 1) \\
&= \phi(N) \times \phi(M)
\end{aligned}$$

Euler's Theorem

For every P and N, **Euler's theorem** states that P and N that are relatively prime iff:

$$P^{\phi(N)} \cong 1 \quad (\text{mod } N) \tag{2.3}$$

Let's see some examples:

$165 = 15 * 11; \ \phi(165) = \phi(15) * \phi(11) = 80; \ 8^{80} \cong 1 \ (\text{mod } 165)$

$1716 = 11 * 12 * 13; \ \phi(1716) = \phi(11) * \phi(12) * \phi(13) = 480; \ 7^{480} \cong 1 \ (\text{mod } 1716)$

$\phi(13) = 12; \ 9^{12} \cong 1 \ (\text{mod } 13)$

2.1.3   Steps in PKC

The public key algorithm can be better understood in three steps:

1. Key generation
2. Encryption
3. Decryption

Key Generation

In this step, the receiver generates a public and private key and sends the public key to the public channel (or in a public key repository) which can be vital and exposed for attack. This public key of receiver is used by a sender to encrypt a message (Plain-Text) he wants to send. Public key generation is based on the fundamental theorem of Arithmetic i.e.,

> All natural numbers having value more than 1 can be represented as a unique product of prime numbers

Other aspects that make the cryptanalysis task hard is the discrete logarithmic problem (DLP) and integer factorization problem (IFP). When the operand's size is large, then there is no efficient IFP solving approach is present (Brent 2000). Once a try was given at a lab to factorize a 193 digit number (RSA-640) which happens to be solved in 5 months, where 30 Numbers of 2.2 GHz-Opteron-CPUs was used. Most of the cryptographic techniques are based on the difficulty of IFP and DLP (Table 2.1).

There should be trade-off between the key-size that can be theoretically chosen and practically implementation is possible. i.e., it should be as long as to make key-attacks difficult and short enough for real-time use of cryptography techniques.

Encryption and Decryption

Encryption and Decryption steps are specific to the various techniques. *Encryption* is a process of converting the user message (plain-text) such that it can be sent over an insecure channel (public channel) and unauthorized person (intruder) cannot understand it.

Table 2.1 PKC algorithms and their associated computational problems

PKC approaches	Computationally hard problem
RSA	Integer factorization problem (exponential congruent)
Rabin	Integer factorization problem (quadratic congruent)
ElGama	Discrete logarithmic problem
ECC	Elliptic curve discrete logarithmic problem

Decryption is a process of retrieving the user message which has been received in a scrambled format (cipher-text). Message received is an encoded message by encryption process which is not understandable by human. Decryption process over the received message is executed to get the readable original message.

Let us take a *pair:* (e, d) belongs to encryption/decryption algorithms. Here $e \in E$ is an encryption algorithm, and $d \in D$ is the counter-part i.e., decryption algorithm, the key-space is denoted by K (refer Sect. 2.1.1). It is considered that finding plain-text $m \in P$ is not possible by any computation, even if encryption- algorithm $e \in E$ and cipher-text $c \in C$ is known, here $e_k(m) = c$. Similarly, it is also applicable to keys, i.e., having a public key K_e it is computationally hard to find the private key K_d in non-polynomial time. Private key K_d is the counterpart of the public key K_e. It is obvious that K_e and K_d are involved in methods of encryption and decryption respectively. In secret-key decryption K_e and K_d are practically same and kept private but here in PKC reverse of that is being observed here K_e is a publicly known key of one-way door encryption algorithm e and inverse-method d knows the way out with the help of private key K_d. Let there be two entities known as Alice (sender) and Bob (receiver) and they want to exchange some information. Illustration of this communication is given in Fig. 2.1. If Alice wants to send the message then Bob is the one who will create his key-pair (K_{eB}, K_{dB}). After which the public key K_{eB} (will be used for encryption) is made public but he keeps the second key K_{dB} as private key (will be used for decryption). Alice gathers the public key of Bob K_{eB} and uses the publicly known encryption algorithm $e \in E$ to encrypt the information $m \in P$ and compute $c \in C$ as $c = e_{K_{eB}}(m)$. Alice sends c over a public channel and Bob uses his private key K_{dB} to decrypt the cipher-text c using decryption method d as $m = d_{k_{dB}}(c)$.

Notice that for a PKC the encryption-key is sent to Alice using a public network. This public-network will be used again to send the cipher-text. As the encryption-key K_{eB} is not required to save privately, it is distributed publicly. Any other person (e.g. Alice) who wants to send some information to Bob can use this encryption-key K_{eB}. Figure 2.2 describe the concept of how $Alice_1$, $Alice_2$, and $Alice_3$ can send their desired information to Bob. $Alice_1$ encrypt the message m_1 into c_1, if she lost the m_1, then in this case even $Alice_1$ herself is not capable of getting back the information m_1 from encrypted cipher-text c_1.

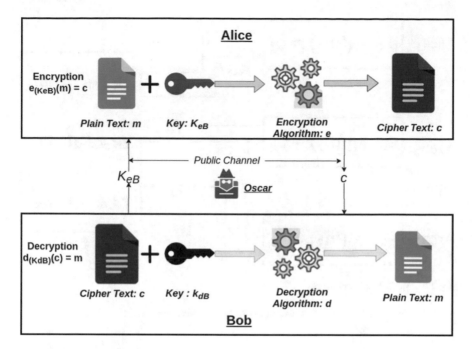

Fig. 2.1 Encryption and decryption

For a real-time example, think of a mail-box of Bob where the inlet is made public by Bob (encryption key K_{eB}) where anyone (e.g. Alice) can drop the mail (plain-text) in the mail-box. Once a mail is inside the mail-box it is secured (like cipher-text). But to open the box only Bob can open it by his private Key (decryption key K_{dB}), even the one who dropped the mail cannot get the mail out of the mailbox. This scenario can be understood as an example of trapdoor i.e., PKC encryption is a one-way method.

> let us assume a scenario that a *cryptography* technique is combination of pair of encryption ($e \in E$) and decryption ($d \in D$) functions. For the technique to be robust, retrieving K_d from K_e needs to be impractical to compute. Where the encryption function e and decryption function d is publicly known and the public key K_e is distributed publicly by receiver. On the other hand the secret key K_d is kept privately by receiver.

Key Exchange

Here in Fig. 2.3 key exchange between two entities Alice and Bob has been given. Initially, both Alice & Bob have their public key and private key with them. The public key of Alice and Bob has been shared over any public network, i.e., Alice has Bob's public-key and Bob has the Alice's public-key such that if Alice wishes to send information to Bob then she will encrypt using public-key of Bob which she already has.

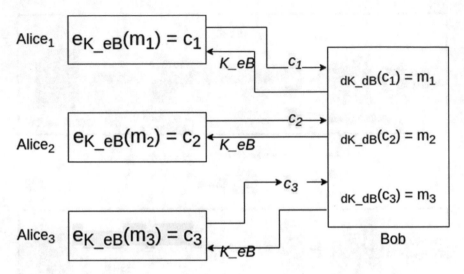

Fig. 2.2 Use of Bob's public key

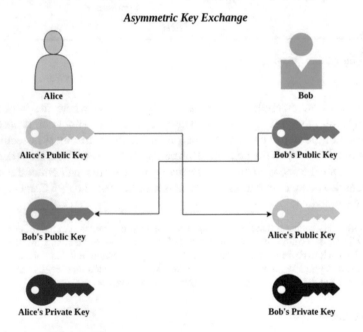

Fig. 2.3 Asymmetric key exchange

Here in this chapter, we are going to discuss these four Public key algorithms.

1. RSA
2. Elgamal
3. Rabin
4. ECC.

2.2 RSA

A very new technique of exchanging information over an insecure channel has been given by Diffie and Hellman (1976), this was a break-through for PKC, it was the origin of a new competition between cryptologists to find new techniques of cryptography, which can satisfy the need of PKC systems. Then on-wards, various approaches for PKC has been researched. In this competition, few seem to be effective initially but soon they found to be easily attacked by intruders.

A year after this break-through in 1977 a group of the competitors' Rivest, Adi Shamir, and Len Adleman at MIT experimented outstanding solutions and published it in the year 1978 (Rivest et al. 1978). The trio Rivest–Shamir–Adleman (RSA *the cryptosystem was named using founder's initials*) given a technique which is used by most of the organizations. It is one of the most trusted PKC techniques implemented by small organizations and also by organizations where a high level of security is required like banking and defense. It is useful for various services to achieve secrecy as well as authenticity. Intractability of the Integer Factorization Problem (IFP) is the main reason for its high security.

RSA Cryptosystem: (P, C, K, E, D)

- P: Set of all possible plain-text/plain-text space and $m \in P$ is a plain-text/message.
- C: Set of all possible cipher-text/cipher-text space and $c \in C$ is a cipher-text/ encrypted message
- K: Set of all possible keys/Keyspace and $n, p, q, e, d \in K$
- E: Set of all variation of RSA encryption algorithm/RSA encryption algorithm space
- D: Set of all variation of RSA decryption algorithm/RSA decryption algorithm space

Here, Alice wishes to send information to Bob over an insecure channel where an intruder Oscar wants to hack the message.

Key Generation

As we know one of the three steps of any PKC algorithm is the key generation. Here the receiver (Bob) is going to set up the key.

Bob's Key generation for RSA

1. Initiate with the selection of two very large prime numbers p and q
2. Compute n such that $n = p \times q$

3. Compute Euler's totient function $\phi(n) = (p - 1) \times (q - 1)$
4. Choose an integer e such that $GCD(e, \phi(n)) = 1$
5. Find d such that $e \times d \cong 1 \pmod{\phi(n)}$

Here we can see that Key for RSA is consist of five elements
$$n, p, q, e, d \in K$$
Public Key set { n, e} $\in e_\beta$
Private Key {p, q, d} $\in d_\beta$ β is the entity who is generating the Keys

Encryption

RSA encryption is performed using the formula:

$$E_{e_\beta}(m) = m^e \quad (\text{mod } n) = C \tag{2.4}$$

where E_{e_β} is RSA encryption algorithm which encrypt message $m \in P$ using key e_β and resultant encrypted message **C** is received by deriving the modulus of m^e by n.

Decryption

RSA decryption algorithm uses private key d for decryption of cipher-text c received from Alice using formula:

$$D_{d_\beta}(C) = C^d \quad (\text{mod } n) \tag{2.5}$$

$$Further - on :$$
$$= (m^e)^d \quad (\text{mod } n)$$
$$= m^{ed} \quad (\text{mod } n)$$
$$\because e \times d = 1 \quad (\text{mod } \phi(n))$$
$$e \times d = k \times \phi(n) + 1$$
$$= m^{k \times \phi(n) + 1} \quad (\text{mod } n)$$

RSA Example

Here we are taking an example to understand the RSA execution.

Key Generation

Key generation part is done by receiver (Bob).

$$p = 7 \text{ and } q = 17$$
$$n = p \times q$$
$$n = 119$$
$$\phi(n) = (p - 1)(q - 1)$$

$$= 96$$
$$e = 5$$
$$e \times d = 1 \quad (\mathrm{mod}\ 96)$$
$$d = 77$$
$$77 \times 5 = 385$$
$$= 4 \times 96 + 1$$

The key pair of e_β, (n, e) is send through public channel. i.e., (119, 5).

Encryption

For encryption we use the formula:

$$E_{e_\beta}(m) = m^e \quad (\mathrm{mod}\ n) = c$$

here let say message $m = 19$

$$E_5(19) = 19^5 \quad (\mathrm{mod}\ 119) = 66$$

Decryption

For decryption we use formula:

$$D_{d_\beta}(c) = c^d \quad (\mathrm{mod}\ n)$$
$$D_{77}(66) = 66^{77} \quad (\mathrm{mod}\ 119)$$
$$D_{77}(66) = 19 = m$$

here we successfully get the original message.

Attack on RSA Algorithm

There exist various known attacks on PKC, most of them target the RSA cryptosystem, out of those 4 common attacks are:

Brute-force method	This method is about iterating all keys from a very large set of possible private keys. By choosing a very long length *key*, we can overcome this attack. But we can't cross a certain threshold, because we need to perform calculations at both the end (sender and receiver) based on the keys. Long length keys can cause slow cryptosystem (Stallings 2006).
IFP attacks	It is one of the oldest problems of mathematical science to find the factors of a very large prime product

	known as the Integer Factorization Problem (IFP). Best algorithm known till now requires exponential time to solve IFP.
Run-Time observing attacks	Intruder can record the running-time of different steps in the publicly known decryption algorithm and by observing them he can guess the key. For example, a con-man can observe the timing of dial-tone to guess the number dialed. This kind of attack can be applied to a task where execution doesn't take a fixed amount of time.
Chosen cipher-text attacks	The publicly transmitted encrypted (cipher-text) information can be collected by an intruder. Later he can perform some analysis on them to guess the private key.

Note: We can observe that *modular exponentiation* is a main and most used operation in RSA algorithm. It is also the costliest operation. In upcoming chapters we will discuss latest and efficient way of computing Modular exponentiation.

2.3   Elgamal

This is historically the pioneer PKC approach that rely on the *discrete logarithm problem (DLP)*. Commercial use of this approach is not preferred as some security issues have been observed. Here we will discuss two variants of Elgamal (Galbraith 2012). The one is termed as *Classic Elgamal* as it is basically the version of basic Elgamal (1985). It requires G to be cyclic and the message $m \in G$. Encoding messages as element of the cyclic group is typical and it is not practical. The second variant has been termed as *Semi-Classic Elgamal*. This is more application-oriented and commercialized because it allows information not to be an element of the group G instead it allows bit-strings. This also leads to the difference in the security level of these two variants.

The receiver runs parameter generation algorithms on a security parameter k, so that all the attackers will need operations more than 2^k (Galbraith 2012). The Sect. 2.3.1 classic Elgamal and the Sect. 2.3.2 gives semi-classic Elgamal. Here the sender is Alice and the receiver is Bob.

2.3.1   Classic Elgamal

Bob runs a parameter generation algorithm over security parameter k that has a large prime p and its corresponding finite field F_p. Then Bob generates cyclic algebraic finite group G over the finite field of F_p. Number of groups G over finite field F_p contain a prime-divisor represented as r. There exist a sub-group represented as G_p, this is a complete group of known techniques for the DLP having the order of r.

Key Generation

1. Calculates α of prime order r $\ldots \alpha \in G$.
2. Bob chooses a random integer a such that $0 < a < r$ and
3. calculates $\beta = \alpha^a \pmod{p}$ same time.

Now the set of public-key has α, β, p and the set private-key has a.
    The message or plain-text space is $M \in G$. The cipher-text space is $C \in G \times G$.

Encryption

As Alice wishes to send some message m to Bob, so first she has to gather the public-key β of the receiver, Bob.
Alice chooses a totally random number k such that $0 < k < r \in G_p$.
Calculate:

$$Y_1 = \alpha^k \pmod{p}$$
$$Y_2 = m \times \beta^k \pmod{p}$$

The cipher-text (encrypted message) Y_1 and Y_2 is sent over a public channel by Alice and Y_1 and Y_2 are $\in C$.

Decryption

Here Bob check whether Y_1 and $Y_2 \in G_p$ and compute:

$$m = Y_2 \times Y_1^{-a}$$

Note: For both variants, k is a security parameter (such that if an intruder (Oscar) wants to attack then he must need to perform a minimum of 2^k bit operations).

2.3.2 Semi-classic Elgamal

Bob selects a large prime p to generate an algebraic group G as previously done in classic Elgamal.

Key Generation

1. Calculate α of prime order r $\ldots \alpha \in G$.
2. Select a message from plain-text space of length l.
3. Select a cryptographic hash-function $H : G \rightarrow \{0, 1\}^l$ and
4. Select an integer, represented as: a $\ldots 0 < a < r$
5. Calculate $\beta = \alpha^a \pmod{p}$.

The public-key set is: H, α, β, p and the private key is a.
Message $m \in M = (0, 1)^l$ Cipher-Text Y_1 and $Y_2 \in C = G \times (0, 1)^l$.

Encryption

This is done by Alice by encrypting message M using Bob's public key.
Choose random k such that $0 < k < r$ and set $Y_1 = \alpha^k \pmod{p}$.
Set $Y_2 = m \oplus H(\beta^k)$
The cipher-text (encrypted message) Y_1 and Y_2 is sent over a public channel by Alice.

Decryption

Here Bob check whether $Y_1 \in G$ and $Y_2 \in 0, 1^l$.
Compute $m = Y_2 \oplus H(Y_1^a)$.

Example

Start with selecting the prime field $G_p(19)$ $\cdots \therefore p = 19.$
Primitive roots of $G_p(19)$: {2, 3, 10, 13, 14, 15}.
Select $\alpha = 10$.
Scenario is that Alice wishes to send some information to Bob.
Generation of key pair is done by Bob

1. Bob selects $a = 5$.
2. Calculate $\beta = \alpha^a \pmod{p} = 10^5 \pmod{19} = 3$.
3. Bob's private key is $a = 5$; Bob's pubic-key set is $\{q, \alpha, \beta\} = \{19, 10, 3\}$.

   For Encryption Information m with the value $m = 17$. Then,

1. Alice selects $k = 6$.
2. Next calculation: $X = \beta^k \pmod{p} = 3^6 \pmod{19} = 729 \pmod{19} = 7$.
3. • $Y_1 = a^k \pmod{p} = a^6 \pmod{19} = 11$
   • $Y_2 = X \times m \pmod{p} = 7 \times 17 \pmod{19} = 119 \pmod{19} = 5$
4. Alice transmit the cipher-text to Bob: $(Y_1, Y2) = (11, 5)$.

   For decryption Decryption is done at Bob's end

1. First calculate $X = (Y_1)^{-\alpha} \pmod{p} = 11^5 \pmod{19} = 161051 \pmod{19} = 7$.
2. Then X^{-1} in $G_p(19)$ is $7^{-1} \pmod{19} = 11$.
3. At last, $m = Y_2 \times X^{-1} \pmod{p} = 5 \times 11 \pmod{19} = 55 \pmod{19} = 17$.

   Random selection of k at the encryption stage enables Elgamal encryption output to be unpredictable. Because of this reason, another encryption of information even with the previous public-key will give different cipher-text naturally.

2.4 Rabin

If we take a special case of RSA with fixed selection of e, specifically $e = 2$ (Rabin 1979). IFP used by any cryptography approach is to make the breaking process difficult for an intruder. It is well known that to find the prime-factor of a large integer is an infeasible task. Similar to IFP the DLP is a equally infeasible task. As it is universally proven that solving IFP and DLP is a difficult task and no such approach has been claimed to solve it efficiently. Therefore cryptosystems that are based on these problems are also believed to be unbreakable. The Rabin PKC cryptosystem was one pioneer approach of secure PKC with proof. The difficulty level for cryptanalysts to recuperate plain-text from the gathered cipher-text is having a similar level of difficulty as finding prime factors of large integer (Menezes Alfred 1997).

Here we first need to deal with the problem of selecting the correct solution in decryption because we get four possible deciphered text and out of that only one is correct. This is because p and q are totally different prime numbers whose squaring is done in encryption stage which leads to four roots. Because of this selection of right answer can be obtained by a certain set of rules as a step of decryption.

Quadratic Residue Modulo p

Let 'p' be a prime and 'a' is an integer then 'a' will be called as a quadratic residue modulo p iff $Y^2 \cong a \pmod{p}$ has a solution in set Z_p e.g. for $p = 11$
$Z_{11} = (\pm 1) = 1, (\pm 2) = 4, (\pm 3) = 9, (\pm 4) = 5, (\pm 5) = 3, (\pm 6) = 3, (\pm 7) = 5,$
$(\pm 8) = 9, (\pm 10) = 1$ here we can see that 1, 3, 4, 5 and 9 are the quadratic residue modulo 11. We can observe for 4 there are two roots ± 2 the $+2$ is simply positive 2 and -2 is basically 9.

Eular Criteria

Let 'p' be a prime and 'a' be a large integer, then 'a' will be called as a quadratic residue of modulo p if and only if:

$$a^{(p-1)/2} \cong 1 \pmod{p} \tag{2.6}$$

This Eq. 2.6 will tell us whether 'a' is quadratic residue or not.

Security Level of Rabin PKC

An intruder who wants to recuperate the information i.e., plain-text m from the encrypted cipher-text c. This is exactly the square root modulo n problem.

> Given a composite integer n, and quadratic residue a modulo with n (i.e., $a \in Q_n$), find a square root of a modulo n (Menezes Alfred 1997).

From this, it is clear that the computing square roots modulo n for Rabin's PKC is having the same level of difficulties in solving as for IFP for an integer n. It is a well-known fact that finding prime factor of a sufficiently large integer n (IFP) is intractable so in the same way the Rabin PKC is also proved to be unbreakable by intruders.

Key Generation

1. Select two random prime integer of size $k/2$ 'p' and 'q' such that $p \cong q \cong 3$ (mod 4).

2. Now, any integer can be in the form of $4k$, $4k + 1$, $4k + 2$, $4k + 3$.
3. Here $4k$ and $4k + 2$ is not prime so we cannot choose them rest two option give us $p = 1 \pmod 4$ or $p = 3 \pmod 4$ we will consider $3 \pmod 4$ because for this there is deterministic polynomial time algorithm to calculate the quadratic residue for it.
4. Compute $N = p \times q$, here N is public key where as set $\{p, q\}$ is private key.

Encryption

Plain-text space $M \in Z_n$ and cipher-text space $C \in Z_n$
$Y = m^2 \pmod N$ ...$Y \in C$ and $m \in M$.
here we ensure m and N are relatively prime.

Decryption

For decryption we need to compute $\sqrt{Y} \pmod N$ for which we need to follow these steps:

1. Compute $m_p = Y^{(p+1)/4} \pmod p$ and $m_q = Y^{(q+1)/4} \pmod q$
2. From Euler criteria, check $m_p^2 \cong Y \pmod p$ and $m_q^2 \cong Y \pmod q$
3. If not then return *NULL*.
4. The 4 possible values of m can be: $m \cong \pm m_p \pmod p$ and $m \cong \pm m_q \pmod q$
5. After calculating the 4 roots we go for redundancy method (discussed later) to determine the right one or else we return *NULL*.

*Note: **Rules for eliminating redundancy:** In order to be certain about getting right plain-text from a unique solution approach for decryption. Achieving this can require us to send a few extra bits (redundancy).*

Example

Let Alice wishes to communicate an information to Bob, so Bob has to generate the key.

Key Generation

Bob selects two large prime integers $i = 277$, $j = 331$, and calculates $n = i \times j = 91687$.

   public-key of Bob: $n = 91687$, and Bob keeps his private keys: $i = 277$, $j = 331$.

Encryption

In this case, as modified Rabin PKC redundancy property the $6\text{-}bits$ at the end of the information are needed to be cloned before actual encryption begins. For encrypting the $10\text{-}bits$ information $m = 1001111001$, Alice clones the $6\text{-}bits$ at the end of the information m such that it gets the $16 - bit$ information $m = 1001111001111001$, the decimal value will be $m = 40569$.
After this Alice calculates $c = m^2 \pmod n = 40569^2 \pmod{91687} = 62111$ and transmit this cipher-text c to Bob.

Decryption

In the process of decrypting c Bob execute the Rabin PKC's decryption algorithm (discussed above) plus the previously known formula for calculating the quadratic factors of n.

In order to calculate the 4-square roots $c \pmod{n}$: $m_1 = 69654, m_2 = 22033$, $m_3 = 40569, m_4 = 51118$, binary representation will be
$m_1 = 10001000000010110$,
$m_2 = 101011000010001$,
$m_3 = 1001111001111001$,
$m_4 = 1100011110101110$.
It can be observed that the m_3 is having the exactly needed redundancy. Bob will select m_3 as correct decrypted information of cipher-text c and recuperate the information $m = 1001111001$.

2.4.1 Draw-Back of Rabin PKC

In particular, cipher-text decryption process includes selection of one out of four possible output of a Rabin's decryption function. This is a major issue with Rabin's cryptosystem to identify the plain-text in unambiguous and deterministic way. This also increases the complexity as well as redundancy.

Chosen Cipher-Text Attack

Rabin PKC is certain about it's unbreakable encryption from intruder. It surrender in front of choosen cipher-text attack. Steps for this attack is:

1. An intruder chooses an arbitrary integer $m \in Z_n$ & calculates $c = m^2 \pmod{n}$
2. Then the intruder send c to Bob's decryption machine
3. Bob decrypts c and gives output let say $y \in plain\text{-}text$
4. Since Bob has no prior knowledge of m, and m is arbitrary selected, the y is need not to be equal as m.
5. With 50% chance $y ! \cong \pm m \pmod{n} \ldots where \ GCD(m - y, n)$ is being one possible prime factor of n.
6. Intruder will again perform the same attack if $y \cong \pm m \pmod{n}$.

Use of Redundancy

The major overhead of Rabin PKC is while recuperating the plain-text the receiver has to select the right plain-text out of 4 possible plaint-texts. In order to remove this problem we can add already known bits as post-fix or prefix into the original information $m \in plain\text{-}text$ before performing the encryption task.

Consider a scenario if we copy the last 64-bits of the information and post-fix it at the end of the information. Then, there is a high chance of preservation of redundancy by one of the decrypted plain-text i.e., four square roots m_1, m_2, m_3, m_4. The receiver can choose it easily as the correct plain-text. Whereas it can also identify the faulty cipher-text by an intruder if no redundancy is present in any-one of the square roots of cipher-text c.

Analysis of Using Redundancy

As discussed in the above paragraph that if redundancy removes the unpredictability of selecting correct plain-text from Rabin PKC. If an intruder chooses information m possessing the needed redundancy and sends $c = m^2$ (mod n) to Bob's decryption algorithm. There is a certain chance that the algorithm's output the plain-text m correct information back to the intruder (as the rest of the 3 resulted in square roots of received cipher-text c will not possess the needed redundancy). But if the intruder chooses information m without possessing the needed redundancy, then there is a certain chance that not a single one out of the four output of Bob's decryption algorithm i.e., the square roots of $c = m^2$ (mod n) will contain the needed redundancy. In the second scenario, Bob's decryption algorithm will not be able to select the correct plain-text m and therefore it will not give any reply to the intruder. *One point can be noted that the chosen cipher-text against the modified Rabin PKC is no longer holds good.*

Result of Using Redundancy

Nonetheless, The general approach for Rabin PKC is defined to be a combination of two tasks:

1. Initially the calculation of the four square roots of c (mod n)
2. Choosing the correct square root out of those 4 square root as the plain-text

Commercialization of modified Rabin PKC (with added redundancy) is a better choice.

2.5   Elliptic Curve Cryptography

The researcher Victor Miller and Neal Koblitz invented Elliptic curve cryptography (ECC) in year 1985. ECC proposed as an alternative to established public-key systems such as DSA and RSA. It has recently gained a lot of attention in industry and academia. If an elliptic curve is selected with proper precautions then there should not exist any sub-exponential approach which can solve the DLP, this is the main reason because of which many researchers are doing research in ECC. Even if the size of input keys and parameters are sufficiently smaller in comparison with RSA and DSA, similar level of information security is achieved by ECC. Nowadays smaller devices are gaining more popularity such as mobile phones, smart cards, IoTs & WSNs. These are the devices that require high security but have resource limitations. The ECC has emerged as a solution because of the small input parameters. ECC benefiting in quick calculations, consumption of less power for execution, save memory, and transmission bandwidth. There is another perk in the process of implementing ECC, We have various internal options (Lopez and Dahab 2000):

- Finite field which is initially chosen,
- Approach to implement the finite field computation,
- The type of elliptic curve,
- Technique for elliptic group operation, and
- Rules for the elliptic curve.

There are basically two fields for well defined ECC

1. Prime integer fields F_p.
2. Binary polynomial fields F_{2^m}.

Based on finite fields inner basic computations like point addition and point multiplication of ECC are described. Fast execution of these finite field computations including elliptic scalar multiplication is directly proportional to the performance of ECC. Even if we select the best approach for the finite field computations we can still improve the overall efficiency by selecting the appropriate finite fields (F_p or F_{2^m}) and corresponding elliptic curve. Finite field F_{2^m} is preferred in particular case of the hardware implementations. Another field F_p, is preferred when distinguished prime p is needed (e.g., a Mersenne prime or a generalized Mersenne prime) (Hoque and Saikia 2014; Solinas et al. 1999). If the requirement needs better scalar multiplication then one should choose a group of curves that can provide better computing performance to compute a scalar multiplication like Koblitz curves defined over F_{2^m}.

The above discussion shows that ECC provides various attribute selection in order to achieve better performance. In different scenarios, we can select various underlying choices to get overall improved performance.

2.5.1 Finite Fields

Here we will briefly discuss finite field arithmetic.

2.5.1.1 The Finite-Field F_p

Consider p is representing a large prime number then finite field F_p, termed as *prime field*, will have following set of numbers:

$$\{0, 1, 2, 3, \ldots, p - 1\}$$

Underlying arithmetic operations:

Addition

We have two elements $a, b \in F_p$, then $a + b$ (mod p) $= r$,
Value of r is equal to the remainder remaining after the division of $a + b$ by p
$\because 0 \le a \le p - 1$ and $0 \le b \le p - 1 \therefore 0 \le r \le p - 1$.

Above operation is termed as *addition-modulo-p*.

Multiplication

We have two elements $a, b \in F_p$, then $a \times b$ (mod p) $= s$, value of s is equal to the
remainder remaining after the division of $a \cdot b$ by p
$\because 0 \le a \le p - 1$ and $0 \le b \le p - 1 \therefore 0 \le s \le p - 1$.

Above operation is termed as *multiplication-modulo-p*.

2.5.1.2   The Finite-Field F_{2^m}

The finite field F_{2^m} termed as a *binary finite-field*, can be understood as a vector space
with m dimension $\in F_2$. Which means, m elements set $\alpha_0, \alpha_1, \ldots, \alpha_{m-1} \in F_{2^m}$ where
for each $a \in F_{2^m}$ 'a' can be uniquely defined as:

$$a = \sum_{i=0}^{m-1} \alpha_i a_i; \ldots where \ a_i \in 0, 1$$

The set $\alpha_0, \alpha_1, \ldots, \alpha_{m-1} \in F_{2^m}$ can be termed as basis of m over F_{2^m}. Next a can
also be represented as a base-2 elements $(a_0, a_1, \ldots, a_{m-1})$.

Second option of customization for cryptographer to design suitable a cryptography technique is bases of F_{2^m} over F_2:

- *Polynomial bases*
- *Normal bases*

Polynomial Basis

This can be understood by following formula:

$$f(x) = x^m + \sum_{i=0}^{m-1} f_i x^i \ldots here \ f_i \in 0, 1; \ for \ i = 0, 1, \ldots, m - 1$$

The function $f(x)$ is an exclusive polynomial with degree m over F_2. The function
$f(x)$ can be termed as a *reduction polynomial* function. There is one to one mapping
for every polynomials basis representation to reduction polynomial function. In this
type of scenario every binary polynomial (having *degree* $< m$) is projected by each
member of F_{2^m}. E.g. if $a \in F_{2^m}$ then it consist of sum of m numbers where $a_i \in 0, 1$:

$$a = a_{m-1}x^{m-1} + \cdots + a_1 x + a_0$$

a is also termed as field element where $a \in F_{2^m}$ can be represented as the string of m-bits $(a_{m-1} \ldots a_1 a_0)$.

Addition and multiplication are the two basic operation which needs to be discussed for polynomial representation having reduction polynomial function $f(x)$. In order to define the operations two elements are considered $a = (a_{m-1}, \ldots a_1 a_0)$ and $b = (b_{m-1} \ldots b_1 b_0)$

Addition bit-wise exclusive-or is performed for addition of $a + b$ the result is c and c can be represented as the string of m-bits: $c = (c_{m-1} \ldots c_1 c_0)$, the value of c bits is $c_i = (a_i + b_i) \pmod 2$.

Multiplication can be defined as a remainder of the division of the polynomial function $f(x)$ such that:

$$\left(\sum_{i=0}^{m-1} a_i x_i \right) \left(\sum_{i=0}^{m-1} b_i x_i \right)$$

is divided by $f(x)$. The multiplication over operators can be represented as $a \cdot b = c$ and c can be represented as the string of m-bits: $(c_{m-1} \ldots c_1 c_0)$, the value of c can be again given as $c(x)$ as the remainder of the division of the polynomial $c(x) = \sum_{i=0}^{m-1} c_i x_i$.

Normal Basis

This can be defined as F_{2^m} over F_2 which is in the form of $\beta, \beta^2, \ldots, \beta^{2m-1}$, where $\beta \in F_{2^m}$ (Hankerson et al. 2006). It is well informed by McEliece et al. that there will be always a basis will be available for finite groups (McEliece 2012). Which implies that, all the member a of F_{2^m} have representation like $a = \sum_{i=0}^{m-1} a_i \beta^{2^i} \ldots a_i \in 0, 1$. The member a can be represented as the string of m-bits $(a_0, a_1, \ldots, a_{m-1})$. We can get mathematical benefits from a normal basis description of F_{2^m} for example the squaring of a member's vector representation can be done by an easy step of shifting in circular, this operation can have another advantage of better hardware implementation. Whereas, multiplying various members becomes a more difficult task in comparison to squaring. Luckily, *Gaussian normal bases (GNB)* is a saver which is a sub-class of normal bases, GNB is capable of performing field arithmetic operations in a better way. In order to know the running time to multiplication of two members belonging to the basis an integer *type T* of the GNB, a cryptographer aims to design and select the finite group such a way that he can achieve a smaller value of the *type T*. It is obvious that smaller the value of T, the time for multiplying-task will be less. The use of GNB is more useful when the length of the operand is not in the multiplication of 8 (i.e., one byte). Moreover, if operands are multiple of 8 and $T > 0$ in that case *type T* GNB for F_{2^m} is valuable source and iff $p = Tm + 1$ has prime value and $Tm \div k$ is relatively prime to m i.e., $GCD(Tm/k, m) = 1$, The parameter k is having the value that is multiplicative order of 2 *modulo p*. *For more details on GNB one should refer* (Ash et al. 1989; Mullin et al. 1988).

Addition, Squaring and Multiplication are the three basic finite field operations which needs to be discussed for F_{2^m}, with the help of GNB having $type\ T$, are defined as follows. For operation definition two elements are considered $a = (a_{m-1} \ldots a_1 a_0)$ and $b = (b_{m-1} \ldots b_1 b_0)$

Addition Similar to polynomial-base bit-wise exclusive-or is performed for addition of $a + b$ the result is c and c can be represented as the string of m-bits: $c = (c_{m-1} \ldots c_1 c_0)$, the value of c bits is $c_i = (a_i + b_i) \pmod 2$.

Squaring: Since the operation square can be performed linearly over F_{2^m},

$$a^2 = \left(\sum_{i=0}^{m-1} a_i \beta^{2^i} \right)^2 = \sum_{i=0}^{m-1} a_i \beta^{2^{i+1}} = \sum_{i=0}^{m-1} a_{i-1} \pmod m \beta^{2^i} = (a_{m-1} a_0 a_1 \ldots a_{m-2}).$$

i.e., squaring of a member's vector representation can be done by an easy step of shifting in circular.

Multiplication: Here p and u be the member having order T where $p = Tm$ & $u \in F_p$. We can describe a series $F(1), F(2), \ldots, F(p-1)$ as:

$$F(2^i u^j \pmod p) = i \qquad for\ 0 \le i \le m-1;\ \ 0 \le j \le T-1$$

For each $l, 0 \le l \le m-1$, defined A_l and B_l by

$$A_l = \sum_{k=1}^{p-2} a_{F(k+1)+l} \cdot b_{F(p-k)+l},\ and$$

$$B_l = \sum_{k=1}^{m/2} (a_{k+l-1} \cdot b_{m/2+k+l-1} + b_{k+l-1} \cdot a_{m/2+k+l-1}) + A_l.$$

Then $a \cdot b = c = (c_0 c_1 \ldots c_{m-1})$, where:

$$c_l = \begin{cases} A_l\ if\ T\ is\ even & (2.7) \\ B_l\ if\ T\ is\ odd & (2.8) \end{cases}$$

The mapping of all possible value of l lies between $0 \le l \le m-1$, having the index values reduced to modulus m.

The elliptic curve parameters for cryptographic schemes should be carefully chosen in order to resist all known possible attacks.

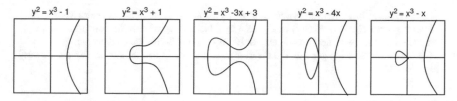

Fig. 2.4 Various elliptic curves

2.5.2 Elliptic Curve

In-general, the elliptic curve is a subsection of cubic curve and its solutions can be limited to a finite space which is topologically limited to a cyclic group.

Specifically, an elliptic curve defined over a finite field F is based on a non-singular *cubic curve* defined using two different parameters: $f(X, Y) = 0$, here the points can be defined at infinity. The finite-field F belongs to any one of the following fields:

- Real numbers
- Prime numbers
- Rational numbers
- Complex numbers

If the setting of field characteristics are set not equal to 2 or 3, and proper tuning of variables we can define a cubic curve as given in Eq. 2.9

$$C_1x^3 + C_2x^2y + C_3xy^2 + C_4y^3 + C_5x^2 + C_6xy + C_7y^2 + C_3x + C_8y + C_9 = 0$$

(2.9)

In Eq. 2.9 the constants $C_1, C_2, \ldots, C_9 \in F$, and the equation can be reformulated as Eq. 2.10

$$y^2 = x^3 + c_1x + c_2$$

(2.10)

The various elliptic curve for various values of c_1 and c_2 based on Eq. 2.10 is given in Fig. 2.4.

2.5.3 Elliptic Curve Public-Key Cryptography

After understanding the elliptic curve and related finite fields operations now, its time to discuss the Elliptic curve cryptography (ECC).

DLP for the ECC

The complexity for cryptanalysts to break the ECC is high because of the use of DLP in all elliptic curve cryptographic techniques (Hankerson et al. 2005). DLP for ECC can be defined as:

Let E_c be an elliptic curve such that $E_c \in F_p$ *or* $E_c \in F_{2^m}$ finite fields, consider a base point P in the curve E_c, $P \in E_c(F_p)$ or $P \in E_c(F_{2^m})$ having degree as n, and one more point Q in the curve, then we select an integer $l \in [0 : n - 1]$ which fulfill the condition: $Q = l \cdot P$. We can define this integer l as the discrete logarithm of Q to the base P, represented as $l = log_P Q$.

Domain Parameter

Elliptic curve cryptography over a curve E_c has the domain-parameters as F_p or F_{2^m} finite fields, and a point in the curve E_c, $P \in E_c(F_p)$ or $P \in E_c(F_{2^m})$ having degree as n, also termed as *base point*. The selection of parameters should be done with the motif of making ECC more robust and unbreakable by cryptanalysts-techniques that are already known. We can also apply other rules based on information security requirements or implementation requirements. Mostly, the domain-parameters are distributed inside a class of individuals or distributed to the users of specific application. All the elliptic curve E_c is over either a prime field F_p or a binary field F_{2^m}.

Domain-Parameters $D = (q, FR, a, b, P, n, S, h)$:

- The degree of field q.
- The representing parameter FR (field representative) for representing the members of F_p or F_{2^m}.
- Two coefficients $a, b \in F_p$ or F_{2^m} for the description of the formulation of the elliptic-curve E_c over F_p or F_{2^m} e.g.

$$y^2 = x^3 + ax + b \ldots for \; the \; curve \; over \; the \; prime \; field \; F_p \qquad (2.11)$$

$$y^2 + xy = x^3 + ax^2 + b \ldots \; for \; the \; curve \; over \; the \; prime \; field \; F_{2^m}. \tag{2.12}$$

- Two field elements or base point x_P and y_P in F_p or F_{2^m} that represent a finite point $P = (x_P, y_P) \in E_c(F_p$ or $F_{2^m})$ in positive coordinates and P has prime order.
- The order n of P.
- $S \leftarrow seed$ for the arbitrary generated elliptic curve in agreeing with algorithms to generate an elliptic curve E_c.
- The cofactor $h = \#E_c(F_p)/n$ or $h = \#E_c(F_{2^m})/n$.

Generating an Arbitrary Elliptic Curve E_c for a Prime Field F_p

The Algorithm 1 is given in Fig. 2.5 which shows the steps involved in generating the elliptic curve E_c over prime field (ECOPF).

Generating an Arbitrary Elliptic Curve E_c for a Prime Field F_{2^m}

Elliptic curve over a Binary Field F_{2^m} (ECOBF) Algorithm 2 is illustrated in Fig. 2.6.

Now we will discuss the basic three steps of the cryptography technique.

Algorithm 1 ECOPF algorithm

Input: Select $p > 3$, H of length $l - bit$ where $p \leftarrow prime\ H \leftarrow hash\ function$.
Output: a, b in F_p defining an elliptic curve $E_c : y^2 = x^3 + ax + b$.

1: Initialize $t \longleftarrow \lceil log_2 p \rceil, s \longleftarrow (t-1)/l, v \longleftarrow t - sl$ and $i \leftarrow 0$.
2: Choose a random bit string seed S having length $g \geq l$ bits.
3: Calculate $h = H(S)$, and assume r_0 is the bit string having v bits length which is acquired by taking the v rightmost bits of h.
4: Let R_0 be the bit string acquired by setting the leftmost bit of r_0 to 0.
5: Let z be the integer whose base-2 representation is S.
6: **while** $i \leq s$ **do**
7:     assuming s_i be the $g - bit$ base-2 representation of the integer $(z + i)$ $(mod\ 2^g)$.
8:     calculate $R_i = H(s_i)$ and $i = i + 1$.
9: **end while**
10: Let $R = R_0 || R_1 || \ldots || R_s$.
11: Let r be the integer whose base-2 representation is R.
12: **if** $r = 0\ or\ 4r + 27 \cong 0(\ (mod\ p))$ **then**
13:     go to step 2.
14: **end if**
15: Select arbitrary $a, b \in F_p$, not both 0, such that $r \cdot b^2 \equiv a^3(\ (mod\ p))$.
16: **Return** (S, a, b).

Fig. 2.5 ECOPF algorithm

Algorithm 2 ECOBF algorithm

Input: Select $m\ and\ H$ where $m > 0$ and H is l-bit hash function.
Output: S is a Seed, and $a, b \in F_{2^m}$ describe an elliptic curve $E_c : y^2 + xy = x^3 + ux^2 + b$.

1: Set $s \longleftarrow (m-1)/l, v \longleftarrow m - sl$ and $i \leftarrow 1$.
2: Choose a random bit string S of having $g \geq l$ bits.
3: Compute $h = H(S)$, and let b_0 be the bit string of length v bits obtained by taking the v rightmost bits of h.
4: Let z be the integer whose binary representation is S.
5: **while** $i \leq s$ **do**
6:     Let s_i be the $g - bit$ binary representation of the integer $(z + i)$ $(mod\ 2^g)$.
7:     Compute $b_i = H(s_i)$ and $i = i + 1$.
8: **end while**
9: Assume $b = b_0 || b_1 || \ldots || b_s$.
10: **if** $b = 0$ **then**
11:     go to step 2.
12: **end if**
13: Choose random $a \in F_{2^m}$.
14: **return** (S, a, b).

Fig. 2.6 ECOBF algorithm

Algorithm 3 ECC Encryption

> **Input:** Domain-parameters $D = (q, FR, S, a, b, P, n, h)$, public-key Q_B and plain-text m.
> **Output:** Ciphertext (K, C, t).

1: Choose random integer $r \in R[1, n-1]$.
2: Compute $K = rP$ and $Z = hrQ_B$.
3: **if** $Z = \infty$ **then**
4:     go to step 1.
5: **end if**
6: $(r_1, r_2) \longleftarrow KDF(x_Z, K)$, where x_Z is the $x-coordinate$ of Z.
7: Compute $C = E_{NC_{r_1}}(m)$
8: Compute $t = MAC_{r_2}(C)$.
9: **Return** (R, C, t).

Fig. 2.7 ECC encryption

Key Generation

For creation of Public and Private key for the receiver (Bob) under domain-parameters $(q, FR, a, b, P, n, S, h)$ for elliptic curve E_C. Below given steps are followed by Bob:

- Choose an arbitrary positive integer d_B in the range $[1, n-1]$
- Calculate $Q_B = d_B P \ldots . d_B \in R[1, n-1]$.
- Bob's public-key will be Q_B and Bob's private key will be d_B.

Encryption

The input parameters of ECC encryption is domain-parameter D, public-key Q_B and a message m(plain-text), whereas the output is a cipher-text c. In order to encrypt a message m for Bob, Alice performs certain steps which is given in the Algorithm 3 (refer Fig. 2.7):

At last the encrypted message is sent through send function: *Send* (K, C, t) to Bob.

Decryption

The decryption algorithm which is performed by receiver Bob the algorithm takes three parameters as input Domain-Parameter D, the private key d, a cipher-text C, as an output the Algorithm 4 is shown in Fig. 2.8 performs a validation check on cipher-text c as valid or invalid if valid then gives a plain-text m, as output.

To decrypt a cipher-text $(K; C; t)$, Bob performs certain steps which is given in Algorithm 4 in Fig. 2.8:

Algorithm 4 ECC Decryption

Input: Domain parameters $D = (q, FR, S, a, b, P, n, h)$, private key d_b, ciphertext (K, C, t).
Output: Plaintext m or rejection of the ciphertext.

1: Perform a partial key validation on K.
2: Compute $Z = hd_B K = (x_Z; y_Z)$.
3: **if** $K = \infty$ **then**
4:    Reject C.
5: **end if**
6: Compute $r_1 \| r_2 = KDF(x_Z)$.
7: Verify that $t = MAC_{r_2}(C)$.
8: Compute $m = ENC_{r_1}^{-1}(C)$.

Fig. 2.8 ECC decryption

Example

If we consider elliptic curve arithmetic for finite fields then geometric analysis of this arithmetic is not generalized. Whereas, analyzing of the elliptic curve arithmetic for real numbers with the help of algebraic analysis is straightforward, so we choose this approach. This approach also has some constrains because we are using real numbers. There is a limitation of equation format like Eq. 2.11. Whereas, for this scenario the coefficients and variables are having finite field F_p and we define curve E_c over it i.e., $E_c(F_p)$:

$$y^2 \ (\text{mod } p) = (x^3 + ax + b) \ (\text{mod } p) \tag{2.13}$$

Let us take an example which meets the requirements of parameters of Eq. 2.13.

$$a = 1$$
$$b = 1$$
$$x = 9$$
$$y = 7$$
$$\alpha = 1$$
$$p = 23$$
$$7^2 \ (\text{mod } 23) = (9^3 + 9 + 1) \ (\text{mod } 23)$$
$$49 \ (\text{mod } 23) = 739 \ (\text{mod } 23)$$
$$3 = 3$$

After this we create a set $S_p(a, b)$ having each possible combination of integers (x, y) such a way in which it meets all the requirements of the parameters of the Eq. 2.13, including a points up to infinity ∞. Parameters a, b are the coefficients of the equation and parameters x and y are capable to hold the points in the curve that belongs to F_p.

Table 2.2 Elements of set S_{23} for eliptic curve

(0, 1)	(6, 4)	(12, 19)
(0, 22)	(6, 19)	(13, 7)
(1, 7)	(7, 11)	(13, 16)
(1, 16)	(7, 12)	(17, 3)
(3, 10)	(9, 7)	(17, 20)
(3, 13)	(9, 16)	(18, 3)
(4, 0)	(11, 3)	(18, 20)
(5, 4)	(11, 20)	(19, 5)
(5, 19)	(12, 4)	(19, 18)

Consider a scenario where the finite field's prime base is $p = 23$ and we construct an elliptic curve E_c based on Eq. 2.13 i.e., $y^2 = x^3 + x + 1$. This equation has the coefficients $a = b = 1$ and the set S_{23} will be created having all possible values for (x, y). The coefficients $(a, b) = (1, 1)$, but we will consider only positive values in the quadrant in range from $(0, 0)$ to $(p - 1, p - 1)$. This consideration will also fulfill the requirements of the modulus (mod p). The Table 2.2 tabulates all the positive points (except 0) which belongs to the set S_{23} for coefficients $(a, b) = (1, 1)$.

Note: All points but one, are symmetric around the axis y = 11.5.

We observed for a finite abelian group the set S_p having coefficient (a, b) of Eq. 2.13 is having unique factors. This scenario is similar for the:

$$4a^3 + 27b^2 \quad (\text{mod } p) \neq 0 \quad (\text{mod } p) \tag{2.14}$$

Now, for the value of Q such that $Q = kP$ $\because Q, P \in S_P$ having coefficient (a, b) and $k < p$. This is one way process i.e., one can compute Q if he has the value of k and P, but it is intractable to find k if having the value of Q and P. This is known as the discrete logarithmic problem (DLP) for elliptic curves (Keller et al. 2009).

Let us take a point $(9, 17)$ from the set S_{23}. we can rewrite the Eq. 2.13 using this point pair as:

$$y^2 \quad (\text{mod } 23) = (x^3 + 9x + 17) \quad (\text{mod } 23)$$

Now, the next question is What will be the discrete logarithm value of k if $Q = (4, 5)$ having the base point $P = (16, 5)$?

There is a brute-force approach that will calculate by multiplying P to itself until Q is found.

$P = \{16, 5\}; P \times P = 2P = \{20, 20\}; 2P \times P = 3P = \{14, 14\};$

$3P \times P = 4P = \{19, 20\}; 4P \times P = 5P = \{13, 10\}; 5P \times P = 6P = \{17, 32\};$

$6P \times P = 7P = \{18, 72\}; 7P \times P = 8P = \{12, 17\}; 8P \times P = 9P = \{4, 5\}$

Table 2.3 Elements of set $S_{2^4}(g^4, 1)$ for eliptic curve

(0, 1)	(g^5, g^3)	(g^9, g^{13})
$(1, g^6)$	(g^5, g^{11})	(g^{10}, g)
$(1, g^{13})$	(g^6, g^8)	(g^{10}, g^8)
(g^3, g^8)	(g^6, g^{14})	$(g^{12}, 0)$
(g^3, g^{13})	(g^9, g^{10})	(g^{12}, g^{12})

Table 2.4 Exponent values of generator g

$g^0 = 0001$	$g^4 = 0011$	$g^8 = 0101$	$g^{12} = 1111$
$g^1 = 0010$	$g^5 = 0110$	$g^9 = 1010$	$g^{13} = 1101$
$g^2 = 0100$	$g^6 = 1100$	$g^{10} = 0111$	$g^{14} = 1001$
$g^3 = 1000$	$g^7 = 1011$	$g^{11} = 1110$	$g^{15} = 0001$

We got the value $9P = \{4, 5\} = Q$, which is the discrete logarithm of Q having the base point $P = (16, 5)$ which means $k = 9$. The above given was just an example but in a real-world scenario, the value of k would be so large which will not allow the brute force technique to be computationally feasible in time.

Example curve over F_{2^m} Based on the requirements of cryptographic applications we select finite field either prime finite field F_p or binary finite field F_{2^m}. The elliptic curves E_c over binary finite field F_{2^m} is created with a cubic equation. The parameters (variables and coefficients) of this cubic equation belongs to the binary finite field F_{2^m}. There exist some value of m for the arithmetic operations (multiplication or addition) are done based on the rules of arithmetic in binary finite field F_{2^m}. From implementation point of view, the cubic equation is more suitable for binary finite field F_{2^m} than for prime finite field F_p. The representation of the equation is:

$$y^2 + xy = x^3 + ax^2 + b$$

Here the parameter's values are clearing the fact that variables (x, y) and coefficients (a, b) belongs to binary finite field F_{2^m} moreover, the results of the arithmetic computations also belongs to the binary finite field F_{2^m}.

We assume that set S_{2^m} for coefficient (a, b) has each possible pairs of variables (x, y) which is fulfilling the requirements of the Eq. 2.12, along with a point at infinity.

The Table 2.3 illustrates an example of the binary finite field F_{2^4} along with the exclusive polynomial equation $f(x) = x^4 + x + 1$. We can get the value of a generator variable g which fulfils the condition $f(g) = 0$ using $g^4 = g + 1$, or in base-2, $g = 0010$. Generation of the exponent values of generator g can be done as given in Table 2.4.

Key Exchange

We consider a scenario where base point $p = 211$ and seed is $S_p(0, -4)$, This assumption satisfy the curve $E_c : y^2 = x^3 - 4$; let us take generating point $g = (2, 2)$.

We can compute that $240g = \infty$.
Now the key-pair for Alice:

- Private key: $n_A = 121$,
- Public key: $P_A = 121(2, 2) = (115, 48)$

And the key-pair of Bob:

- Private key: $n_B = 203$,
- Public key: $203(2, 3) = (130, 203)$.

now both will calculate the common key as secret-key: $121\ (130, 203) = 203$ $(115, 48) = (161, 69)$.

Encryption

As Alice is the one who wants to send the message therefore she uses the generator g using which they have calculated the common secret key. She uses the set over base point called an elliptic set S_p with coefficients (a, b). Sender Alice has the private key n_A and she wants to communicate a message m to Bob.

1. First of all, she chooses an arbitrary integer k where $k > 0$
2. Computes the encrypted message c (cipher-text) with the help of shared common keys.
3. The encrypted message c is consists of points which can be computed as:

$$c = kg, m + kP_B$$

Alice hides the original message m by summation of a product kP_B with m. The main feature is the arbitrary integer k which is known to Alice only. The public-key P_b is known to all, but getting the hidden message because of the product kP_B is an intractable task. The one who knows the private-key n_B is the only one who is capable of decoding the encrypted message c. If an intruder wants to break the cipher-text to obtain the original message, the intruder needs to find the k (which was arbitrary selected by Alice) and calculate kg given g, which is infeasible in non-polynomial time.

Decryption

As Bob knows that his public-key P_B is used to encrypt the message m and he received the encrypted message c. In the process of decryption Bob follows these simple steps,

1. He calculate the product of the 1st part in the pair (kg) and his secret-key(n_B):
   $V1 = n_B \cdot (kg)$
2. Then he deduct that product from the 2nd part of the received cipher-text: $V2 - V1$ where $V2 = m + kP_B$

$$V2 - V1 = m + kP_B - n_B(kg) = m + k(n_Bg) - n_B(kg) = m.$$

2.6   PKC in Wireless-Sensor-Networks (WSN)

Secret-key cryptography is mostly used for information security by small devices and networks which has hardware constraints like wireless sensor networks. As the secret-key cryptography has less computational complex algorithms which is a strong point to use it. It is also desirable to have session keys to be embedded in the sensor devices prior to the installation. There is an overhead of updating this session key because, a proper communication and memory space is needed. The communication should be governed by a proper protocol that is responsible for synchronizing the session-keys of all the nodes in the network. During this synchronization secrecy of session-key is not ensured by secret-key cryptography, this is a disadvantage which cannot be ignored (Quirino et al. 2012; Sen 2012).

On the other hand, it is a general perception that PKC approaches are comparatively not so fast and also require much power for execution, as a result the architectural overhead is high. With the help of a hardware/software co-design technique, the PKC based technique can be implemented for a number of WSNs. The aim of the designer should be the light-weight hardware architecture with efficient use of limited resources for implementing PKC.

2.7   Possible Attacks on PKC

As we already know there are two sides of Cryptology, one is cryptography and another is cryptanalysis. While cryptography is the task of constructing a robust PKC, on the other hand, the Public-Key Cryptanalysis the cryptanalysts try to perform analysis on cipher-text, encryption algorithms or maybe on complete cryptosystems (whatever accessible). Their goal is to break or find weak-links in the established cryptosystems. In this process, they also tend to get knowledge of the working cryptosystem as much as possible and improve their own approaches to discover the defects. A cryptanalyst aims to get more useful information about the plain-text source, secret-key, or the approach using which the cipher-text is prepared. The target of cryptanalysts is not only PKC it also aims to break secret-hashing, DSS, and other cryptography approaches.

The counter effect of cryptanalysis is a positive point for cryptographers as they can use the defects found by cryptanalysts to remove the weak-links or any flaws present in their cryptographic approach, such that they can design a more robust cryptosystem. Both the parties (the cryptographer and cryptanalysts) studies under one umbrella i.e., cryptology, which is all about the arithmetic of programs, encoding, and other cryptosystem related algorithms. In the process of breaking a cryptography technique the cryptanalysts can achieve either of two things:

- He can totally break the encryption code, i.e., get the original message without any proper knowledge of the private key.

- He can reduce the size of the possible key set, such that try and hit method can have a small size of key-set.

The first achievement by cryptanalyst is to completely destroy the cryptographer design where-as the second one weakens the design. Most of the time the cryptanalyst achieves the second and helps the cryptographer to improve their design.

Let us take an encryption scheme of a 128-bit private-key having 2^{128} different keys.

Now if we apply, a brute force attack to break this encryption it can achieve the break-through just by trying 50% of these different keys. In the process of breaking the encryption scheme, the cryptanalyst can also achieve a reduction in the size of the key-set 2^{40} which is needed to be tried for getting the plain-text. In this way, the cryptanalyst shows weak-links of the algorithm. Once a brute-force approach is capable of breaking the cryptosystem then commercial implementation is not an option.

Cryptanalysis has its significance in the information security world and many other important fields such as, the country's army are trying to decode the private information of the other nation's army. Information security companies hire cryptanalysts for the development and testing of their information security products, whereas independent entities like hackers, academicians and researchers are continuously trying to find the weak-links in cryptosystems. There is a continuous competition where the cryptographers are making more robust cryptosystems and cryptanalysts are giving their efforts to break that cryptosystems and the overall technology of cryptology is growing ahead.

The task of cryptanalyst is to acquire as much as possible information about the cipher-text, encryption algorithm and private-key. Depending on the acquired information the cryptanalysis attacks are classified. Few crypt-analytic techniques are:

Cipher-Text Only Attack	In this attack the intruder has information only about the few cipher-text but has no information about the original message or encryption method or private-key. This type of analysis is performed by the organizations that intercept private information from a secure channel.
Known Plain-Text Attack	In this type of attack the intruder has the information about some original message i.e., plain-text and it's encrypted cipher-text. The intruder aims to guess the right private key, in a process so that he can retrieve the original message from an upcoming cipher-text. Most of the time the public-key is easily available but the tracking of private-key is hard. If an intruder succeed in his aim of finding the private-key then the intruder can retrieve all original messages from cipher-text which was

	encrypted with the help of that key. An example of this class is *Linear cryptanalysis* which takes the help of a linear approximation technique that defines how this attack is guessing the original message from the cipher-text. Just for a scenario if the intruder knows the name of the receiver then he can treat the name of that person as plain-text.
Chosen Plain-Text Attack	Intruder has temporary access to *encryption machinery* without revealing the key K, using which intruder has some plain-text and cipher-text (P_i, C_i) pair values. Here the goal is to get Key K and to guess new plain-text p* from new cipher-text c*. In this case, the cryptanalyst has one of the two ways of getting the plain-text and corresponding cipher-text both from an encryption algorithm i.e., 1st is that he has knowledge of the encryption algorithm or 2 is that he has some privilege of the system using which encryption can be performed. The analyst will gather enough number of plain-text and cipher-text pair and then he will try to guess the private key.
Chosen Cipher-Text Attack	Similar to chosen plain-text attack here the attacker has temporary access of decryption machinery to attack and obtain some (C_i, P_i) pair values. The goal is to get key K and guess new plain-text p* from new cipher-text c*.
Differential Crypt-Analysis Attack	In this attack the analysis is done on the pair of plain-texts and tries to get some information about the working mechanism of the encryption algorithm. The intruder tries to learn how the encryption algorithm responds to different types of text input. This attack is a sub-class of the chosen plain-text attack on block ciphers when it encounters different types of data.
Integral Cryptanalysis Attack	This type of attack is somehow equal to differential cryptanalysis attacks. In this case, the intruder uses sets of plain-text in place of pairs of plain-texts, The set is treated in two parts one part of this set is kept unchanged whereas the other part of the plain-text is altered. If the encryption algorithm is based on substitution-permutation then this type of attack is useful.

Side Channel Attack	In this type of attack the intruder collects the information by the physical means. Intruders can install a bug into a cryptosystem. The bug is capable of measuring the power and running time of the encryption algorithm. Here the intruder is not concern about the cipher-text, plain-text, or algorithm but he wants the information about the time and power fluctuation of the system while responding to a particular input. The bug can observe the level of power used by the cryptographic system, or electromagnetic radiation which is coming out of the cryptographic system.
Dictionary Attack	This is the attack that usually comes into consideration when the target is user's password. By analyzing the human nature of choosing the password, which is usually the daily used words or series which can be guessed without so much effort. The working of this attack is like it keeps the record of all the possible words with its encrypted cipher-text. When some new queries come then the mapping is done with the stored cipher-texts.
Man In The Middle Attack	This type of attack is done by an intruder who is capable of playing the role of one entity between communicating entities. The entities can communicate either by PKC or by symmetric-key cryptography. If the intruder gets himself inside the network and started to play the role on behalf of one entity then entities exchange keys with intruders by believing him to be a trusted entity. Then two entities unknowingly share the keys with an intruder.

Still, few more cryptanalysis attacks are there which can use the above attacks as base or combination of those. It can be used for hacking the private-key or making users reveal their passwords. Examples are:

- Planting the Trojan horse programs
- Convincing the user for installing a weak cryptosystem.

The Side-channel attacks can be termed as timing or differential power analysis attack. These attacks gain popularity during the last decade of the 19th century when cryptographer Paul Kocher was analyzing the outcome of his work done for timing-attacks and differential-power-analysis for PKC. The smart-card use was mostly effected by this approach.

Another way to attack is based on a mathematical approach that is, if one can break the IFP and DLP. Which to date not proved to be unbreakable but, there is no efficient approach that has been found to solve the problem. The most widely used PKCs are based on these problems only like RSA, ECC, DSA, etc.

One more attack is there which is particular for PKC. This attack concentrates on the probability of occurring a message in a communication. Let us consider a scenario where the message, which needs to be communicated is made up of only 56-$Bits$ DES this is encrypted and communicated over the network. If the intruder is capable of encrypting all possible 56-$Bits$ DES keys using the same public key and he can match the same with the communicated encrypted message. Therefore the attack size is decreased to a brute-force attack on 56-$Bits$ key-length. It can be overcome by appending a few arbitrary bits to every message.

There are few more cryptanalysis technique based on software and hardware implementation of PKC, we will see those in next chapters.

Trade-off Between Key Size and Practical Implementation
The use of long-length keys is required to overcome the brute force approach for breaking any PKC or any secret-key cryptography. But the use of the long-length key is having its own disadvantage as the practical implementation of these long-length keys causes computational overhead. The PKC has its encryption and decryption is composed of complex arithmetic operations, also that it has few invertible arithmetic methods. The complexity of these encryption functions is not linear it increases exponentially with respect to the length of the key. Therefore, the length of the key needs to be as long as it should be hard for a brute-force attack to break the code. At the same time it should be small that can satisfy the practical implementation needs of the algorithms. The longer length keys in real-world problems make it unbreakable for brute-force attack but also results in decreasing the execution speed. It makes the encryption & decryption operation to take more time for completion. Key-length management is one of the limitations of PKC which is a continuous field of research.

References

Ash DW, Blake IF, Vanstone SA (1989) Low complexity normal bases. Disc. Appl. Math. 25(3):191–210

Brent RP (2000) Recent progress and prospects for integer factorisation algorithms. In: International computing and combinatorics conference, Springer, pp 3–22

Diffie W, Hellman M (1976) New directions in cryptography. IEEE Trans. Inf. Theory 22(6):644–654

ElGamal T (1985) A public key cryptosystem and a signature scheme based on discrete logarithms. IEEE Trans. Inf. Theory 31(4):469–472

Galbraith SD (2012) Mathematics of public key cryptography. Cambridge University Press, Cambridge

Hankerson D, Menezes AJ, Vanstone S (2005) Guide to elliptic curve cryptography. Comput. Rev. 46(1):13

Hankerson D, Menezes AJ, Vanstone S (2006) Guide to elliptic curve cryptography. Springer Science & Business Media, Berlin

Hoque A, Saikia HK (2014) On generalized mersenne prime. SeMA Journal 66(1):1–7

Keller M, Byrne A, Marnane WP (2009) Elliptic curve cryptography on fpga for low-power applications. ACM Trans. Reconfig. Technol. Syst. (TRETS) 2(1):1–20

Lopez J, Dahab R (2000) An overview of elliptic curve cryptography

McEliece RJ (2012) Finite fields for computer scientists and engineers, vol 23. Springer Science & Business Media, Berlin

Menezes Alfred J (1997) Handbook of applied cryptography/alfred j. menezes, paul c. van oorschot, scott a. vanstone

Mullin RC, Onyszchuk IM, Vanstone SA, Wilson RM (1988) Optimal normal bases in gf (pn). Discr. Appl. Math. 22(2):149–161

Quirino GS, Ribeiro AR, Moreno ED (2012) Asymmetric encryption in wireless sensor networks. In: Wireless sensor networks-technology and protocols, InTech, pp 219–232

Rabin MO (1979) Digitalized signatures and public-key functions as intractable as factorization. Technical report, Massachusetts Institute of Technology, Cambridge Lab for Computer Science

Rivest RL, Shamir A, Adleman L (1978) A method for obtaining digital signatures and public-key cryptosystems. Commun. ACM 21(2):120–126

Sen J (2012) Security in wireless sensor networks. In: Wireless sensor networks: current status and future trends, pp. 407–408

Solinas JA, et al (1999) Generalized mersenne numbers. Citeseer

Stallings W (2006) Cryptography and network security, 4/E. Pearson Education India

Part II
Modular Exponentiation

Chapter 3
Modular Exponential Techniques

1. Left-to-Right binary modular exponential technique
2. Right-to-Left binary modular exponential technique
3. Sliding window techniques
4. Bit forwarding techniques

The solution of the problem *"what is the least number of multiplications for calculating g^e, if we already know that we can only perform multiplication operation of two already computed exponentiation of g?"* is kept in the set of NP-complete problem set (Nedjah et al. 2007). It is hard to prove that this problem is not in the set by giving any perfect solution. Eventhough, researchers have attempted to decrease the number of multiplications needed to get the final exponent value. Algorithms following this approach mostly perform some pre-computation on base-2 bit-wise representation of the exponent e, to arrange the bits in such a way that it can efficiently get the repeating pattern and use it as square-and-multiply calculation to get the final result of the modular exponent.

3.1 Binary Modular Exponential Technique

Various approaches for calculating g^e for a random and considerably large integer e where $e > 0$ has been proposed. It is observed that all the approaches with binary framework fits into one of two prevailing classes, these classes will be discussed in this section. The binary representation of *Exponent e* is given in Eq. 3.1.

$$e = \sum_{i=0}^{l} b_i \times 2_i \tag{3.1}$$

© The Author(s), under exclusive license to Springer Nature Switzerland AG 2021
S. Vollala et al., *Energy-Efficient Modular Exponential Techniques*
for Public-Key Cryptography, https://doi.org/10.1007/978-3-030-74524-0_3

The two classes based on binary representation are left-to-right approach and right-to-left approach. These approaches are adopted by most of the modular exponentiation techniques (Möller et al. 2003). Here the Left-to-right approach operates on bits b_i from b_l i.e., most significant bit (MSB) and proceed towards the b_0 i.e., least significant bit (LSB). Whereas the right-to-left approaches begin with b_0 i.e., LSB and proceed towards b_l i.e., MSB. These two classes can remove the overhead of storing the binary-representation b_i prior to the actual exponentiation operation by calculating them at the time of requirement.

3.1.1 Left-to-Right Binary Exponential Technique

The evaluation of a left-to-right approach can have the already stored values of base-2 representation of exponent e in bits as b_i which is easy to access. Another way of getting the bits is during run time while computing the exponentiation. The given Algorithm 1 shown in Fig. 3.1 performs the computation of the asked exponentiation having the already computed value of g_b here b is $base = 2$. In this approach, we move from MSB to LSB.

In the given left to right exponent Algorithm 1 shown in Fig. 3.1 we compute the output of g^e exponentiation. First, we check that if MSB is non zero or not if it is non-zero then we initialize the Result R with base g, or if MSB is zero then we initialize the Result R with 1. Then we enter the loop which will run until the LSB is processed. Here in the loop we square the result R for each bit but multiply with the base g only if the bit of this exponent e_i is having non-zero value. At last, we return the final result.

Algorithm 1 Left to Right Binary Exponentiation algorithm

    Input: g, e
    Output: $S = g^e$

1: *Initialize* $i = l - 2$ ▷ Exponent is having length of l
2: **if** $e_{l-1} = 1$ **then**   ▷ If MSB is non-zero element
3:     $R = g$
4: **else** $R = 1$
5: **end if**
6: **while** $i \geq 0$ **do**
7:     $R \leftarrow R^2$
8:     **if** $e_i = 1$ **then**
9:         $R = R \times g$
10:     **end if**
11: **end while**
12: Return R

Fig. 3.1 Left to right binary exponentiation algorithm

Table 3.1 Example for exponent e = 55 using left-to-right binary exponentiation method

i	4	3	2	1	0
e_i	1	0	1	1	1
for MSB: $R = g$	$R = R \times R$ $R = R^2 \times g$	$R = R^3 \times R^3$	$R = R^6 \times R^6$ $R = R^{12} \times g$	$R = R^{13} \times R^{13}$ $R = R^{26} \times g$	$R = R^{27} \times R^{27}$ $R = R^{54} \times g$
Result $R = g$	g^3	g^6	g^{13}	g^{27}	g^{55}
					Final Result: $R = g^{55}$

Consider a scenario where the exponent is calculated by Left to Right binary exponentiation Algorithm 1 shown in Fig. 3.1. The base g is an integer where the exponent is $e = 55 = (110111)$. The length of the exponent is 6 i.e., $l = 6$ since the last bit e_{l-1} i.e., $e_5 = 1$, the algorithm will initialize the result R with base g ($R = g$), processing of rest of the bits is given in the Table 3.1. The values of R, i & e_i at each iteration of the loop in Algorithm 1 shown in Fig. 3.1.

Note that in the Algorithm 1 shown in the Fig. 3.1, we have omitted square function to execute for the first iteration using the conditional statement in *Step 1*, In the same way, the multiplication can be performed by an assignment and division assignment followed by inversion of exponent e.

3.1.2 Right-to-Left Binary Exponential Technique

In left-to-right binary exponential technique we can compute the bits of exponent on the fly. Whereas, for the calculation of a right-to-left approach we have two ways first one is to have the already stored values of base-2 representation of exponent e in bits which is easy to access but increases the space complexity, or another way is to calculate the bits on the fly while computing the exponentiation similar to left-to-right approach. The given Algorithm 2 shown in Fig. 3.2 performs the computation of the asked exponentiation having the already computed value of g_b here b is $base = 2$. In this approach, we move from LSB to MSB. Here we use one extra memory register termed as *accumulator A*. With the help of accumulator precomputation steps which was required by the left-to-right algorithm can be ignored. Accumulators A_i are used to store intermediate values inside the loop and then at last all the values of accumulators are combined in order to get the final result. The right-to-left binary exponential Algorithm 2 is shown in Fig. 3.2.

The aim is to minimize the number of multiplications required for calculation of g^e. The brute force approach will calculate the same by multiplying the base g for e times. It is observed if we perform the same by alternate approach going bit-wise and calculate $g^1 \times g^2 \times g^4$. We can easily compute $g^2 = g \times g$ or $g^4 = g^2 \times g^2$ and so using less number of multiplications. Let us take an example where the base is g and exponent $e = 283$. The brute force approach will calculate the result in 283

Algorithm 2 Right to Left Binary Exponentiation algorithm

Input: g, e
Output: $R = g^e$

1: *Initialize $R = 1, A = g, i = 0$*
2: **while** $i \leq l - 2$ **do** $\triangleright$ l is the length of exponent's binary string
3:      **if** $e_i = 1$ **then**
4:          $R = R \times A$
5:      **end if**
6:      $A = A \times A$
7:      $i = i + 1$
8: **end while**
9: **if** $e_{l-1} = 1$ **then** $R = R \times A$
10: **end if**
11: return R.

Fig. 3.2 Right to left binary exponentiation algorithm

Table 3.2 Example for exponent e = 283 using right to left binary exponentiation method

i	e_i	for LSB: $A = g$	Intermediate Result $R = 1$
0	1	$R = R \times A$ $A = A \times A$	$R = g$; $A = g^2$
1	1	$R = R \times A$ $A = A \times A$	$R = g^3$; $A = g^4$
2	0	$A = A \times A$	$R = g^3$; $A = g^8$
3	1	$R = R \times A$ $A = A \times A$	$R = g^{11}$; $A = g^{16}$
4	1	$R = R \times A$ $A = A \times A$	$R = g^{27}$; $A = g^{32}$
5	0	$A = A \times A$	$R = g^{27}$; $A = g^{64}$
6	0	$A = A \times A$	$R = g^{27}$; $A = g^{128}$
7	0	$A = A \times A$	$R = g^{27}$; $A = g^{256}$
			Final Result: $R = g^{283}$

multiplications. The discussed right-to-left Algorithm 2 shown in Fig. 3.2 can achieve the same with a lot of reduced amount of multiplication. Binary representation of e would be $(100011011)_2$ i.e., the length $l = 9$ and loop will run for $l - 1$ times i.e., 8 times. The given Table 3.2 gives the values of i, e_i, A, R at each iteration of the loop in the Algorithm 2 shown in Fig. 3.2.

With-Out Pre-Computing the Exponent's Binary Values

The Algorithm 2 shown in Fig. 3.2 is using pre-computed exponent e binary values. There is another approach where we can perform the same without any pre-computation i.e., compute the same while calculating multiplication (Tandrup et al.

Algorithm 3 Right to Left Exponentiation algorithm With-Out Pre-Computing Exponent's Binary Representation

---

Input: g, e
Output: $R = g^e$

1: *Initialize* $R = 1, A = g$
2: **while** $e \neq 0$ **do**
3:     **if** e is odd **then**   ▷ That means MSB is 1
4:         $R = R \times A$
5:         $e = \lfloor \frac{e}{2} \rfloor$
6:     **end if**
7:     **if** $e \neq 0$ **then**
8:         $A = A \times A$
9:     **end if**
10: **end while**
11: return R.

Fig. 3.3 Right to left exponentiation algorithm with-out pre-computing exponent's binary representation

2004). This algorithm uses the knowledge of relation between LSB and even-odd integer. If integer is odd the LSB is 1 and if integer is even the LSB is 0. The Algorithm 3 is shown in Fig. 3.3.

3.1.3 Applying Modulus Operation in Exponential Technique

The two techniques i.e., *left-to-right and right-to-left binary exponential techniques* calculates the exponent for a given number. Whereas, for PKC we need to evaluate modular exponentiation. We can apply modulus operation in between the stages given in the Algorithms 1 and 3 given in Figs. 3.1 and 3.3 respectively.

Property of modular multiplication which is stated in Eq. 3.2

$$a^N \pmod{m}$$
$$= [(a^{N/2} \pmod{m}) \times (a^{N/2} \pmod{m})] \pmod{m} \qquad (3.2)$$
$$= [(a^P \pmod{m}) \times (a^Q \pmod{m})] \pmod{m}$$

$$... N = P \times Q$$

From given Eq. 3.2 we can modify the Algorithms 1 and 3 (refer Figs. 3.1 and 3.3) such that the size of any intermediate result will not exceed more than modular m which will help in computing the modular exponential value of large numbers in less space and time.

First modify the Left to Right Binary Exponentiation algorithm:

Algorithm 4 Left to Right Binary Modular Exponentiation algorithm

---

Input: g, e, m
Output: $R = g^e$ (mod m)

1: *Initialize i = l − 2*   ▷ Exponent is having length of *l*
2: **if** $e_{l-1} = 1$ **then** $R = g$
3: **else**
4:      $R = 1$
5: **end if**
6: **while** $i \geq 0$ **do**
7:      $R \leftarrow R^2$ (mod m)   ▷ applying modulus operation.
8:      **if** $e_i = 1$ **then**
9:          $R = R \times g$ (mod m)   ▷ applying modulus operation.
10:     **end if**
11:     $i = i - 1$
12: **end while**
13: return R

Fig. 3.4 Left to right binary modular exponentiation algorithm

Table 3.3 Example for exponent e = 55, modulus m = 10, base g = 7 using left-to-right binary modular exponentiation algorithm

i	e_i	For MSB: $R = 7$	Intermediate Result $R = 7$
4	1	$R = 7 \times 7 \, mod \, 10$ $R = 9 \times 7 \, mod \, 10$	$R = 3$
3	0	$R = 3 \times 3 \, mod \, 10$	$R = 9$
2	1	$R = 9 \times 9 \, mod \, 10$ $R = 1 \times 7 \, mod \, 10$	$R = 7$
1	1	$R = 7 \times 7 \, mod \, 10$ $R = 9 \times 7 \, mod \, 10$	$R = 3$
0	1	$R = 3 \times 3 \, mod \, 10$ $R = 9 \times 7 \, mod \, 10$	$R = 3$
			Final Result $= R = 3$

Let us take an example and try to solve with the given Algorithm 4 (refer Fig. 3.4). e.g. for $g = 7, m = 10, e = 55 = (110111)$. The length of the exponent is 6 but MSB $e_5 = 1$, the initialization of modified LR algorithm is same as previous and it begins with $R = 10$, and proceeds as given in Table 3.3.

Now, let us modify the Right to Left Binary Exponentiation Algorithm 2 shown in Fig. 3.2, by applying modular m to the intermediate steps.

Let us take an example and solve with the Algorithm 5 shown in Fig. 3.5. E.g. for $g = 7, m = 10, e = 283 = (100011011)$. The length of the exponent is 9 but MSB $e_8 = 1$, the initialization of modified RL algorithm is same as previous and it begins with $R = 1$ and $A = 7$, and proceeds as given in Table 3.4.

Algorithm 5 Right to Left Binary Modular Exponentiation algorithm

Input: g, e, m
Output: $R = g^e \pmod{m}$

1: *Initialize $R = 1, A = g, i = 0$*
2: **while** $i \leq l - 2$ **do**   ▷ l is the length of exponent's binary string
3:     **if** $e_i = 1$ **then**
4:         $R = R \times A \pmod{m}$ ▷ applying modulus operation.
5:     **end if**
6:     $A = A \times A \pmod{m}$ ▷ applying modulus operation.
7:     $i = i + 1$
8: **end while**
9: **if** $e_{h-1} = 1$ **then** $R = R \times A \mod m$ ▷ applying modulus operation.
10: **end if**
11: return R.

Fig. 3.5 Right to left binary modular exponentiation algorithm

Table 3.4 Example for exponent e = 283, modulus m = 10, base g = 7 using right to left binary modular exponentiation method

i	e_i	for LSB: $A = 7$	Intermediate Result $R = 1$
0	1	$R = 1 \times 7 \bmod 10$ $A = 7 \times 7 \bmod 10$	$R = 7; A = 9$
1	1	$R = 7 \times 9 \bmod 10$ $A = 9 \times 9 \bmod 10$	$R = 3; A = 1$
?	0	$A = 1 \times 1 \bmod 10$	$R = 3; A = 1$
3	1	$R = 3 \times 1 \bmod 10$ $A = 1 \times 1 \bmod 10$	$R = 3; A = 1$
4	1	$R = 3 \times 1 \bmod 10$ $A = 1 \times 1 \bmod 10$	$R = 3; A = 1$
5	0	$A = 1 \times 1 \bmod 10$	$R = 3; A = 1$
6	0	$A = 1 \times 1 \bmod 10$	$R = 3; A = 1$
7	0	$A = 1 \times 1 \bmod 10$	$R = 3; A = 1$
		Final Result = $R = 3 \times 1 \bmod 10$	

3.2 Sliding Window Technique

After analyzing the long bit-strings of an exponent it is observed that if we create a group of bits i.e., partition the strings into small bit-strings and termed it as words. Words can be of constant or variable length. Many of these words are found to be containing zeros only, for which we can escape the multiplication task and perform the multiplication only for non-zero words. Variable-length partitioning strategies are keen to find more number of words with zeros therefore has fewer non-zero words which in result reduces the number of multiplications (Koç 1995).

Consider the string $e_{l-1}e_{l-2} \ldots e_1 e_0$ be the base-2 representation of e. For constant length partition we divide the exponent's binary string into k words each having the length = d.

$$l = k.d \tag{3.3}$$

Suppose that l is not a perfect multiple of d then it requires padding of some extra zeros. A maximum of $d - 1$ bits will be needed for padding. Padding is done with zero bits.

For each word k we have value:

$$0 < S_i \leq 2^d - 1$$

$$S_i = e_{id+d-1}, e_{id+d-2}, \ldots e_{id}$$

$$= \sum_{j=0}^{d-1} e_{id+j} 2^j \tag{3.4}$$

$$Exponent \qquad e = \sum_{i=0}^{k-1} S_i . 2^{id}$$

3.2.1 M-Ary Method

In order to understand the basics of sliding window technique, we first go through M-Ary method. Here we first compute and store $g^w \ for \ w = 2, 3, \ldots 2^{d-1}$. Then we decompose exponent e into k words of length d, by scanning bits of e from most significant bit to least significant bit. Finally for all k partial results the exponentiation of 2^d is performed and multiplication with g^{S_i} is performed in the case where S_i is a non-zero word.

For computing the number of multiplication required in Algorithm 6 shown in Fig. 3.6.

Storing the array required $2^d - 2$ multiplications.

in step 8 multiplication required is : $(k - 1).d = l - d$.

in step 9 multiplication required is : $(k - 1)(l - 2^{-d})$ $\qquad \ldots k = l/d$.

We can calculate the multiplication required in average case:

$$T(n, d) = 2^d - 2 + l - d + \left(\frac{l}{d} - 1\right)(l - 2) \tag{3.5}$$

We can find optimal average multiplication value by substituting d with 1 which will give an average number of multiplication as $1.5(l - 1)$. We can also find an optimal value d^* for $T(n, d)$ to be minimized by enumeration (Koc 1991).

Algorithm 6 m-ary

> **Input:** g, e
> **Output:** $R = g^e$
> Let $d \leftarrow$ window size and to $l \leftarrow$ number of bits in binary representation of e (refer Equation 1.3).

1: **for** $w \leftarrow 2 \, to \, 2^d - 1$ **do** $A[w - 2] \leftarrow g^w$ ▷ storing array
2: **end for**
3: **for** $i \leftarrow 0 \, to \, k - 1$ **do** $S_i = 0$ ▷ decomposing into words
4:    **for** $j \leftarrow 0 \, to \, d - 1$ **do** $S_i + = 2^{id + j}$
5:    **end for**
6: **end for**
7: $R = g^{S_{k-1}}$ ▷ initializing result with last word
8: **for** $i \leftarrow k - 2 \, to \, 0$ **do** $R = R^{2^d}$
9:    **if** $S_i \neq 0$ **then** $R = R.g$
10:    **end if**
11: **end for**
12: return R.

Fig. 3.6 M-ary

3.2.2 Use of M-Ary in Sliding Window Technique

Till now we have discussed binary modular exponentiation Algorithms 4 and 5 shown in Figs. 3.4 and 3.5 respectively and M-ary Algorithm 6 shown in Fig. 3.6. During iteration of the loop whenever the non-zero word is encountered then only the modular multiplication is executed. Therefore the aim is to divide the exponent's bit string in such a way that we can maximize the number of zero-words in order to minimize the number of modular multiplications (Nedjah et al. 2007).

A binary string of length l is divided into $k - words$ of d size where the probability of a word to be a zero-word can be given as 2^{-d}. and we can say:

$$Number \; Of \; Modular \; Multiplication \; Required \propto 1/d. \qquad (3.6)$$

The sliding window protocol is adaptable for variable-length windows i.e., word of different length d. Which helps to have a minimum number of non zero words (NZW) and a maximum number of zero words (ZW).

Procedure
In sliding window modular exponentiation algorithm we partition binary representation of exponent e into two forms i.e., either zero words (ZW) or non zero words (NZW). Consider S_i for variable length $L(S_i)$, as the size of each word (window) is not fixed so the Eq. 3.3 does not hold good here. We consider value of d as maximum length of words. $d = Max(L(S_i)) \ldots i = 0, 1, 2, \ldots k - 1$.

If S_i is NZW then LSB of $S_i = 1$.

Algorithm 7 Sliding Window Method

Input: g, e
Output: $R = g^e$
Let: $d \leftarrow$ window size and l is number of bits in binary representation of exponent e.

1: **for** $w = 3, 5, \ldots 2^d - 1$ **do** $A[((w+1)/2) - 2] \leftarrow g^w$ ▷ storing array A from index 0
2: **end for**
3: Decompose e into variable length words ZW and NZW windows for $S_i of length L(S_i) : i = 0, 1 \ldots k - 1$
4: $R = g^{S_{k-1}}$ ▷ initializing with last word
5: **for** $i = k - 2\, down to\, 0$ **do** $R = R^{2^{L(S_i)}}$
6:     **if** $S_i \neq 0$ **then** $R = R \times g^{S_i}$
7:     **end if**
8: **end for**
9: return R.

Fig. 3.7 Sliding window method

The number of modular multiplications required by step 1 of the Algorithm 6 shown in Fig. 3.6 is reduced to half as only for odd numbers we need to calculate the value of g^w.

From the Algorithm 7 shown in Fig. 3.7 for the third step we have various partitioning techniques. Basically, this is the key step which determines the number of multiplications needed.

One of the ways to categorize various techniques is the length of the NZ window (Koc 1991) i.e., it can be fixed of it can be variable in either case however it will be $\leq d$ as d = Max of the length of NZW.

Constant Length Non Zero Window (CLNZW)
We traverse the binary representation of e and form the words ZW and NZW on the go, considering that we start with ZW and follow the given definition for labeling the windows.

1. For *ZW* check the next bit if the bit value is equal to zero then continue labeling as ZW else switches to NZW.
2. For *NZW* first cover d bits without checking for 1 or 0 then check for next bit if it is zero go to ZW labeling or go to NZW labeling.

As the name suggests the length of the NZ window(d) is fixed. Whereas ZW is variable (however $\leq d$). Two ZW needs to be concatenated if they are adjacent to each other. But a concatenation of two NZW is optional. For example $d = 3, e = 9815 = (10011001010111)_2$.

The CLNZW follows the exponentiation Algorithm 7 shown in Fig. 3.7. As per step 1 pre compute the exponentiation of g for $3, 5, 7$ where $d = 3$ and store it in an array. Then as per step 3 and following rule of CLNZW the value of e is decomposed as:

$$E = \underline{001}\,0\,\underline{011}\,00\,\underline{101}\,0\,\underline{111}$$

there are total 7 words.

Table 3.5 Example for CLNZW

i	S_i	$L(S_i)$	Step 5 $R = R^{2^{L(S_i)}}$	Step 6 $R = R \times g^{S_i}$
5	0	1	$(x)^2$	x^2
4	011	3	$(x^2)^8$	$x^{16} \times x^3$
3	00	2	$(x^{19})^4$	x^{76}
2	101	3	$(x^{76})^8$	$x^{608} \times x^5$
1	0	1	$(x^{613})^2$	x^{1226}
0	111	3	$(x^{1226})^8$	$x^{9808} \times x^7$

Now, step 4, $R = x^1$ ∵ $S_6 = x^1$ and for remaining steps tabular representation is given in the Table 3.5.

Final result $R = x^{9815}$

Variable Length Non Zero Window (VLNZW)

The CLNZW partitioning approach begins with a NZ word when it sees the bit 1, irrespective of upcoming $d - 1$ bits values is zero or one. The CLNZW approach carries on to join them into the ongoing NZ word. Let us take an example, where $d = 3$, the exponent $E = (111001010001)$ is partitioned as

$$E = 111\,00\,101\,0\,001.$$

Whereas, The same exponent $E = (111001010001)$ can be partitioned into more efficient way if the Variable Length NonZero Window technique is applied, e.g.

$$E = 111\,00\,101\,000\,1.$$

The key change is that in the variable-length NZ window (VLNZW) approach for partitioning the binary string, it checks for upcoming $d - 1$ bits. The values can be zero or one. It switches to ZW if the upcoming $d - 1$ bits are having value as zero. This approach decreases the average number of NZ words.

Suppose we start with ZW then to carry on with ZW or NZW the VLNZW approach works as given steps:

1. ZW: Examine the upcoming one bit, if it has value as 0 then carry on with ZW or else switch to NZW.
2. NZW: Examine the upcoming q bits, if all of them are having value as 0 then switch to ZW or else carry on with NZW.

Note: $q \leftarrow$ Required number of zeros to switch to ZW Where as $d \leftarrow$ maximum length of NZW

This VLNZW approach arises a question, i.e., for how long one should check for upcoming bits to be zero or one. For answering this question let us consider a variable u. The relation between window size d and u can be given as :

$$d = 1 + kq + u \quad Where \; 1 < u < q$$

We check for $1 + kq$ bits to carry on with NZW whereas at the last step the variable $'u'$ will give us the number of upcoming bits. Check for all upcoming u bits if they are having zero-bits, then switch to ZW, otherwise carry on with NZW. At last, if the word is full that is all d bits are accumulated then check for next bit if it is a zero-bit, then switch to ZW, otherwise switch to NZW.

3.2.3 Attacks on Sliding Window Exponential Technique

This technique reduces the number of multiplications required by the exponentiation method by a huge margin. As a result, it also gets the attention of cryptanalysts, who intend to find flaws in this approach. In this process C.D. Walter et al. shows that Big Mac is a special kind of cryptanalysis that is capable of deducing the private key bits separately or can decrease the possible key set (Walter 2001) (refer Sect. 2.7). It uses differential power analysis (DPA) as observed that if the k-bit multiplier is used and bits are sequentially computed one by one then using DPA one can steal the private information. The requirements to break the code and acquire the private key is very nominal, few exponentiations which have no relation with key-length and plain-text is executed over an adequately capable monitoring device is enough. This approach works where the security product is running over uni-processor and it can't mask the bit's multiplication with the help of other running processes. This type of attack is more simple when the key size is more, as longer bit strings carry more relevant information. Intruder knows a fact that a constant value of k is used for all information encryption and the execution time is proportional to window-size.

The intruder patiently gathers adequate exponentiation and wait for correct exponent calculation. Then uses DPA to analyse the private key. The task of intruder becomes simple if the same exponent is processed twice or more. This cryptanalysis approach is targeting a single exponent which suggests that blinding techniques can be helpful but it cannot be so much of help as if the intruder's target is only single exponentiation.

Walter et al. has given following countermeasures (Walter 2001):

- Use of processors/co-processor hardware designed in such a way that they can mask each other.
- A parallel processing using a pipelined $k - bit$ multiplier having various stages can be helpful.
- Parallel execution of exponentiation on 2 independent multipliers.
- All the digits can be multiplied separately and simultaneously using a systolic modular multiplier.

Two basic techniques are used by many cryptanalysts to attack the cryptosystems based on RSA.

1. Simple Power Analysis (SPA) and
2. Differential Power Analysis (DPA).

These two analysis are very helpful, whereas Fouque et al. shows that private-information stealing from sliding window modular exponentiation technique using SPA (Fouque et al. 2006). These attacks are suitable if the large module and long length key are used (Bernstein et al. 2017).

3.3 Bit Forwarding Techniques

We have seen two basic techniques of modular exponentiation

1. Algorithm 4: left-to-right binary modular exponential algorithm shown in Fig. 3.4 and,
2. Algorithm 5: right-to-left binary modular exponential algorithm shown in Fig. 3.5.

Both of them use the binary representation of their exponent. The input is base g, exponent e and mod m whereas the expected output is g^e (mod m). The average amount of modular multiplications required to compute g^e (mod m) is $l + k$, where $l \leftarrow$ bit-length of exponent's binary string and $k \leftarrow$ number of non-zero bits present in the exponent e.

It is observed that in the left-to-right binary modular exponential technique, the bits are processed from MSB to LSB of the exponent e. In the loop, the result is squared every time but base g is multiplied only if we get a non-zero bit i.e., $e_i \neq 0$. That's why it is also termed as the square and multiply method (Vollala et al. 2016).

Therefore, the efficiency of processing of all these cryptosystem products mainly relies on the efficient execution of modular exponential techniques. The square and multiply approach is widely being used for the same as it is adequate for hardware. The efficiency of the earlier discussed techniques is increased by the Bit Forwarding(BFW) approach. In this section, we will discuss the BFW approach and how it is improving the performance of modular exponential algorithms. But there are challenges faced for direct hardware implementation. The hardware implementation of modular exponentiation is comprised of trial divisions, so the BFW approaches are modified in such a way that it can be implemented in hardware with a little extra overhead.

The key logic behind the BFW techniques is that if there are t successive ones in the binary string of exponent e, then this technique skips the $t - 1$ multiplications and directly multiply the result with base g to the exponent 2^{t-1} (mod m). This technique finds the successive ones while traversing from MSB to LSB i.e., from left to right. Each time when skip for $t - 1$ $bits$ is done $t - 1$ modular multiplications is saved. Therefore performance is increased and power consumption is saved. This approach requires some amount of pre-computation like $A_{2^{t-1}} = g^{(2^{t-1})}$ (mod m) needs to be computed and stored (cause memory overhead). The BFW techniques are compatible for hardware implementation. Here in this section, we will see three different bit forwarding algorithms.

1. BFW-1 algorithm ($t = 2$)
2. BFW-2 algorithm ($t = 3$)
3. BFW-3 algorithm ($t = 4$).

3.3.1   Bit Forwarding 1-Bit Algorithm

The two parameters are pre-computed and stored:

1. $A_1 = AMM(g, PC, m)$
2. $A_3 = AMM(A_1, A_2, m)$ Where $A_2 = AMM(A_1, A_1, m)$

While traversing MSB to LSB if two successive ones are encountered in the exponent $e's$ binary string then one bit is forwarded *(1-bit-BFW)*. Then the pre-computed parameter A_3 is multiplied with the result. The Algorithm 8 is shown in Fig. 3.8. one multiplication is saved for two successive ones in the binary string of exponent e i.e., Algorithm 8 shown in Fig. 3.8 helps in reducing the multiplication required by a factor of 1.

Note: The bit forwarding algorithms are using one procedure Adaptable Montgomery Multiplication(AMM) which will be discussed in detail in Chap. 9.

Algorithm 8 BFW1:Bit forwarding 1-bit algorithm

Input: $g, E, m \ldots E = (e_{k-1}, \ldots, e_1, e_0)_2$
And a new constant referred to as the proposed constant PC
Output: $Res = g^E \pmod{m}$

1: *Precompute the value of A_1, A_3*
2: $A_1 = AMM(g, PC, m)$;
3: $A_2 = AMM(A_1, A_1, m)$;
4: $A_3 = AMM(A_2, A_1, m)$;
5: $R[k-1] = A_1$;
6: **for** $i = k - 2 \, Down to \, 0$ **do** $R[i] = AMM(R[i+1], R[i+1], m)$
7:     **if** $((e_i \neq 0) \, and \, (e_{i-1} \neq 0))$ **then**
8:         $i = i - 1$;   ▷ Forwarding one bit
9:         $R[i] = AMM(R[i+1], R[i+1], m)$;
10:        $R[i] = AMM(R[i], A_3, m)$;
11:    **else if** $(e_i \neq 0)$ **then**
12:        $R[i] = AMM(R[i], A_1, m)$;
13:    **end if**
14: **end for**
15: $Res = AMM(R[0], 1, m)$;
16: **Return** Res.

Fig. 3.8 BFW1: bit forwarding 1-bit algorithm

3.3.2 Bit Forwarding 2-Bits Algorithm

Here 3 parameters are pre-computed and stored:

1. $A_1 = AMM(g, PC, m)$
2. $A_3 = AMM(A_1, A_2, m)$ where $A_2 = AMM(A_1, A_1, m)$
3. $A_7 = AMM(A_6, A_1, m)$ where $A_6 = AMM(A_3, A_3, m)$

As in the BFW-1bit algorithm, we were searching for 2 successive ones here we search for three successive ones in the binary string of the exponent e, if encountered then we can skip the 2-bits. Then the pre-computed parameter A_7 is multiplied with result R. Whereas similar to the BFW-1 Algorithm 8 shown in Fig. 3.8, BFW-2 Algorithm 9 shown in Fig. 3.9 also consider the 2 successive 1's in the exponent's binary string and also take care of overlapping of the same with 3 successive 1's. If 2 successive ones are encountered then 1-bit is skipped, and the pre-computed parameter A_3 is multiplied with the result. Two multiplications are saved for three successive ones in the binary string of exponent e i.e., the Algorithm 9 shown in Fig. 3.9 helps in reducing the multiplications required by a factor of 2.

Algorithm 9 BFW2:Bit forwarding 2-bit algorithm

Input: $g, E, m \ldots E = (e_{k-1}, \ldots, e_1, e_0)_2$
And a new constant referred to as the proposed constant PC
Output: $Res = g^E \pmod{m}$

1: *Precompute the value of A_1, A_3, A_7*
2: $A_1 = AMM(g, PC, m)$;
3: $A_2 = AMM(A_1, A_1, m)$;
4: $A_3 = AMM(A_2, A_1, m)$;
5: $A_6 = AMM(A_3, A_3, m)$;
6: $A_7 = AMM(A_6, A_1, m)$;
7: $R[k-1] = A_1$;
8: **for** $i = k - 2\ Down to\ 0\ do$ **do** $R[i] = AMM(R[i+1], R[i+1], m)$
9:    **if** $((e_i \neq 0)\ and\ (e_{i-1} \neq 0)\ and\ (e_{i-2} \neq 0))$ **then**
10:       $i = i - 1$;   ▷ Forwarding one bit
11:       $R[i] = AMM(R[i+1], R[i+1], m)$;
12:       $i = i - 1$;   ▷ Forwarding 1 - bit
13:       $R[i] = AMM(R[i+1], R[i+1], m)$;
14:       $R[i] = AMM(R[i], A_7, m)$;
15:    **else if** $((e_i \neq 0)\ and\ (e_{i-1} \neq 0))$ **then**
16:       $i = i - 1$;   ▷ Forwarding one bit
17:       $R[i] = AMM(R[i+1], R[i+1], m)$;
18:       $R[i] = AMM(R[i], A_3, m)$;
19:    **else if** $(e_i \neq 0)$ **then**
20:       $R[i] = AMM(R[i], A_1, m)$;
21:    **end if**
22: **end for**
23: $Res = AMM(R[0], 1, m)$;
24: **Return** Res.

Fig. 3.9 BFW-2: bit forwarding 2-bits algorithm

3.3.3   Bit Forwarding 3-Bits Algorithm

Here 4 parameters are pre-computed and stored:

1. $A_1 = AMM(g, PC, m)$
2. $A_3 = AMM(A_1, A_2, m)$ Where $A_2 = AMM(A_1, A_1, m)$
3. $A_7 = AMM(A_6, A_1, m)$ Where $A_6 = AMM(A_3, A_3, m)$
4. $A_{15} = AMM(A_{14}, A_1, m)$ Where $A_{14} = AMM(A_7, A_7, m)$

Algorithm 10 BFW3: Bit forwarding 3-bit algorithm

Input: $g, E, m \dots E = (e_{k-1}, \dots, e_1, e_0)_2$
And a new constant referred to as the proposed constant PC
Output: $Res = g^E \pmod{m}$

1: *Precompute the value of A_1, A_3, A_7, A_{15}*
2: $A_1 = AMM(g, PC, m)$;
3: $A_2 = AMM(A_1, A_1, m)$;
4: $A_3 = AMM(A_2, A_1, m)$;
5: $A_6 = AMM(A_3, A_3, m)$;
6: $A_7 = AMM(A_6, A_1, m)$;
7: $A_{14} = AMM(A_7, A_7, m)$;
8: $A_{15} = AMM(A_{14}, A_1, m)$;
9: $R[k-1] = A_1$;
10: **for** $i = k - 2 \, Down to \, 0$ **do** $R[i] = AMM(R[i+1], R[i+1], m)$
11:     **if** $((e_i \neq 0) \, and \, (e_{i-1} \neq 0) \, and \, (e_{i-2} \neq 0) \, and \, (e_{i-3} \neq 0))$ **then**
12:         $i = i - 1$;   ▷ Forwarding one bit
13:         $R[i] = AMM(R[i+1], R[i+1], m)$;
14:         $i = i - 1$;   ▷ Forwarding one bit
15:         $R[i] = AMM(R[i+1], R[i+1], m)$;
16:         $i = i - 1$;   ▷ Forwarding one bit
17:         $R[i] = AMM(R[i+1], R[i+1], m)$;
18:         $R[i] = AMM(R[i], A_{15}, m)$;
19:     **else if** $((e_i \neq 0) \, and \, (e_{i-1} \neq 0) \, and \, (e_{i-2} \neq 0))$ **then**
20:         $i = i - 1$;   ▷ Forwarding one bit
21:         $R[i] = AMM(R[i+1], R[i+1], m)$;
22:         $i = i - 1$;   ▷ Forwarding 1 - bit
23:         $R[i] = AMM(R[i+1], R[i+1], m)$;
24:         $R[i] = AMM(R[i], A_7, m)$;
25:     **else if** $((e_i \neq 0) \, and \, (e_{i-1} \neq 0))$ **then**
26:         $i = i - 1$;   ▷ Forwarding one bit
27:         $R[i] = AMM(R[i+1], R[i+1], m)$;
28:         $R[i] = AMM(R[i], A_3, m)$;
29:     **else if** $(e_i \neq 0)$ **then**
30:         $R[i] = AMM(R[i], A_1, m)$;
31:     **end if**
32: **end for**
33: $Res = AMM(R[0], 1, m)$;
34: **Return** Res.

Fig. 3.10   BFW3: bit forwarding 3-bits algorithm

As in BFW-1 bit and BFW-2 bit algorithms, we were searching for 2 and 3 successive ones here we will search for four successive ones in the binary string of the exponent e. If encountered, then we can skip 3 bits. Then the pre-computed parameter A_{15} is multiplied with the result R. Whereas similar to BFW-1 bit and BFW-2 bit Algorithms 8 and 9 shown in Figs. 3.8 and 3.9 respectively, this Algorithm 10 is shown in Fig. 3.10. This algorithm also consider the 3 and 2 successive 1's in the exponent's binary string and also take care of overlapping of the same. If 2 successive ones are encountered then 1 bit is skipped, and the pre-computed parameter A_3 is multiplied with the result. Whereas if 3 successive ones are encountered then 2 bits are skipped, and the pre-computed parameter A_7 is multiplied with the result. Three multiplications are saved for four successive ones in the binary string of exponent e i.e., Algorithm 10 shown in Fig. 3.10 helps in reducing the multiplication by a factor of 3 for every four consecutive ones.

Note: Hardware implementation of all Bit-Forwarding techniques will be in discussed in depth in Chap. 10.

References

Bernstein DJ, Breitner J, Genkin D, Bruinderink LG, Heninger N, Lange T, van Vredendaal C, Yarom Y (2017) Sliding right into disaster: Left-to-right sliding windows leak. In: International conference on cryptographic hardware and embedded systems, Springer, pp 555–576

Fouque PA, Kunz-Jacques S, Martinet G, Muller F, Valette F (2006) Power attack on small rsa public exponent. In: International workshop on cryptographic hardware and embedded systems, Springer, pp 339–353

Koc CK (1991) High-radix and bit recoding techniques for modular exponentiation. Int J Comput Math 40(3–4):139–156

Koç CK (1995) Analysis of sliding window techniques for exponentiation. Comput & Math Appl 30(10):17–24

Möller B, et al (2003) Public key cryptography: theory and practice. PhD thesis, Darmstadt University of Technology, Germany

Nedjah N, de Macedo Mourelle L, da Silva RM (2007) Efficient hardware for modular exponentiation using the sliding-window method. In: Fourth international conference on information technology (ITNG'07), IEEE, pp 17–24

Tandrup MB, Jensen MH, Andersen RN, Hansen TF (2004) Fast exponentiation in practice

Vollala S, Geetha K, Ramasubramanian N (2016) Efficient modular exponential algorithms compatible with hardware implementation of public-key cryptography. Secur Commun Netw 9(16):3105–3115

Walter CD (2001) Sliding windows succumbs to big mac attack. In: International workshop on cryptographic hardware and embedded systems, Springer, pp 286–299

Chapter 4
Review of Algorithmic Techniques for Improving the Performance of Modular Exponentiation

These algorithms also have to minimize the running time, even for a single modular multiplication while computing modular exponentiation. The better efficiency can be obtained with the help of multi-core cryptosystems that can be understood with the help of *Amdhals' law*. The factors which affect the complete system performance are:

- Utilization of power
- Emission of heat
- Clock rate
- Ideal time of the processor

Performance for a single processor can be enhanced by enhancing the frequency, but the frequency is proportional to power consumption i.e., the more we enhance the frequency more power will be utilized and more emission of heat. These factors are not desirable for any PKC system. This relation between frequency, power utilization, and emission of heat motivates researchers to concentrate on reducing the clock cycle count instead of increasing the frequency.

The single task is divided into threads and distributed among different cores of a multi-core processor to run simultaneously in a given clock cycle. Here the frequency is the same as the unicore processor. i.e., no extra power requirement and heat emission. This works on the divide and conquer approach (Burger 2005; González and Fraguela 2010). All the applications which have the capability of distributing one task into threads can take advantage of this architecture, which can avail different and ingenious advantages.

The radix and clock cycles are inversely proportional to each other and radix and memory space is directly proportional. i.e.,

© The Author(s), under exclusive license to Springer Nature Switzerland AG 2021
S. Vollala et al., *Energy-Efficient Modular Exponential Techniques*
for Public-Key Cryptography, https://doi.org/10.1007/978-3-030-74524-0_4

$$Radix \propto \frac{1}{Clock\ Cycles}$$

$$Radix \propto Memory\ Space$$

That is if we increase the radix we can minimize the clock cycles, on the other hand, it also needs the extra memory space. Adequate value of radix is selected as per the need. Based on the constraint we can select one of the algorithms:

- If there is no constraint of memory and fast running devices are priority over the web servers e.g. organizations like banking sectors the Adaptable High-Radix Montgomery Multiplication (AHRMM) is an optimal choice.
- Whereas for devices like sensors that are having memory constraints the algorithm Adaptable Montgomery Multiplication (AMM) is a more optimal choice.

We have already seen the various algorithms in the previous chapter there are many more left for discussion. This chapter discusses the common basic insight of these algorithms i.e., on what area they focus on to improve the overall performance.

4.1   Montgomery Multiplication

As we have already studied the Diffie–Hellman key-exchange technique for cryptography. The most popular PKC is RSA and ECC which uses modular exponentiation as the main operation. Modular exponentiation is the most expensive operation of complete cryptographic arithmetic. Many academicians and organizations have given solutions to increase the performance of modular exponentiation. Different aspects of modular exponentiation are targeted to reduce complexity. The basic formula is:

$$C = g^e \quad (\text{mod } m) \tag{4.1}$$

In Modular exponentiation, there is a sequence of modular multiplications (MMs). If the operand is large then running time is too high as it increases exponentially. Binary modular exponentiation is a common and simple approach is to calculate the long length (≥ 1024) exponent bits modular exponentiation, termed as the "Square and Multiply" (refer Chap. 3 Sect. 3.1). This technique follows a simple approach of processing each bit of the exponent's binary string. Processing each bit involves squaring for each bit whereas depending on the value of bit multiplication operation is done. In order to reduce the complexity of binary methods, Many researchers have selected the right to left binary modular exponentiation technique which scans the bit from LSB to MSB. The reason for selecting this technique is that it allows squaring and multiplication to execute simultaneously. For reducing the running time of MM they use the Montgomery algorithm (Koc et al. 1996), which is capable of replacing division by the sequence of shift and addition operations.

Algorithm 1 Montgomery's Method

Input X, Y and m
Output $X \times Y$ (mod m)

Initialization Select R such that $R > m$ and $GCD(R, m) = 1$
1: Compute: N^{-1} (mod m)
   Now
2: $X' = X.R$ (mod m) and $Y' = Y.R$ (mod m)
3: $C' = (X'Y')R^{-1}$ (mod m)
4: $C = C'R^{-1}$ (mod m)
   We claim $C = X.Y$ (mod m)
   from 2 and 3:
   $C'.R^{-1}$ (mod m) $= (X'Y')R^{-1}R^{-1}$ (mod m)
5: $C'.R^{-1}$ (mod m) $= (X'R^{-1})(Y'R^{-1})$ (mod m)
   $\therefore C = X.Y$ (mod m)...   ▷ Refer Equation 4.2

Fig. 4.1 Montgomery method

Montgomery first changes the operand into another form within its own defined domain. The division operation is performed in the converted form with the help of addition and shift operation. After calculating the product the operands are restored to their original form. Operands in Montgomery domain is given as $x' = x \times R$ (mod m). Here R is the value in the form of 2^k and k is the size of the operand in bits. Using the operand in Montgomery domain primary operation i.e., MM is performed (Bansal et al. 2015). With some pre and post-computation, the combination of Right to Left binary modular exponentiation and Montgomery multiplication can achieve an optimal solution by replacing the modular division with easy shift operation (refer Algorithm 1 shown in Fig. 4.1).

In order to get MM of two operands X and Y of k bits and modulus m, the Montgomery algorithm gives the output as shown in the Eq. 4.2

$$C = MM(X, Y) = X \times Y \times R^{-1} \quad (\text{mod } m) \tag{4.2}$$

Montgomery Reduction

In order to implement the Montgomery multiplication, we need to reform the equation from (mod N) to (mod R) where R is the value in the form of 2^k. If $R = 2^k$ i.e., power of 2

- Multiplication of R is left shift k-bit i.e., performing multiplication with 2^k
- Division of R is right-shift k-bit i.e., performing division by 2^k

The mathematical explanation of Montgomery Reduction which proves the conversion of operands into and from Montgomery Domain in order to compute MM is illustrated here.

$$let\ R > N\ and\ GCD(R, N) = 1$$
$$0 \le T < NR$$

The Montgomery Reduction of T modulo N wrt R is defined as

$$T R{-}1 \quad (\mathrm{mod}\ N)$$
$$Now,$$
$$m = T \times N^{-1} \quad (\mathrm{mod}\ R)$$
$$t = (T + mN)/R$$
$$if\,(N \le t)$$
$$t = t - N$$

here we claim $: t = T R^{-1} \quad (\mathrm{mod}\ N)$

we can see there is no $(\mathrm{mod}\ N)$ *in algorithm but we have* $(\mathrm{mod}\ N)$ *in our claim*

$$t R = T R^{-1} R(\mathrm{mod}\ N)\ multiplying\ R\ to\ our\ claim$$
$$t R = R \quad (\mathrm{mod}\ N)\ here \ldots 0 \le t < N$$
$$\because t = (T + mN)/R$$
$$\therefore t R = T + mN$$
$$t R = T \quad (\mathrm{mod}\ N)$$
$$\because m = T \times N^{-1} \quad (\mathrm{mod}\ R)$$
$$\therefore we\ can\ say\ 0 \le m < R$$
$$0 \le mN < RN\ \ Multiply\ N$$
$$from\ definition\ 0 \le T \le NR$$
$$0 \le mN + T < 2NR$$
$$0 \le (T + mN)/R < 2N$$
$$\therefore 0 \le t < N$$
$$\therefore T R^{-1} = (T + T(-N)^{-1} \quad (\mathrm{mod}\ R)N)/R \quad (\mathrm{mod}\ N)$$

4.2   High-Radix Modular Multiplication

Today's PKC uses a long length operand and modulus (longer than 1 KByte) for modular exponentiation. The modular exponentiation operation is subdivided into modular multiplications (MMs) i.e., by series of iteration of MMs one can calculate modular exponentiation. This encourages the new and efficient algorithms for MM which is capable of handling long length modulus. This is the key logic of a high-performance encryption/decryption procedure of efficient PKC.

Higher Radix versions of MM methods are more efficient, if implemented with proper hardware architecture. Factors of modulus and multiplicand can be computed for residue calculation. This computation can be done by complement operation or shift operation over them. Another way is to apply a combination of both the operations i.e., complement operation and shift operation. But, this type of approach needs to have the operands in a non-redundant representation.

Inside the loop, the intermediate result is in a redundant form. Because of this, the running time of each loop is increased. Because base-transformation is a time-consuming process that includes a carry propagate addition of long numbers. This base-transformation operation is required at each multiplication. The product (the result of the previous iteration) is needed as an operand of the next multiplication.

For a better understanding a *Radix-4* modular multiplication method is discussed (Takagi 1992). This method is a kind of division-during-multiplication method. Most of the MM algorithms have been classified into two methods i.e., "division after multiplication" and "division during multiplication". One of the key factors of getting an efficient algorithm is that the representation of the partial products is more redundant than that for the operands and the product. We consider the following notation and representation for radix-4 modular multiplication algorithm:

Consider residue class for multiplication is:

$$Z_Q = 0, 1, \ldots, Q - 1 \ \text{where} \ 2^{n-1} \leq Q < 2^n$$

Representation 1 (REP1)
For the product, multiplier and the multiplicand we represent $\alpha \in Z_Q$ by n-digit redundant binary number X, which satisfies $-d_1.Q < X < d_1.Q$ and $X \cong \alpha$ (mod Q).

Representation 2 (REP2)
For the partial products we represent $\beta \in Z_Q$ by an $(n + 1) - digit$ redundant binary number Y, which satisfies $-d_2.Q < Y < d_2.Q$ and $Y \cong \beta$ (mod Q).

Consider a scenario, where X and Y are a power of 2, this makes the computation task much simpler. To reduce the number of cycles one can use the techniques known from high-radix multiplication and division, e.g. the multiplier is given in the power of 2 i.e., $radix = 2^k$ and quotient digits are determined in that base also. The system modulus must satisfy $2^k \leq m < 2^{kn}$ (cases, where m is a power of 2, are much simpler), and the algorithm will proceed through n + 2 cycles. Algorithm 2 shown in Fig. 4.2 (Interleaved Modular Multiplication) is suitable for modular exponentiation.

Note that we allow X and Y to be negative, $-m < X; Y < m$, and assume Y is represented in a redundant digit set. Since we shall prove that the resulting S is in the same interval, and may also be in redundant representation.

4.2.1 Radix-4 Modular Multiplication

This subsection discusses the radix-4 Montgomery algorithm. As the representation of exponent is switched from binary to radix-4 representation. Therefore the number of iterations and the number of MM is reduced by half. If k number of iterations are required to perform the partial product by Montgomery algorithm, whereas the

---

Algorithm 2 Interleaved Modular Multiplication

Input X , Y , m
Output An integer S such that : $m < S < m$ and $S \equiv XY \pmod{m}$.

1: *Initialization* $S := 0; i := n - 1$;
2: **while** $i \geq -(1 + \frac{r}{k})$ **do**
3:      L determine integer q_i such that $|S - q_i 2^r m| \leq \alpha 2^r m$
4:      $S := 2^k(S - q_i 2^r m) + y_i X$
5:      $i := i - 1$
6: **end while**
7: $S := S \div 2^{(k+r)}$
8: **Return** S

Fig. 4.2 Interleaved modular multiplication

given algorithm 3 shown in Fig. 4.3 minimize the value of n to $\frac{(k+3)}{2}$ i.e., required iterations, as well as partial products to be accumulated, is also minimized. Booth's multiplier is used in the radix-4 Montgomery algorithm 3.

Let X and Y be integers where X is having $(k + 3) - bit$ and Y is having $(k + 1) - bit$ and another k bit odd integer $m = (m_{k-1}, \ldots, m_{k_1}, m_{k_0})$, in such a way that $-m \leq X, Y < m$. If X and Y are negative integers then we take there 2's complement. For the given radix-4 Montgomery algorithm we consider a radix-4 booth partial product variable PP and for ith iteration PP_i stores the value $PP_i = (pp_{i(k+1)}, \ldots, pp_{i1}, pp_{i0})$. If we are switching to radix-4 and for booth partial product, we consider that $PP_{\lceil(k+1)/2\rceil} = 0$ and $-2m \leq PP_i \leq 2m$ $\because 0 \leq i < [(m + 1)/2]$. Modular reduction value (i.e., $m_i = 2m$, $\pm m$, or 0) can be obtained with the help of the two LSBs of T_i (i.e., t_{i1} and t_{i0}) where $T_i = S[i] + PP_i$. The Radix-4 Montgomery multiplication algorithm (Hong and Wu 2000) shown in Fig. 4.3.

Algorithm 3 given in Fig. 4.3 reduced the iteration to half i.e., $\frac{k}{2}$ instead of unlike previous algorithms needed k or $2k$. If we observe this algorithm 3 and the previous algorithm 1 (Fig. 4.1) uses similar steps in each iteration, i.e., as the half of iterations are required so this algorithm 3 is quicker than the previous algorithm 1. The value of $S[(k + 3)/2]$ falls in the range $[-m, m]$, The range is the same as it was, at the beginning i.e., there is no need for subtraction or addition of final result from modular value m.

4.2.2   Modular Exponentiation Using Radix-4 Montgomery Multiplication

The Modular Exponentiation algorithm 4 shown in Fig. 4.4 is modified form of left to right binary modular exponentiation algorithm (refer Chap. 3 algorithm 4 shown in Fig. 3.4). Assume a variable $R = 4^{\lceil\frac{k+3}{2}\rceil}$ such that $C = R^2 \pmod{m}$, the modular

Algorithm 3 Radix-4 Modular Multiplication Algorithm Using Montgomery's Concept(R4MMM)

Input X,Y,m
Output XY mod m

1: *IntializationS*$[0] = 0$
2: **for** $i = 0 to [(k+3)/2]$ **do**
3:     $(t_{i1}, t_{i0}) = (S[i] + PP_i)(mod 4)$
4:     **if** $t_{i0} = 0$ **then**
5:         **if** $t_{i1} = 0$ **then**
6:             $S[i+1] = (S[i] + PP_i)/4$
7:         **else**
8:             $S[i+1] = (S[i] + PP_i + 2m)/4$
9:         **end if**
10:     **else**
11:         **if** $t_{i1} = k_1$ **then**
12:             $S[i+1] = (S[i] + PP_i - m)/4$
13:         **else**
14:             $S[i+1] = (S[i] + PP_i + m)/4$
15:         **end if**
16:     **end if**
17: **end for**
18: **Return** $S([(k+3)/2])$

Fig. 4.3 Radix-4 modular multiplication algorithm using montgomery multiplication concept(R4MMM)

Algorithm 4 Radix-4 Modular Exponentiation Algorithm Using Montgomery's Concept

---

Input g,e, m
Output g^e (mod m)

1: *Initialization* $g_0 = R4MMM(g, C, m)$ and $P_0 = 1$
2: **for** $i = 0 to k - 1$ **do**
3:     $g_{i+1} = R4MMM(g_i, g_i, m)$
4:     **if** $e_i = 1$ **then**
5:         $P_{i+1} = R4MMM(g_i, P_i, m)$
6:     **else**
7:         $P_{i+1} = P_i$
8:     **end if**
9: **end for**
10: **if** $P_k < 0$ **then**
11:     $P_k = P_k + m$
12: **end if**
13: Return P_k

Fig. 4.4 Radix-4 ME algorithm using MMM concept

Table 4.1 Intermediate value for algorithm 3

i	0	1	2	3	…	n
g_i	$g \times R$	$g^2 \times R$	$g^4 \times R$	$g^8 \times R$	…	–
P_i	1	g^{e_0}	$g^{2e_1+e_0}$	$g^{4e_2+2e_1+e_0}$	…	g^e

exponentiation algorithm (Hong and Wu 2000) have the final value stored in P_k i.e., $P_k = g^e \pmod{m}$. The range of the variables (g_i's and P_i's) during the iteration remain inside the range i.e., $[-m, m]$ because the algorithm 4 is used.

Note that the variables g_i and P_i are in the range $[-m, m]$ inside the iteration but conversion of the final result P_k is needed so we add m to final result only if $P_k < 0$. Also the intermediate values of g_i and P_i are shown in the Table 4.1. This approach allows us to encrypt one plain-text and read another plain-text simultaneously moreover we can also write back the previously encrypted cipher-text at the same time (Hong and Wu 2000).

4.3 Chinese Remainder Theorem (CRT)

Chinese remainder theorem is an old theorem which defines the solution for more than one equation which are having simultaneous results. In the context of cryptography, we can understand it as a method to minimize MMs or exponentiation required. CRT is useful when a large modulus operation is needed and there is more than one similar computation is required, for each of the (mutually co-prime) factors of the modulus (Cankaya 2011). Finally, the results of the sub-computations are accumulated in order to get the final result. The basic benefit here is that intermediate computations are consist of smaller integers e.g. $24 \times 32 \pmod{35}$ can be sub-computed if we perform the product $24 \times 32 \pmod{5}$ and $24 \times 32 \pmod{7}$ where $5 \times 7 = 35$. These integers are mutually co-prime i.e., they don't have any common factor (in fact, in this case, both are prime themselves). So performing the sub computation which can be performed in parallel:

$$24 \times 32 \cong 4 \times 2 \cong 8 \cong 3 \quad (\text{mod } 5)$$
$$24 \times 32 \cong 3 \times 4 \cong 12 \cong 5 \quad (\text{mod } 7)$$

There is a unique relation between the pair (p, q) and integers i such that $0 \le i < 35$, here $0 \le p < 5$ and $0 \le q < 7$. Let i be an integer between 0 and 35. Then the relation between pair (p, q) and integer i is the mod value from prime factors of modulus. Consider a scenario for $i = 24$ and the factors of modulus 35 are 5 and 7, and then the pair (p, q) will be (4, 3) i.e., 24 $(\text{mod } 5) = 4$ and 24 $(\text{mod } 7) = 3$.

The value of i can be given as $i = a \times p + b \times q$. The multipliers a, b can be given as:

$$a \cong q^{-1} \quad (\text{mod } p)$$
$$b \cong p^{-1} \quad (\text{mod } q)$$

$$\vdots$$

$$a \cong 1 \quad (\text{mod } 5) \text{ and } a \cong 0 \quad (\text{mod } 7)$$
$$a \cong 1 \quad (\text{mod } 7) \text{ and } b \cong 0 \quad (\text{mod } 5)$$

In this example $a \cong 21$ (mod 35) and $b \cong 15$ (mod 35) can be calculated. Now accumulating the sub-computation results for final result:

$21 \times 3 + 15 \times 5 \cong 33$ (mod 35)

First generalize the mathematics of *Chinese Remainder Theorem*.

Let $m_0, m_2, \ldots, m_k$ be pairwise relatively prime positive integers and let $a_0, a_1, \ldots a_k$ & $b_0, b_1, \ldots b_k$ be any pair of integers which satisfy the linear congruence system in one variable given by:

$$a_0 X \cong b_0 \quad (\text{mod } m_0')$$
$$a_1 X \cong b_1 \quad (\text{mod } m_1')$$

$$\vdots$$

$$a_k X \cong b_k \quad (\text{mod } m_k')$$

i.e., $GCD(a_i, m_i') \cong 0$ (mod b_i) so the final and unique solution will have modulo $m_0' \times m_1' \times \ldots m_k'$.

We can increase the efficiency of the calculation of RSA up to 4 times by introducing the *Chinese Remainder Theorem (CRT)* (Dingyi et al. 1996) method. CRT uses the divide & conquer approach to minimize the computation.

As we know modular exponentiation algorithms use the Square and Multiply technique which can be used with the block interleaving method to minimize the ideal time of the processing unit of the systolic array and achieve 100% utilization (Wu et al. 2001).

We can minimize the running time of the RSA decryption and signature process with the help of the CRT. Suppose relatively prime positive factors (m_1, m_2) of modulus m are already available. By CRT, the computation of $C = g^e$ (mod m) and $M = C_D$ (mod N) can be partitioned into two parts:

$$C_{m_0} = g_{m_0}^{e_{m_0}} \quad (\text{mod } m_0),$$
$$C_{m_1} = g_{m_1}^{e_{m_1}} \quad (\text{mod } m_1),$$

where

$$g_{m_0} = g \quad (\text{mod } m_0), \; e_{m_0} = e \quad (\text{mod } m_0 - 1),$$
$$g_{m_1} = g \quad (\text{mod } m_1), \; e_{m_1} = e \quad (\text{mod } m_1 - 1)$$

The running time is minimized i.e., e_{m_0} , e_{m_1} < e and g_{m_0} , g_{m_1} < g, not even less actually it may be of half of the original modulus m. For the best-case scenario, we can minimize the running time by a factor of 4. Finally, we calculate R with the help of the CRT using the Eq. 4.3.

$$R = [R_{m_0}(m_1^{-1} \quad (\text{mod } m_0))m_1 + R_{m_1}(m_0^{-1} \quad (\text{mod } m_1))m_0] \quad (\text{mod } m) \quad (4.3)$$

... *Remember* m_0, m_1 *are relatively prime positive factors of modulus m.*

To achieve the minimum number of clock cycles m_0 and m_1 needs to be of same length, i.e., $k/2$. But it is not possible as per the constraints i.e., (m_0 *and* m_1 should be relatively prime and $m_0 \neq m_1$). For better information security the length of the two should be close enough. It is desired that, the length of m_0 and m_1 is in the range of $n/3$ to $2n/3$.

4.4   Enhancement in the Montgomery Multiplication

Till now Montgomery multiplication algorithm has been known as the best performing MM (Montgomery 1985). This approach is efficient because it is capable of replacing the trial divisions for modulus with a sequence of shift operations and summation. Therefore, it is an optimal choice of hardware implementation and widely used in the latest known RSA hardware architectures.

One of the main tasks in the addition process is carry-propagation, if one can bypass carry-propagation then it increases the overall performance of MM. Therefore many researchers have proposed various techniques to bypass carry-propagation. In the same process, Elbirt and Paar (1999) successfully implemented an approach on FPGA where a fast carry chain is available and then they select an adequate x such that the benefit from this fast carry chain of the latest FPGA can be maximized. Based on the selected x they break the additions process into x-bit stages. However, this approach requires the highly complex implementation of circuits that is application-specific. This is a shortcoming as it is very less likely that the same design can be compatible with any other technology. That is if we wish to migrate our work to some other latest FPGA, or new ASIC or PLD then the same performance cannot be guaranteed.

4.4.1   Residue Number System in Montgomery Multiplication

All the number systems like binary, octal, decimal, etc are positional number systems i.e., where each digit is carrying the weight of their base to the power of their positions. But unlike these positional number system, the *residue number system (RNS)* digits does not carry any obvious weight. Therefore, basic mathematical operations like comparison, division, and MM are complex to perform. Montgomery multiplication is strongly based on the positional number system and LSB/MSB are used in intermediate steps in the loop. These requirements of the Montgomery multiplication method suggest that the use of RNS is not suitable for it. If we want to incorporate RNS with the Montgomery multiplication method then we need to take the help of few operands in a mixed-radix representation linked with the RNS. The key logic of the modified approach is that if two or more residue systems are based on the same modulus then we can select the least significant digit of a mixed-radix representation as to any one of the residues of the RNS. The modified algorithm performs a multiplication interleaved with reduction steps, executed simultaneously on each residue of the RNS. Each step requires an exact division by one of the moduli, which makes the algorithm a little bit complex. Since one of the residues then becomes undefined. By performing all computations also in an auxiliary (redundant) base, the result is still available in the extended base. Alternatively, the lost residue can be recovered through a base extension using the Chinese Remainder Theorem (Bajard et al. 1998).

RNS can be understood as a special representation of an integer in such a way that it consists of a set of residues in different Radix elements of it. This allows us to execute basic mathematical operations separately for different base residues. Whereas Montgomery multiplication is an approach of calculating modular multiplication by replacing multiplication and division by series of shift and addition operations. It would be a good idea to combine both of them i.e., RNS and Montgomery multiplication to achieve a better and parallel processing environment to calculate modular exponentiation. One of the key step and also time-consuming steps in the RNS and Montgomery combination is *base-transformation*. Many researchers have done study on the base transformation (Nozaki et al. 2001).

This section first discusses the RNS and Montgomery separately in short & then, their combination will be discussed.

Residue Number System

$$x \leftarrow an\ integer\ to\ be\ expressed\ in : RNS$$
$$a \leftarrow set\ of\ n\ bases.$$
$$set\ a = \{a_1, a_2, \ldots, a_n\}$$
$$n \leftarrow base\ size$$
$$here\ the\ expression\ of\ x\ is :$$
$$\langle x \rangle_a = (x[a_1],\ x[a_2],\ \ldots,\ x[a_n])$$

The relation between x and a_i is such that

$$x[a_i] = x \quad (\text{mod } a_i) \tag{4.4}$$

where as the members of set of bases should posses the mutually prime relation i.e.,

$$GCD(a_i, a_j) = 1 \tag{4.5}$$

$$here \ 0 < i, j \leq n \ \& \ i \neq j.$$

From Chinese remainder theorem (CRT) the Eqs. 4.4 and 4.5 and if integer x is such that $0 \leq x < A$ then

$$A = \prod_{i=1}^{n} a_i \tag{4.6}$$

Using the Eq. 4.6 we can uniquely represent the integer $\langle x \rangle_a$.

Using the given expressions of RNS the basic mathematical operations (addition, subtraction, and multiplication) can be efficiently represented in their modular operation form (i.e., modular addition, modular subtraction, and modular multiplication). For any two integer x, y :

$$\langle x \pm y \rangle_a = ((x[a_1] \pm y[a_1])[a_1], \ldots, (x[a_n] \pm y[a_n])[a_n])$$

$$\langle x \cdot y \rangle_a = ((x[a_1] \cdot y[a_1])[a_1], \ldots, (x[a_n] \cdot y[a_n])[a_n]) \tag{4.7}$$

Equation 4.7 is enabling us to perform the parallel processing using n processing elements. As the few basic mathematics for RNS expression has been derived (Refer Eq. 4.7 but other operations like division and comparison are still don't have any efficient formulation to perform. To fulfill this gap we can take the help of the Montgomery multiplication method.

Montgomery Multiplication

The basic of Montgomery multiplication is discussed in Sect. 4.1. In the algorithm 1 shown in Fig. 4.1, the input parameters were operand X, Y and modulus m where $(X, Y < m)$ whereas the result was $C \cong XYR^{-1}$ (mod m)) where $(C < m)$, where R and modulus m are co-prime $GCD(R, m) = 1$ where $m < R$. We select R in such a way that it has value in $2's$ power in a radix 2 representation. This enables the RNS formulation to perform MMs efficiently with the help of shifting and addition operations. From Eq. 4.7 the parallelism is achieved in basic mathematical operations (addition, subtraction, and multiplication) and the combination of this RNS expression and Montgomery multiplication is believed to achieve the better parallel processing performance.

Algorithm 5 RNS Montgomery Multiplication

Input $\langle X \rangle_{a \cup b}, \langle Y \rangle_{a \cup b} (X, Y < m)$
Output $\langle C \rangle_{a \cup b} (C \equiv XYB^{-1} \pmod{m}, C < 2m)$

1: $\langle s \rangle_a \leftarrow \langle XY \rangle_a$ ▷ base a operation
2: $\langle s \rangle_b \leftarrow \langle XY \rangle_b$ ▷ base b operation
3: $\langle t \rangle_b \leftarrow \langle s(-m^{-1}) \rangle_b$ ▷ base b operation
4: $\langle t \rangle_a \leftarrow BT(\langle t \rangle_b, 0)$ ▷ base transformation operation
5: $\langle u \rangle_a \leftarrow \langle tm \rangle_a$
6: $\langle v \rangle_a \leftarrow \langle s + u \rangle_a$
7: $\langle C \rangle_a \leftarrow \langle vB^{-1} \rangle_a$
8: $\langle C \rangle_b \leftarrow BT(\langle C \rangle_a, 0.5)$ ▷ base transformation operation
9: **Return** $\langle C \rangle$

Fig. 4.5 RNS montgomery multiplication

RNS Montgomery Multiplication

Based on the RNS the Algorithm 5 shown in Fig. 4.5 is given. For the formulation of the combined RNS and Montgomery algorithm, few parameters are needed to be pre-defined such as :

- Two bases a, b and the base size n is same for a&b.
- B :Montgomery constant, similar to Eq. 4.6 i.e., $(B = \prod_{i=1}^{n} b_i)$
- x based on a and b by $\langle x \rangle_{a \cup b}$ or simply by $\langle x \rangle$
- The bases a and b satisfy A, $B > 8m$, $GCD(A, B) = 1$, and $GCD(B, m) = 1$.

Steps 4 and 8 in the algorithm 5 are the base transformation between a and b. Most of the research is going on in this field i.e., base transformation. This is the key step, and efficiently executing this step means improving the overall algorithm.

4.4.2 Adaptable Montgomery Multiplication for Radix-2 (AMM)

Modular exponentiation is performed by a series of MMs. MM requires trial division processes, which are time-consuming, and cannot be directly implemented in hardware. The Montgomery multiplication method is a powerful algorithm to compute MM. In this section, the Montgomery multiplication method is customized according to the needs of BFW algorithms and termed as AMM (Vollala et al. 2016), listed an Algorithm 6 shown in Fig. 4.6. All the costlier operations, namely, trial divisions, are replaced by additions and shift operations as mentioned in Algorithm 6. Whenever AMM is invoked, it multiplies the result with $2^{-n} \pmod{N}$. After all the iterations are over in the modular exponential algorithm, invoking the AMM with the three parameters i.e., updated result, 1 and modulus, provides the required modular exponentiation value. Modular exponentiation is performed by a series of MMs. MM has

---

Algorithm 6 Adaptable Montgomery Multiplication

    Input: X, Y, m

    Output: $R = X \cdot Y \cdot 2^{-n} \pmod{m}$,   ▷ n is the length of m

  1: *Intialization $H = X.Y; P = 0; i = 0$*   ▷ Assigning of values to the registers

  2: $P = 0$

  3: **while** $i < n$ **do**

  4:     **if** $((H[i] \neq 0) \, and \, (P[0] \neq 1))$ **then**

  5:         $P = (P + m + 1) >> 1$

  6:     **else if** $((H[i] \neq 0) \, and \, (P[0] \neq 0))$ **then**

  7:         $P = (P + 1) >> 1$

  8:     **else if** $((H[i] \neq 1) \, and \, (P[0] \neq 0))$ **then**

  9:         $P = (P + m) >> 1$

10:     **else**

11:         $P = P >> 1$

12:     **end if**

13:     $i = i + 1$

14: **end while**

15: $R = P[n] + H[2n-1, n]$

16: **Return** R

Fig. 4.6 Adaptable montgomery multiplication (AMM)

a basic step termed the trial division which is responsible for increasing the running time, the implementation of this division operations cannot be implemented directly to the hardware.

Montgomery multiplication gives the solution to this problem. This section discusses how the Montgomery multiplication procedure is modified in order to achieve the requirements of Bit forwarding algorithms that are customized according to the needs of BFW algorithms (Vollala et al. 2016). The modified algorithm is termed Adaptable Montgomery Multiplication (AMM) by Vollala et al. The Algorithm 6 is capable of converting the costlier steps, known as trial divisions, into series of additions and shift steps. Whenever the algorithm 6 AMM is executed, it gives the product of the result and $2^{-m} \pmod{m}$. In order to obtain the final modular exponentiation result when all loops have executed the algorithm 6 AMM is again called with parameters updated result and digit 1.

4.4.3 Adaptable High-Radix Montgomery Multiplication (AHRMM)

As we know that, in the calculation of modular exponentiation, increase the radix results in minimizing the clock cycles (refer Sect. 4.2). To support the higher radix modular exponentiation algorithms *adaptable high-radix Montgomery multiplication (AHRMM)* can be used (Vollala et al. 2016). Similar to the AMM algorithm the

AHRMM algorithm is also adaptable because of its compatibility with all the BFW techniques.

For high-radix representation:

- $k \leftarrow$ Length of an integer which need to be represented in higher radix
- $w \leftarrow$ Number of parts(blocks) length k can be divided
- $r \leftarrow$ Length of each words (w) in bits

it means for an integer of k bit length:

$$k = w \times r$$

The k-bit integer can be represented by w number of r-bit words C_i as $A = \sum_{i=0}^{w-1} (2^r)^i . C_i$, where $0 \leq i < w$. Before defining the algorithm AHRMM consider some parameters:

$$Integer\ X = (x_{w-1}, x_{w-2}, x_{w-3}, \ldots, x_2, x_1, x_0)_{HR}$$
$$Integer\ Y = (y_{w-1}, y_{w-2}, y_{w-3}, \ldots, y_2, y_1, y_0)_{HR}$$
$$High - Radix\ HR = 2^r \ \ldots \because r > 1$$
$$Modulus\ m = (m_{w-1}, m_{w-2}, m_{w-3}, \ldots, m_2, m_1, m_0)_{HR}$$
$$A\ New\ High - Radix\ Constant \alpha_{HR} = -m^{-1} \quad (mod\ HR)$$

Based on above given pre-defined parameters AHRMM algorithm 7 is shown in Fig. 4.7.

Initially, the Montgomery Product (MP) is assigned zero value. Then MP is updated at step 4 for each bit of modulus m. where t_i is the temporary variable that has assigned values at step 3 in each iteration. The modular operation involved in step 3 for the calculation of t_i is replaced with right-shift operations as high-radix is always

---

Algorithm 7 Adaptable High-Radix Montgomery Multiplication

Input X, Y, m, HR and α_{HR}
Output Montgomery product $MP = X.Y.2^{-wr} \pmod{m}$ $\triangleright$ w is the length of m

1: *Initialization* $MP = (p_{w-1}, p_{w-2}, p_{w-3}, \cdots p_2, p_1, p_0)_{HR} = 0; i = 0$
2: **while** $i < w$ **do**
3:      $t_i = (p_0 + x_i.y_0).\alpha \pmod{HR}$
4:      $MP = (MP + x_i.Y + t_i.m) >> r$ $\triangleright$ right shift
5:      $i = i + 1$
6: **end while**
7: **if then**$(MP \geq m)$
8:      $MP = MP - m$
9: **end if**
10: return MP;

Fig. 4.7 Adaptable high-radix montgomery multiplication (AHRMM)

represented in powers of 2. If the modulus α is expressed as an exact power of 2, say $\alpha = 2^{\gamma}$, then $\beta \pmod{\alpha}$ can be expressed as $\beta \pmod{\alpha} = \beta - ((\beta >> \gamma) << \gamma)$, where right shift ($>>$) performs division by 2^{γ} and left shift ($<<$) performs multiplication with 2^{γ} .

The proposed constant PC used in BFW techniques has been redefined as $PC = 2^{(2wr+2)} \pmod{m}$ to invoke Algorithm 7 AHRMM instead of Algorithm 6 AMM for calculating MM. The total number of clock cycles required to evaluate one MM of the w-bit modulus concerning Algorithm AHRMM is $10w + 3$. It is obvious that the increase in radix reduces the clock cycles, but with a tradeoff of increased space. The optimal value for the radix can be fixed based on requirements. For high-speed computing systems used in web servers and banking sectors, which are not having any memory constraint, Algorithm 7 AHRMM is the optimal choice. Embedded systems that impose memory constraints can select Algorithm 6 AMM as an optimal choice.

References

Bajard JC, Didier LS, Kornerup P (1998) An rns montgomery modular multiplication algorithm. IEEE Trans Comput 47(7):766–776

Bansal M, Kumar A, Devrari A, Bhat A (2015) Implementation of modular exponentiation using montgomery algorithms. Int J Sci Eng Res 6(11)

Burger TW (2005) Intel multi-core processors: Quick reference guide. cache www.intel.com/cd/00/00/23/19/231912_231912.pdf

Cankaya EC (2011) Chinese wall model

Dingyi P, Arto S, Cunsheng D (1996) Chinese remainder theorem: applications in computing, coding, cryptography. World Scientific

Elbirt AJ, Paar C (1999) Toward an fpga architecture optimized for public-key algorithms. Reconfig Technol: FPGAs Comput Appl Inter Soc Optics Photon 3844:33–42

González CH, Fraguela BB (2010) A generic algorithm template for divide-and-conquer in multi-core systems. In: 2010 12th IEEE international conference on high performance computing and communications (HPCC), IEEE, pp 79–88

Hong JH, Wu CW (2000) Radix-4 modular multiplication and exponentiation algorithms for the rsa public-key cryptosystem. In: Proceedings of the 2000 Asia and South Pacific design automation conference, pp 565–570

Koc CK, Acar T, Kaliski BS (1996) Analyzing and comparing montgomery multiplication algorithms. IEEE Micro 16(3):26–33

Montgomery PL (1985) Modular multiplication without trial division. Math Comput 44(170):519–521

Nozaki H, Motoyama M, Shimbo A, Kawamura S (2001) Implementation of rsa algorithm based on rns montgomery multiplication. In: International workshop on cryptographic hardware and embedded systems, Springer, pp 364–376

Takagi N (1992) A radix-4 modular multiplication hardware algorithm for modular exponentiation. IEEE Tran Comput 8:949–956

Vollala S, Geetha K, Ramasubramanian N (2016) Efficient modular exponential algorithms compatible with hardware implementation of public-key cryptography. Secur Commun Netw 9(16):3105–3115

Wu CH, Hong JH, Wu CW (2001) Rsa cryptosystem design based on the chinese remainder theorem. In: Proceedings of the 2001 Asia and South Pacific Design automation conference, pp 391–395

Chapter 5
Review of Hardware Techniques for Improving Performance of Modular Exponentiation

5.1 Pipeline

The Modular Exponentiation (ME) is achieved by a sequence of modular multiplications (MMs). In order to achieve a better ME the fast performing MM method is needed. In the traditional MM method (repeated multiply-addition) there are two drawbacks:

- It needs precise comparison which requires more running time as well as hardware overhead.
- *Addition* and *Subtraction* steps have data dependency, therefore they have to be executed sequentially.

These two operations were performed for each bit of multiplier. Sheu et al. have given an option which helps to overcome these two drawbacks (Sheu et al. 1998). The basic logic is to break the multiplier into the number of equal-length segments and then calculate the multiplication of the current segment, whereas simultaneously calculate the residue of its preceding segment. This pipelined approach can minimize the running time.

$$X \leftarrow multiplier$$
$$Y \leftarrow multiplicand$$
$$m \leftarrow modulus$$
$$n \leftarrow size\ of\ multiplier,\ multiplicand\ and\ modulus$$

Formulation of modular multiplication for the pipelined environment, where the multiplier X can be divided into k equal-sized parts (*each with* $n \div k$ *bits, parts can be represented from* X_{k-1} *to* X_0) is:

$$R = (\dots(YX_{k-1} \pmod{m})2^{n/k} + YX_{k-2} \pmod{m})2^{n/k} + \dots + YX_0) \pmod{m} \quad (5.1)$$

© The Author(s), under exclusive license to Springer Nature Switzerland AG 2021
S. Vollala et al., *Energy-Efficient Modular Exponential Techniques*
for Public-Key Cryptography, https://doi.org/10.1007/978-3-030-74524-0_5

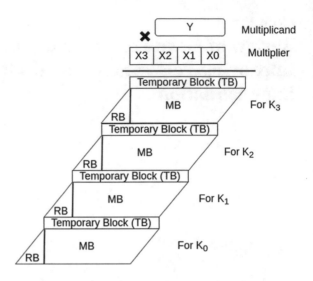

Fig. 5.1 Pipelined framework for k = 4

From the Eq. 5.1 it is clear that the dependency of addition and subtraction is removed for different parts. This means that the multiplication of the current part and the residue calculation of its preceding part can be calculated simultaneously. Therefore, the algorithm can be executed in the pipelined manner.

Based on the given formula in the Eq. 5.1, MM task can then be performed in pipelined fashion with the help of two different blocks:

1. The **Residue Block (RB)**: Computes the residue
2. The **Multiplication Block (MB)**: Computes $Y.X_i$ in (n/k) clock-cycles and balance the load with some extra clock-cycle.

For partition variable $k = 4$ the Fig. 5.1 gives the conceptual framework for implementing the RB and the MB. The total clock-cycles of the RB are the same as those of the MB. The RB and MB can run simultaneously and minimize the running time using only $(n/k + 4)(k + 1)$ clock cycles. Another **Temporary Block (TB)** is used in between two segments, to accumulate *residue value*, by shifting the value of the old residue in RB and then add it to the value from MB. The design has to execute the segments k times to compute the MM.

Carr et al. have also given a pipelined hardware implementation for Montgomery multiplication algorithm (Carr and Badamo 2020). It is known that Montgomery multiplication is a key operation in ME. Using their approach number of cycles and components has been minimized. The use of a lookup table and multiplexer for selecting terms to be added during computation was very helpful. They created segments of operands and then addition and shifting were done using pipelined modules which are arranged in a series.

Carr et al. has given the conceptual framework of the working of Montgomery multiplication without pipeline (refer Fig. 5.2) (Carr and Badamo 2020). The pipelined architecture for the adder of Montgomery multiplication is given in Fig. 5.3. We

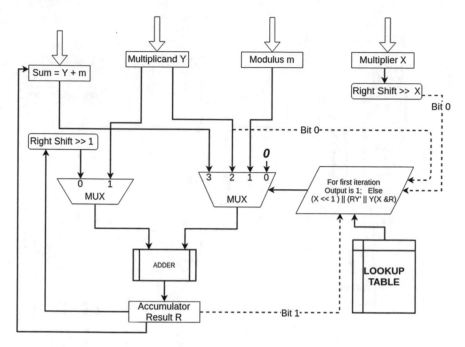

Fig. 5.2 Montgomery Multiplication without Pipeline

can see that there are four registers at the top for holding operands, modulus, and summation of multiplicand and modulus.

1. **Register X:** holding the multiplier
2. **Register Y:** holding the multiplicand
3. **Register m:** holding the modulus
4. **Register Y+m** holding the sum for multiplicand and modulus.

The shift register takes multiplier X as input and shifts multiple bits of it. Whereas, another shift register takes the result R as input and shifts it for 4 times and gives the output which is given as input to the *ADDER 1*. All four adders are arranged in a pipelined manner and chained together such that they have the following inputs:

1. Result of the previous pipelined adder (except the ADDER 1 as it receives the shifted Result)
2. Has a multiplexer to select one of (*zero, m, Y, or Y + m*) coming as input via delay module
3. Input from *Adder control logic*.

Delay module is framed in such a way that the first Delay module receives the input from $Y, m, Y + m$ registers and shift the received values and give the output to sequentially chained adders. The Result Accumulator receives the input from *Adder 4* and gives the output to second shift register.

The *Adder control logic* receives the input in the form of multiple bits from:

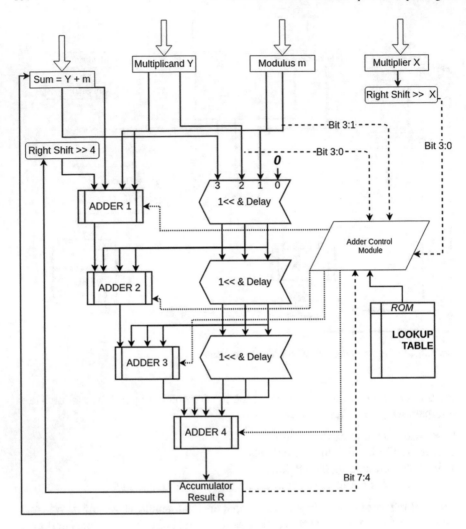

Fig. 5.3 Pipelined Architecture for Montgomery Multiplication

1. Modulus m (bits 3:1)
2. Multiplicand Y (bits 3:0)
3. Fist shift register shifting multiplier X (bits 3:0)
4. Result R (bits 7:4)

Adder control logic has a lookup table stored in ROM. Lookup table for the same is given in the Table 5.1: Algorithm 1 shown in Fig. 5.4 for performing Montgomery multiplication is based on the hardware configuration given in Fig. 5.3. For the Algorithm 1 shown in Fig. 5.4 the binary representation of X, Y, R, and m are:

- $X = x_0, x_1, \ldots, x_n$

Algorithm 1 Pipelined Montgomery's Modular Multiplication

Input: X, Y , m
Output: $R = X.Y \pmod{m}$

1: *Intialization:* $R = 0, i = 0$
2: **while** $i < n$ **do**   ▷ n is the length of binary representation of X,Y and m
3:      **if** $x_0 = 0$ and $r_0 = 0$ **then**
4:          $R = (R + 0) >> 1$ ▷ dividing the result by 2
5:      **else if** $x_0 = 0$ and $r_0 = 1$ **then**
6:          $R = (R + m) >> 1$
7:      **else if** $x_0 = 1$ and $r_0 = y_0$ **then**
8:          $R = (R + Y) >> 1$
9:      **else if** $x_0 = 1$ and $r_0 \neq y_0$ **then**
10:        $R = (R + Y + m) >> 1$
11:      **end if**
12:      *FirstShiftRegister* $= X >> 1$
13:      $i = i + 1$
14: **end while**
15: **if** $R > m$ **then**
16:      $R = R - m$
17: **end if**
18: **Return** Result **R**

Fig. 5.4 Pipelined Montgomery Multiplication

Table 5.1 LookUp Table for Adder Control Logic

Y	X	R	MUX
0	0	0	00
0	0	1	01
0	1	0	10
0	1	1	11
1	0	0	00
1	0	1	01
1	1	0	11
1	1	1	10

- $Y = y_0, y_1, \ldots, y_n$
- $R = r_0, r_1, \ldots, r_n$
- $m = m_0, m_1, \ldots, m_n$

Binary representation length of them are n-bit.

Algorithm 2 Montgomery Multiplication Algorithm

Input: X, Y, m
Output: $X \times Y$ (mod m)

1: *Initialization:* $R[0] = 0; i = 0$
2: **while** $i < n$ **do**
3:     $q_i = (R[i]_0 + x_i * y_O)$ (mod 2)
4:     $R[i+1] = (R[i] + x_i * Y + q_i * m) \div 2;$
5: **end while**
6: **Return** $R[k]$

Fig. 5.5 Montgomery Multiplication Algorithm

5.2 Carry Save Adder (CSA)

Several approaches have been discovered such as one can bypass the carry propagation during the *addition* steps of algorithms. Because the *addition* step is one of the main aspects of performance evaluation. Initially, one technique was proposed where addition is divided into k stages. The value of k is an optimal bit length. The selection of k is done in such a way that it can take full advantage of modern FPGA's carry chain features. But this approach has an unavoidable fault, that is the designed architecture will be application dependent and very much complex. It is obvious that one developed design will not be accessible by other devices with the same efficiency. Moreover, migration of the same design to a modern ASIC technology or indeed an alternative type of FPGA or PLD is difficult.

Another approach to avoid long carry propagation is using carry-save adders (CSAs). CSA can be used to execute the *addition* steps of Montgomery's algorithm. These CSAs have one benefit inherently i.e., their parallel structure. This property of CSA enables it to provide shallow combinational logic depth, without any concern of the implementing platform. This distinguishing feature of CSA attracts the developer of RSA and ECC Cryptosystems.

The CSAs are capable of performing additions for large operands which is a key requirement of the MM algorithms. These algorithms use either of the two architecture of CSA and the combination of any one of the CSA with a multiplexer can improve the performance of MM algorithms.

1. Five-to-two CSA and
2. Four-to-two CSA

This section discusses and compares both the modular multiplier approaches, First with a five-to-two CSA and then second with four-to-two CSA having 2 extra registers. The five-to-two CSA takes $n + 1$ clock cycles whereas four-to-two CSA takes $n + 2$ clock cycles. First, a different version of Montgomery multiplication which is compatible with CSA implementation is illustrated:

The unavoidable carry propagation resulting from the very large operand additions. Because of the computation of the R having 3 parameters during addition in

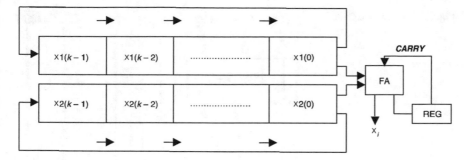

Fig. 5.6 The BRFA

step 4 of Algorithm 2 shown in Fig. 5.5. Therefore the main reason for the extra clock cycle is:

$$R[i + 1] = R[i] + x_i * Y + q_i * m \tag{5.2}$$

Barrel Register Full Adder (BRFA):

The inputs and outputs to the modified algorithms remain in redundant carry-save format, a full *addition* of the X1 and X2 input operands needs to be performed in order to determine the correct X_i values in various modified algorithms being discussed in this section. This is achieved by using the **barrel register full adder (BRFA)** (McIvor et al. 2004). The determination of the correct X_i values are calculated dynamically using the BRFA shown in Fig. 5.6. The desired X_i value is available when required with the help of only one full adder which adds the LSB of X_1 and X_2 two input parameters. For the second desired value, when the computation of the current X_i value is completed, the BRFA performs the right shifting of the input parameters X_1 and X_2 in order to obtain the next desired X_i. In this way, the BRFA saves the additional critical delay which can be caused because of the modification done in algorithms to make it compatible with CSAs. This saving of time is done by adding a single-bit with a full adder, which can be simultaneously performed with the CSAs in the same clock cycle. Therefore, saving additional clock-cycles for the computation of $X_1 + X_2$ is achieved.

5.2.1 Five-to-Two CSA

This carry-save architecture has 3 levels of carry save logic where they implement the Eq. 5.2 in two steps:

$$Sum = \alpha_1 \oplus \alpha_2 \oplus \alpha_3; \quad \& \quad Carry = (\alpha_1 \wedge \alpha_2) \vee (\alpha_2 \wedge \alpha_3) \vee (\alpha_1 \wedge \alpha_3) \tag{5.3}$$

The 3 input-bit vectors α_1, α_2, α_3 are added to obtain the Sum and Carry bit-vectors. With the help of the implementation of Eq. 5.3 using a five-to-two CSA approach

Fig. 5.7 Five to Two CSA

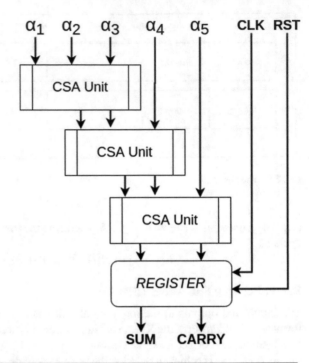

Algorithm 3 Montgomery's Modular Multiplication using Five-to-Two CSA

Input: $X1, X2, Y1, Y2, m$
Output: $R1, R2$ as Sum and Carry respectively

1: *Initialization:* $R1[0] = 0, R2[0] = 0, i = 0$
2: **while** $i < n$ **do**
3:     $a_i = (R1[i]_0 + R2[i]_0) + X_i \times (Y1_0 + Y2_0) \pmod 2$
4:     $R1[i+1], R2[i+1] = CSR(R1[i] + R2[i] + X_i \times (Y1 + Y2) + q_i \times m) \div 2$ ▷ CSR : Carry Save Representation
5:     $i = i + 1$
6: **end while**
7: **Return** $R1[n], R2[n]$

Fig. 5.8 Montgomery Multiplication using Five-to-Two CSA

shown in Fig. 5.7 we can get the output of 5 input operands in the register only in 1 clock cycle.

In Algorithm 3 shown in Fig. 5.8 the critical delay is cause due to the five to two carry save addition given in Eq. 5.4.

$$R1[i+1],\ R2[i+1] = CSR(R1[i] + R2[i] + X_i \times (Y1 + Y2) + q_i \times m) \div 2$$
$$(5.4)$$

Fig. 5.9 Four to Two CSA

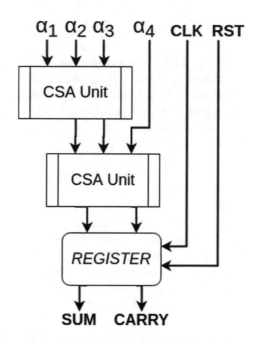

Algorithm 4 Montgomery Multiplication using Four-to-Two CSA

Input: $X1, X2, Y1, Y2, m$
Output: $R1, R2$ as Sum and Carry respectively

1: *Initialization:* $R1[0] = 0, R2[0] = 0, i = 0, Z1, Z2 = CSR(Y1 + Y2 + m + 0)$
2: **while** $i < n$ **do**
3:    $q_i = (R1[i]_0 + R2[i]_0) + (X_i \times (Y1_0 + Y2_0)) \pmod 2$
4:    **if** $X_i = 0$ and $q_i = 0$ **then**
5:       $R1[i+1], R2[i+1] = CSR(R1[i] + R2[i] + 0 + 0) \div 2$
6:    **else if** $X_i = 1$ and $q_i = 0$ **then**
7:       $R1[i+1], R2[i+1] = CSR(R1[i] + R2[i] + Y1 + Y2) \div 2$
8:    **else if** $X_i = 0$ and $q_i = 1$ **then**
9:       $R1[i+1], R2[i+1] = CSR(R1[i] + R2[i] + m + 0) \div 2$
10:    **else**
11:       $R1[i+1], R2[i+1] = CSR(R1[i] + R2[i] + Z1 + Z2) \div 2$
12:    **end if**
13: **end while**
14: **Return** $R1[n], R2[n]$

Fig. 5.10 Montgomery Multiplication using Four-to-Two CSA

The Eq. 5.4 require exact value of X_i. The exact value of X_i can be obtain by adding two parameter X1 and X2. This addition can be done by BFRA (refer paragraph in Sect. 5.2) simultaneously without any extra clock cycle within the loop (McIvor et al. 2004).

5.2.2 Four-to-Two CSA

Instead of 5-input this architecture supports 4-input which in result saves one level of CSA logic. Similar to five-to-two CSA this architecture also performs the Sum and Carry vector calculation in one clock cycle only (McIvor et al. 2004). The block diagram of four-to-two CSA architecture is given in Fig. 5.9.

In the Algorithm shown in Fig. 5.10 the critical delay is caused due to the four to two carry-save addition given in Eq. 5.5.

$$R1[i + 1], R2[i + 1] = CSR(R1[i] + R2[i] + a + b) \tag{5.5}$$

The variable a and b in Eq. 5.5 is derived from the current state of X_i and q_i in the loop of Algorithm 4 shown in Fig. 5.10. This derivation of variables a, b are done with the help of a multiplexer control logic. The overhead of this multiplexer should be considered while deciding the critical delay. But even after this consideration the Algorithm 4 shown in Fig. 5.10 takes lesser clock cycles than the previous Five-to-Two CSA Algorithm 3 shown in Fig. 5.8. This minimization of the clock-cycle in the step shown in Eq. 5.5 is done with the help of two extra memory registers (Z1, Z2). In the very first step of the Algorithm 4 shown in Fig. 5.10. The value of $Z1$ and $Z2$ is calculated during initialization only with the expense of one extra clock cycle. Similar to the previous Algorithm 3 shown in Fig. 5.8 (Five-to-Two CSA) the Algorithm 4 shown in Fig. 5.10 (Four-to-Two CSA) also requires the exact value of X_i. The exact value of X_i can be obtained by adding two-parameter X1 and X2. This addition can be done by BFRA (refer to the paragraph in Sect. 5.2) simultaneously without any extra clock cycle within the loop. Therefore, Algorithm 4 is shown in Fig. 5.10 takes only $n + 2$ clock cycles for complete execution.

5.3 Field-Programmable Gate Array (FPGA)

Field programmable the term *Field* refers to Programming in the field i.e., we can modify the device function in the lab or the site where the device will be installed. FPGA can be used for addition, multiplication, it is an inexpensive, easy realization of logic networks in hardware. *FPGA hardware* contains PLDs, Logic Gates, RAM, clock manager and other components. FPGA has a layout of a unit representation in matrix form where a user can configure the function of each logic block, Input/Output and interconnection between them.

FPGA can be also understood in a simple way as a silicon chip that has re-programmable digital circuitry, i.e., it has thousands of configurable logic blocks and they are connected with re-configurable wiring. We can have a certain section of FPGA dedicated to one task and another section for some other task, and we can run all those tasks in parallel. Which helps single-point control for multiple programs running in parallel.

Family of FPGAs (Betz and Rose 1995)

- Hard-Wired Logic Blocks
- Experimental Methodology
- Area and Delay Models
- Experimental Results

This family differs in physical means for implementing a program, Interconnection arrangements and Basic functionality of Logic blocks.

As discussed, an FPGA is interspersed wiring of logic blocks which is developed in a way that the user can configure the wired logic blocks as per his need (refer Fig. 5.11 (Rose et al. 1993). The user can configure the device after the development, which justifies the term "field-programmable". The language needed to configure the FPGA is known as hardware description language (HDL). The same language is also used by an application-specific integrated circuit (ASIC). The all-new generation automation tools for designing electronic devices like FPGA has outdated the circuit diagrams which were previously used for configuration of the same.

FPGAs are a new generation electronic device used for making a breadboard or small sample of any target product. It is used by many researchers for Proof of Concept (POC). The single FPGA can be used again and again for different POCs targeting various applications. FPGA is preferred where the designs are small production demand is low, in comparison to ASIC where the designs are big and production is on a large scale.

There are some FPGAs available in the market e.g. a Spartan FPGA from Xilinx FPGAs has lots of logic blocks connected to each other which can be programmed according to requirement. The connection between the logic blocks is linked hierarchically. These Logic blocks are highly scalable from executing basic logic gates like AND/OR to executing complex combinational programs. Another variety of Virtex-4 Series FPGAs has been used by Suzuki et al. to improve the Montgomery multiplication algorithm (Suzuki 2007). In order to maximize the performance of the multiplication unit in FPGA, it uses typical hardware macros such as the DSP48 function of an FPGA. Various FPGAs come with a memory option. Memory can be in the form of basic flip-flops or whole blocks of memory. These memory units can be attached to each logic-blocks or may be shared by them.

If we compare two systems one has a processor-based system like CPU another one system is FPGA.

- Both are configurable units in the context of reprogramming.
- Both are silicon chips.
- FPGA has the option of running the programs in different logic blocks, whereas the CPU finds a way of running the programs sequentially.
- FPGA can run programs simultaneously without sharing any resources.

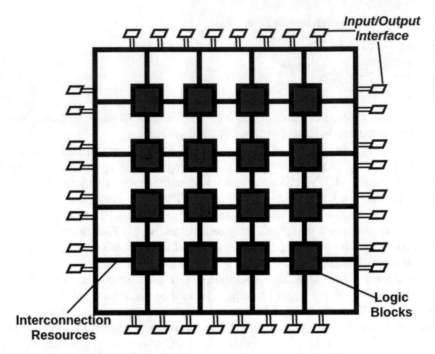

Fig. 5.11 Basic FPGA Architecture

5.4   Application Specific Integrated Circuits (ASIC)

The complexity of various Cryptosystems especially PKC is increasing day by day. The encryption technique uses complex approaches to encrypt information like hashing or exponentiation techniques. Another computation overhead is the use of large size keys. The increasing complexity requires more computing power and generates competition among ASICs, CPUs and GPUs. They all try to provide the best electronic circuit design for the cryptosystem. Specially customized ASICs has been used by some cryptographic devices to save energy and chip size.

ASICs are playing a key role in changing the latest trend of the information security hardware implementations, nowadays the target of new research is not to find better option between ASIC or FPGA or any other technology, instead, researchers are trying to find new ways of integrating ASICs with CPUs and GPUs in order to obtain better performance (Dally and Chang 2000).

According to the need for an application or product, the designer can design a custom ASIC. The designer has full control of the physical structure of the circuit. With the proper design of ASIC, the designers can achieve high speed, better power utilization, and better performance without increasing the design time. A proper design includes the following points:

- Initial stage is to plan the base (floor-planning) and carpeting data bus i.e., the designer first put the critical wires in the correct place.
- After the designing of the basic floor, the logic-circuit design is done.
- Carpeted data-bus and well-structured wiring between logic unit keep local wire short enabling the use of minimum-sized drivers.
- Circuiting the wire at the initial stage benefits the designer to analyze the timing issues, enable designers to minimize the wiring overhead and obtain better performance.

Basically, ASICs are made-up of silicons. It is ideal for devices that perform a very specific task repeatedly. General-purpose chips like GPUs or CPUs or FPGAs are capable of performing various tasks on the same hardware design. They are reconfigurable but less efficient. Whereas ASIC's design is specific to an application only, and runs much faster and more efficiently. Cryptosystems used in information security at large data centers (private data center, public clouds) have repetitive tasks like encryption and decryption.

Once an ASIC is designed then it cannot be reconfigured, this characteristic of ASIC can be expensive in terms of cost. For designing a prototype of a product the FPGA is preferred. Once the design is accepted and large-scale production is required then only ASIC is suitable. Designing a single or few ASIC can be very expensive but one needs to find the break-even point between the production cost and demand.

5.5 Systolic Array

The simultaneous execution of algorithms deviates from conventional Von Neumann architecture. The systolic array is an example of a simultaneous processing approach. The systolic array was first proposed in the 1970s. Intel used this technique to produce CMU's iWarp processor last decade of the 19th century for parallel execution of the program. If we arrange the processors in an interconnecting system such that they can collectively execute a given task. Similar to blood circulation in the biological system, the data flow in the interconnected system can be simulated. A systolic array is that interconnected system that skillfully passes the data between all the processors (or memory) and performs the computation of data. From this explanation, it is clear that parallel computing can be achieved with a Systolic array, but one has to exercise the pipelining concept.

Processing Element (PE) in a systolic refers to a processing unit that is arrayed in a matrix (with one or multiple rows) such that each PE can communicate with other PEs. The PEs can have their own small memory, as well as they share a common memory space (Poornima et al. 2019). This matrix of PEs is also attached to a gateway termed as a *host-station* which is responsible for connecting the systolic array with the outer network.

Some of the qualities of systolic array are:

- **Simultaneous Processing** All PEs are interconnected as well as capable of performing independently. There is no central governing element, which provides a systolic array of simultaneous processing.
- **Pipelining** The independent structure of PEs of the systolic array can minimize the required processing clock cycle results in maximizing the throughput.
- **Synchronized Clock** In a systolic array, all the PEs are synchronized with a single global clock. The clock signal has a fixed length. Communication and computation of data both are triggered by the global clock.
- **Similar PEs** For the ease of programming similar types of PEs are arranged in various positions of the systolic array.
- **Spatial Locality** The PEs are closely interconnected and it is more likely that if a PE is used then PE beside it will be used next.
- **Temporal Locality** All the PEs are connected with the global clock which means it takes a minimum of one unit of clock cycle to transmit the data between PEs.
- **Scalability** The arrangements of PEs in a systolic array is in such a way that it can be extended. The number of PEs are arranged in modular number and the interconnection between them is homogeneous. This enables the systolic array to expandable according to the need.

Some of the benefits of systolic array are:

- It can run various programs simultaneously and provide better throughput.
- It has a compact and strong structure.
- The Global clock eases the communication of data and signal.

Some of the drawbacks of the systolic array are:

- Systolic arrays are specified to the set of problems it can solve. Which makes it inflexible for various problems.
- Making procedure is tough.
- Fabrication cost is also very high.
- Multiple PEs are closely connected which minimize the larger fan-out and the long wired delays for long operands (Walter 1993; Blum and Paar 2001).

The importance of the systolic array in the field of *cryptography* is very crucial. PEs of a systolic array is programmed by Ali Alkar et al. in such a way that it can improve the performance of Montgomery multiplication and square by 20% in comparison to Walter's model (Alkar and Sönmez 2004; Walter 1993). Bit-level systolic arrays are used in hardware presented by Ali Alkar et al. as a hardware version of the RSA, to speed up MM and squaring. This improves the parallelism between the squaring systolic structure and systolic multiplication. For this purpose, the systolic array is organized in a single row manner. To overcome large fanout signals and large wire delays for operands Miyamoto et al. used a systolic array approach for the systematic design of the RSA processor (Miyamoto et al. 2011).

A multiply and square algorithm for ME can be incorporated in a systolic array in three simple steps (Ibrahim et al. 2019):

1. Generate the data dependency graph of the target algorithm.
2. Use special scheduling procedure to allocate a time value to each node in the data dependency graph.
3. Map all the nodes from the data dependency graph to the processing elements (PEs) of the systolic/semi-systolic array.

The designing of modular exponential computing systolic array can be divided hierarchically into three levels (Blum and Paar 2001) .

1. **Processing Element**: Responsible for *bit level* calculation of a MM operation.
2. **Array of PEs:** The array of PEs are combined to compute the full-length *MM* result.
3. **Complete architecture of systolic array:** Merge the computed values of MMs to get final *ME* result.

5.6 Transport Triggered Architecture (TTA)

Transport Triggered Architecture (TTA) is a technology that gives an economical option to choose between the advantages of ASIC and FPGA where ASIC provides features like better size and performance and the FPGA provides customization and programming ability (Hamalainen et al. 2005). The main disadvantage of ASIC is the production period is high and up-gradation is a very tough task in the term of time and cost both. But the positive side is that it offers the highest performance at low energy and low cost (in large production volumes). One classical example can be a defective IEEE 802.11 Wireless Local Area Network (WLAN) ASIC chip if there is an error then a low-cost upgrading option would have been desirable. Whereas the FPGA provides re-programmability and full customization with proper efficiency. Its production period is very short. A classical example of FPGA can be network routers that require an update its routing algorithms from time to time. But it is not an efficient option for light-weight sensitive devices like embedded systems, sensor nodes.

Technology with advantages of both is always desirable and TTA is a solution which is basically a *processor architecture* which can be adopted by both ASIC and FPGAs technologies. The central processing unit (CPU) of TTA is consist of:

- **Functional Units (FUs)**: It can be a very simple logic consist basic gates or a fully functional Arithmetic Logic Unit (ALU), but the TTA architecture requires at least one FU to perform the task as a Load and Store Unit (LSU).
- **Register Files (RFs)**: It is used for storing the integer value and the ports & bus connections can be changed for unlimited number of times.
- **Buses**: Interconnecting buses are responsible for transferring the data between FUs. The number of buses can vary for different TTAs.

There is a vast variety of TTA configurations are available we need an exploring device to find the best suitable TTA for our application. The explorer should be capable of examining and assessing the running time, size and power utilization of a vast number of TTAs available (Hamalainen et al. 2005).

5.7 Cox-Rower Architecture

The motive behind designing the cox-rower architecture is the efficient implementation of Residue Number System (RNS) Montgomery multiplication. cox-rower is comprised of two separate but interconnected units. The *cox* is unit is typically a 7-bit adder and *rower* unit is a single-precision modular multiplier-and-accumulator.

RNS and Montgomery multiplication algorithms are combined to overcome the disadvantage of RNS i.e., RNS is efficient with addition, subtraction and multiplication but consumes time when it comes to division and comparison, whereas the Montgomery algorithm smartly avoids the division process by changing radix representation which helps to effectively avoid division difficulties faced by RNS system.

Cox-Rower architecture targets the RNS representation method because it has an advantage that calculation of each RNS element can be carried out individually i.e., n processing elements can speed up the process by a factor of n.

Some examples for Cox-Rower Architecture implementation for modular multiplication (MM) are:

- Architecture given by Shinichi Kawamura et al. capable of executing RNS based Montgomery multiplication. This architecture supports the base extension algorithm to run in parallel by multiple Rower units which are govern by the Cox unit (Kawamura et al. 2000). The rower unit responsible for executing single-precision MM and accumulation, and the Cox unit is responsible for adding 7-bit at a time. The base extension algorithm running in parallel enables the conversion of RNS to radix and radix to RNS efficiently. Therefore this is capable of handling the existing radix algorithm of RSA cryptography.
- The Cox-Rower architecture for supporting RNS to implement ECC with a high performance given by Bajard et al. This is an improved version of RSA and implemented over FPGA (Bajard and Merkiche 2014).

After the first implementation by Kawamura et al. other modifications are done for various public-key algorithms to achieve better efficiency (Kawamura et al. 2000). Modification in the inner architecture of cox and rower is also performed by Bajard et al. (2014). Most of the cox-rower architecture supports the parallel execution of the Montgomery multiplication algorithm based on RNS. It is not so difficult to design fast ME by applying the Montgomery multiplication algorithm repeatedly. The key improvement of all cox-rower architecture is parallelism supported by the new RNS base extension algorithms.

References

Alkar AZ, Sönmez R (2004) A hardware version of the RSA using the Montgomery's algorithm with systolic arrays. Integration 38(2):299–307

Bajard JC, Merkiche N (2014) Double level Montgomery cox-rower architecture, new bounds. In: International conference on smart card research and advanced applications. Springer, pp 139–153

Betz V, Rose J (1995) Using architectural "families" to increase FPGA speed and density. In: 3rd international ACM symposium on field-programmable gate arrays. IEEE, pp 10–16

Blum T, Paar C (2001) High-radix Montgomery modular exponentiation on reconfigurable hardware. IEEE Trans Comput 50(7):759–764

Carr R, Badamo MJ (2020) Reduced and pipelined hardware architecture for Montgomery modular multiplication. US Patent App. 16/184,139

Dally WJ, Chang A (2000) The role of custom design in ASIC chips. In: Proceedings of the 37th annual design automation conference, pp 643–647

Hamalainen P, Heikkinen J, Hannikainen M, Hamalainen TD (2005) Design of transport triggered architecture processors for wireless encryption. In: 8th Euromicro conference on digital system design (DSD'05). IEEE, pp 144–152

Ibrahim A, Tariq U, Ahmad T, Elmogy A, Bouteraa Y, Gebali F (2019) Efficient parallel semi-systolic array structure for multiplication and squaring in GF (2m). IEICE Electron Express 16:20190268

Kawamura S, Koike M, Sano F, Shimbo A (2000) Cox-rower architecture for fast parallel Montgomery multiplication. In: International conference on the theory and applications of cryptographic techniques. Springer, pp 523–538

McIvor C, McLoone M, McCanny JV (2004) Modified Montgomery modular multiplication and RSA exponentiation techniques. IEE Proc-Comput Digit Tech 151(6):402–408

Miyamoto A, Homma N, Aoki T, Satoh A (2011) Systematic design of RSA processors based on high-radix Montgomery multipliers. IEEE Trans Very Large Scale Integr (VLSI) Syst 19(7):1136–1146

Poornima B, Sumathi A, Premkumar CPR (2019) Memory efficient high speed systolic array architecture design with multiplexed distributive arithmetic for 2D DTCWT computation on FPGA. Inf MIDEM 49(3):119–132

Rose J, El Gamal A, Sangiovanni-Vincentelli A (1993) Architecture of field-programmable gate arrays. Proc IEEE 81(7):1013–1029

Sheu JL, Shieh MD, Wu CH, Sheu MH (1998) A pipelined architecture of fast modular multiplication for RSA cryptography. In: ISCAS'98. Proceedings of the 1998 IEEE international symposium on circuits and systems (Cat. No. 98CH36187), vol 2. IEEE, pp 121–124

Suzuki D (2007) How to maximize the potential of FPGA resources for modular exponentiation. In: International workshop on cryptographic hardware and embedded systems. Springer, pp 272–288

Walter CD (1993) Systolic modular multiplication. IEEE Trans Comput 42(3):376–378

Part III
Modular Multiplication

Chapter 6
Introduction to Montgomery Multiplication

6.1 Montgomery Multiplication

Montgomery Multiplication (MMM) is most useful and interesting when it comes about modular multiplication (MM). Till now MMM has advances the efficiency most. In this section, the operation required in computing MMM is discussed. The Montgomery product:

We need to compute:

$$X.Y \pmod{m}$$

...where $X, Y < m$

We have Montgomery reduction element p such that $GCD(m, p) = 1$

We can have Montgomery product as:

$$MonProd(X, Y) = X \times Y \times p^{-1} \pmod{m} \tag{6.1}$$

It will be preferable if p is chosen to be in the power of 2. In order to increase the speed of mathematical operations such as division and multiplication, the MMM is used. Because it can be performed efficiently with simple shift and addition operation (Omondi 2020).

Similar to multiplication there are various ways to perform Montgomery multiplication. Basically, to understand Montgomery multiplication in a structured manner, methods can be categorized into two categories:

1. First one is when multiplication and reduction is done separately and
2. Second one is when reduction and multiplication is done integrated

Level of integration is depends upon switching between reduction *and* multiplication (Großschädl et al. 2004; Koc et al. 1996). Number of switching can be high or low.

Independent from switching frequency the other factor is scanning the operand and product.

© The Author(s), under exclusive license to Springer Nature Switzerland AG 2021
S. Vollala et al., *Energy-Efficient Modular Exponential Techniques for Public-Key Cryptography*, https://doi.org/10.1007/978-3-030-74524-0_6

- The method designer can run the outer loop by scanning the words of operand one by one
  Or
- The method designer can run the outer loop by scanning the word of products.

Either way, the integration of multiplication and reduction is independent.

1. Independent operand scanning
2. Less switching operand scanning
3. High switching operand scanning
4. High switching product scanning
5. Less switching hybrid scanning

The Montgomery product is further used for Montgomery multiplication (MMM) for the various applications in cryptosystems. In Eq. 6.1 let us choose $p = 2^k$ such that m be a $k - bit$ integer i.e., $2^{k-1} \le m < 2^k$ and p and m should be relatively prime. From third step of Algorithm 1 shown in Fig. 4.1 of Chap. 4 it can be stated as:

$$R' = (X'Y')p^{-1} \pmod{m}$$

$Tp^{-1} = (T + T(-m)^{-1}((\bmod\ p))\ m)/p \pmod{m}$
let $Tp^{-1} = u$ then,
$u = (T + T(-m)^{-1}((\bmod\ p))\ m)/p \pmod{m}$

Applying Modulation Operation in Exponentiation Technique:

Given categorisation of techniques calculate the exponent for a given number, for PKC modular exponentiation is needed. We can apply modulus operation in between the stages given in algorithms.

We know the property of modular multiplication:

$$
\begin{aligned}
a^N &\pmod{m} \\
&= [(a^{N/2} \pmod{m}) \times (a^{N/2} \pmod{m})] \pmod{m} \quad\quad (6.2)\\
&= [(a^P \pmod{m}) \times (a^Q \pmod{m})] \pmod{m}
\end{aligned}
$$

$$...N = P \times Q$$

From given Eq. 6.2 one can modify the Algorithms 1 and 2 given in the Chap. 3 shown in Fig. 3.1 & shown in Fig. 3.2 such that the size of any intermediate result will not exceed more than modular m. Which will help in computing the modular exponential value of large numbers in less space and time.

6.1.1 Independent Operand Scanning (IOS)

Commonly known as Separated Operand Scanning (SOS). The product $X \times Y$ is computed first using this method (McIvor et al. 2004). The Algorithm 1 shown in

---

Algorithm 1 Independent Operand Scanning

Input: X, Y , m, m'.
Output: $t_s = (C, S) = X \times Y$ (mod m)

1: *Initialization* $i = 0$
2: **while** $i < s$ **do** ▷ loop for words
3:     *Initialization* $C = 0; j = 0$
4:     **while** $j < s$ **do**
5:         $(C, S) = t_{i+j} + X_j \times Y_i + C$
6:         $t_{i+j} = S$
7:         $j = j + 1$
8:     **end while**
9:     $t_{i+s} = C$
10:     $i = i + 1$
11: **end while**
12: $i = 0$
13: **while** $i < s$ **do** ▷ loop for words
14:     *Initialize* $C = 0; j = 0, u = t_i \times m'_0$ (mod 2^w)
15:     **while** $j < s$ **do**
16:         $(C, S) = t_{i+j} + u \times m_j + C$
17:         $t_{i+j} = S$
18:         $j = j + 1$
19:     **end while**
20:     $t_{i+s} = t_{i+s} + C$
21:     $i = i + 1$
22: **end while**
23: *Initialization* $j = 0$
24: **while** $j \leq s$ **do**
25:     $t_j = t_j + s$
26:     $j = j + 1$
27: **end while**

Fig. 6.1 Independent operand scanning

Fig. 6.1 is computing $X \times Y \times p^{-1}$ (mod m). Operand and modulus is of size k-bit. We compute s number of words and the size of each word is w.

The reason for two disjoint loops for the calculation of $X \times Y$ and calculation of u is to achieve better efficiency for the Montgomery multiplication algorithm, especially in the case of squaring where $X = Y$. The foremost calculation procedure to be done in the Algorithm 1 shown in Fig. 6.1 involve word size multiplications also numerous additions of not-fixed length variables. The additions are calculated by utilizing the fast carry chains of FPGA. In order to enhance the multiplication operation, the design has been modified to support several word size multipliers. The partial result obtained by these multipliers is added by utilizing the fast look-ahead carry chains of FPGA to get the 64-bit conclusive result.

For analysing IOS procedure, according to a technique given by Koc et al. (1996), which is used for getting the number of operations. For $s - bit$ operand and modulus it require $2s^2 + s$ multiplications, $4s^2 + 4s + 2$ additions, $6s^2 + 7s + 3$ read requests, and $2s^2 + 6s + 2$ write requests. Moreover, where space is a concern,

---

Algorithm 2 Less Switching Operand Scanning

Input: X, Y , m, m'.
Output: $t_s = (C,S) = X \times Y \pmod{m}$

1: *Initialization:* $i = 0$;
2: **while** $i < s$ **do**   ▷ The Outer Loop
3:     *Initialization* $C = 0; j = 0$
4:     **while** $j < s$ **do**
5:         $(C,S) = t_j + X_j \times Y_i + C$
6:         $t_j = S$
7:         $j = j + 1$
8:     **end while**
9:     $(C,S) = t_s + C$
10:     $t_s = S$
11:     $t_{s+1} = C$
12:     $u = t_0 \times m'_0 \pmod{2^w}$
13:     $(C,S) = t_0 + u \times m_0$
14:     *Initialization* $j = 0$
15:     **while** $j < s$ **do**
16:         $(C,S) = t_j + u \times m_j + C$
17:         $t_{j-1} = S$
18:         $j = j + 1$
19:     **end while**
20:     $(C,S) = t_s + C$
21:     $t_{s-1} = S$
22:     $t_s = t_{s+1} + C$
23:     **for** $j = 0\, to\, s$ **do**   ▷ Loop for shifting the result
24:         $t_j = t_{j+1}$
25:     **end for**
26:     $i = i + 1$
27: **end while**

Fig. 6.2 Less switching operand scanning

the IOS procedure needs a total of $2s + 2$ word-space for intermediate results, the $(2s + 1)$ word-spaces are used to save array t and 1 word-space is for reduction parameter u (refer the Algorithm 1 shown in Fig. 6.1).

6.1.2   Less Switching Operand Scanning (LSOS)

Commonly known as Coarsely Integrated Operand Scanning (CIOS). The LSOS upgrades from IOS by combining the multiplication & reduction steps in a single loop. Particularly, rather than calculating the whole product $X \times Y$ before the reduction procedure, it switches between loops of the calculating product and reduction procedure within the main outer loops. This is achievable because there is no dependency on reduction parameter u in the reduction procedure, apart from the value

Algorithm 3 High Switching Operand Scanning

Input: X, Y , m, m'.
Output: $t_s = (C,S) = X \times Y \pmod{m}$

1: *Initialization:* $t = 0; i = 0$
2: **while** $i < s$ **do**   ▷ The outer loop
3:     $(C,S) = t_0 + X_0 \times Y_i$
4:     $\text{ADD}(t_1,C)$
5:     $u = S \times m'_0 \pmod{2^w}$
6:     $(C,S) := S + u \times m_0$
7:     *Initialization:* $j = 0$
8:     **while** $j < s$ **do**   ▷ The inner loop
9:         $(C,S) = t_j + X_j \times Y_i + C$
10:        $\text{ADD}(t_{j+1},C)$
11:        $(C,S) = S + u \times m_j$
12:        $t_{j-1} = S$
13:        $j = j + 1$
14:     **end while**
15:     $(C,S) = t_s + C$
16:     $t_{s-1} = S$
17:     $t_s = t_{s+1} + C$
18:     $t_{s+1} = 0$
19:     $i = i + 1$
20: **end while**

Fig. 6.3 High switching operand scanning

of intermediate result $t[i]$ in the ith iteration of the outer loop. Intermediate result $t[i]$ is entirely calculated by the ith iteration of the outer loop for calculation of the Montgomery product.

The LSOS Algorithm 2 shown in Fig. 6.2 (along with the minor modification) needs $2s^2 + s$ multiplications, $4s^2 + 4s + 2$ additions, $6s^2 + 7s + 2$ read requests, & $2s^2 + 5s + 1$ write requests, involve the concluding multi-precision subtraction. It requires $s + 3$ words of storage space, a compelling development compare to the IOS method.

6.1.3   High Switching Operand Scanning (HSOS)

It is commonly known as Finely Integrated Operand Scanning (FIOS). The HSOS combines the 2 inner loops of the LSOS Algorithm 2 shown in Fig. 6.2 in order to calculate the multiplications and additions in a single loop. The HSOS Algorithm 3 is shown in Fig. 6.3. In LSOS partial results are calculated by performing the multiplication of $X_j \times Y_i$ & $u \times m_j$ in a single loop, followed by performing the addition of the partial results with the final t. The HSOS algorithm requires the

---

Algorithm 4 High Switching Product Scanning

Input: X, Y , m, m'.
Output: $t_s = (C,S) = X \times Y \pmod{m}$

1: *Initialize:* $i = 0$
2: **while** $i < 2s$ **do**
3:      *Initialize:* $j = i - s + 1$
4:      **while** $j < s$ **do**
5:          $(C,S) = t_0 + X_j \times Y_{i-j}$
6:          $\text{ADD}(t_1, C)$ ▷ We assume array t to be set to 0 initially.
7:          $(C,S) = S + u_j m_{i-j}$
8:          $t_0 = S$
9:          $\text{ADD}(t_1, C)$
10:          $j = j + 1$
11:      **end while**
12:      $u_{i-s} = t_0$
13:      $t_0 = t_1$
14:      $t_1 = t_2$
15:      $t_2 = 0$
16:      $i = i + 1$
17: **end while**

Fig. 6.4 High switching product scanning

initialization of t_0 before beginning with the loop, as the value of u relies on the value of t. This resembles the execution of 1st iteration ($i = 0$) of the loop.

The Algorithm 3 shown in Fig. 6.3 majorly performs two tasks, first calculate partial products of $X \times Y$ at each iteration, second it performs addition of calculated product of $u \times m$ with the partial product. Followed by right-shifting of the result of the addition is performed by 1 word such that the value of t is less than modulus m. It then shifts this sum right one word, making t prepared for the upcoming $(i + 1)$th iteration. This approach has a difference from LSOS, here it has only a single inner loop.

The HSOS method shown in Fig. 6.3 needs $2s^2 + s$ multiplications, $5s^2 + 3s + 2$ additions, $7s^2 + 5s + 2$ read requests and $3s^2 + 4s + 1$ write requests. Moreover, it requires total of $s + 3$ temporary words space.

6.1.4 High Switching Product Scanning (HSPS)

It is commonly known as Finely Integrated Product Scanning (FIPS). Unlike the previous Algorithm 3 shown in Fig. 6.3 where interleaving computation of products $X \times Y$ and $u \times m$ was performed here, in HSPS the iteration is done in the form of scanning the product rather than operand. The Algorithm 4 shown in Fig. 6.4 store the values of u & result in array u only, the size of array u is $s - words$.

From the iterating variable j of inner loop it is clear that least significant s words of final result is available in u. Where the MSB is t_0, at the end the value of t_1 and t_2 is zero. The final result is available in $s - words$ of array u. The HSPS Algorithm 4 shown in Fig. 6.4 needs $2s^2 + s$ multiplications, $6s^2 + 2s + 2$ additions, $9s^2 + 8s + 2$ read requests, and $5s^2 + 8s + 1$ write requests. The number of additions, read requests, and write requests is higher in comparison from already discussed algorithms. However, the number of multiplications required is equivalent. The space needed is $s + 3$ words.

6.1.5 Less Switching Hybrid Scanning (LSHS)

This algorithm is an enhancement of the IOS algorithm, demonstrating a different way towards Montgomery multiplication. Commonly known as Coarsely Integrated Hybrid Scanning (CIHS). It is observed that the IOS algorithm needs $2s + 2$ word-space for saving the intermediate values of t and u. The Algorithm 5 shown in Fig. 6.5 demonstrates that using only $s + 3$ word-space for saving intermediate values while keeping the overall execution of the algorithm the same. The algorithm is termed "hybrid scanning" because it combines the product-scanning & operand-scanning approaches for multiplication. But the reduction procedure has still followed the approach of the operand-scanning algorithms. In this algorithm, the procedure starts with partitioning the calculation of $X \times Y$ into two separate loops. The responsibility of the following loop is to perform one-word shifting of the intermediate result at the last of each iteration.

The two excess words calculated in the 1st loop of the Algorithm 5 are utilized in 2nd $j - loop$ responsible for computation of the $(s + i)$th word of $X \times Y$. The number of multiplications needed in this algorithm is $2s^2 + s$. But, the number of additions minimized to $4s^2 + 4s + 2$. The number of read requests are $6s^2 + 6s + 2$ and the number of write requests are $3s^2 + 5s + 1$. We have already discussed about the memory space required by this algorithm i.e., $s + 3$.

Architecture has to deal with trade-offs for parallelizing these five discussed approaches, up to what extent the algorithms can be parallelized.

6.2 An RNS Montgomery Multiplication Algorithm

Unlike the other position-based number systems the Residue Number System (RNS) system doesn't provide specific weight to its digits based on its position (Bajard et al. 1998). The digits in a different position are independent of each other which means some of the arithmetic operations such as addition, subtraction can be performed simultaneously but some other operations like multiplication, division & comparison are not defined for RNS. Montgomery's multiplication method requires a positional based number system to perform modular multiplication. It starts from LSB or MSB

Algorithm 5 Less switching Hybrid Scanning

Input: X, Y , m, m'.
Output: $t_s = (C,S) = X \times Y \pmod{m}$

1: *Initialize: i = 0*
2: **while** $i < s$ **do**
3:     $u = t_0 \times m'_0 \pmod{2^w}$ ▷ The array t is assumed to be set to 0 initially.
4:     $(C,S) = t_0 + u \times m_0$
5:     **while** $j < s$ **do**
6:         $(C,S) = t_j + u \times m_j + C$
7:         $t_{j-1} = S$
8:         $j = j + 1$
9:     **end while**
10:     $(C,S) = t_s + C$
11:     $t_{s-1} = S$
12:     $t_s = t_{s+1} + C$
13:     $t_{s+1} = 0$
14:     *Initialization: j = 0*
15:     **while** $j < s$ **do**
16:         $(C,S) = t_{s-1} + Y_j \times X_{s-j+i}$
17:         $t_{s-1} = S$
18:         $(C,S) = t_s + C$
19:         $t_s = S$
20:         $t_{s+1} = C$
21:         $j = j + 1$
22:     **end while**
23:     $i = i + 1$
24: **end while**

Fig. 6.5 Less switching hybrid scanning

and proceeds bit by bit in each iteration. This makes RNS arithmetic unsupported for Montgomery multiplication at first. In order to use RNS for the Montgomery algorithm, using mixed-radix representation for operands and modulus is more helpful. For this, follow the approach where the least significant digit of a mixed-radix representation is selected arbitrarily from the residues of the RNS representation when the two systems are based on the same set of modulus. The method executes a multiplication in between the reduction procedure, and this method can be simultaneously executed for different residues of the RNS representation. The requirement of even division by any modulus at each iteration increases the complexity of the method. Because at last 1 residue will be left obscure. Secondly, all the calculations are executed in excess base representation therefore, the final result will be also in excess base form. Which requires a format conversion. In order to increase the efficiency of RNS based Montgomery multiplication, an efficient format-conversion approach is required. If any residue is lost in the process, then it can be retrieved by a Chinese remainder theorem (CRT) (Kwon et al. 2013).

RNS System Terminology:

For understanding the mathematics of RNS following are the some assumptions: an integer Z can be expressed as

$$\langle Z \rangle_a = (Z[a_0], Z[a_1], \dots, Z[a_{n-1}]) \tag{6.3}$$

- The least significant digit of a mixed-radix representation is selected arbitrary from the residues of the RNS representation. When the two systems are based on the same set of modulus that means: $Z[a_i] = Z \pmod{a_i}$
- The a is termed as a base set $a = a_0, a_1, \dots, a_{n-1}$
- The elements of the base set are mutually co-prime i.e., $GCD(a_i, a_j) = 1$ for $i \neq j$
- To retrieve the lost residue $\langle Z \rangle_a$ from CRT the integer Z should be such that $0 \leq Z < A \ \because (A = \prod_{i=1}^{n} a_i)$
- Base size means the number of elements present in base set i.e., n

By following CRT condition, any Z where $Z < A$ will have only unique RNS-expression. The mixed RNS expression for two operands have a benefit where apart from modular addition and subtraction ($\pm_{RNS}$), also the multiplication ($\times_{RNS}$) can be calculated as modular multiplication for different RNS elements:

$$\langle C \pm_{RNS} D \rangle_a = (|C_j \pm D_j|a_j) \dots for \ j \in \{0, \dots, n-1\} \tag{6.4}$$

$$\langle C \times_{RNS} D \rangle_a = (|C_j \times D_j|a_j), \dots for \ j \in \{0, \dots, n-1\} \tag{6.5}$$

The formulas given in Eqs. 6.4 and 6.5 enables programmers to run addition, subtraction and multiplication simultaneously on various processing unit (at max n units). Still, comparison and division is a challenging task for RNS. Here the Montgomery method plays an important role and reduces the complexity. For defining "even division" ($\div_{RNS}$) in RNS let there be a modulus a_i that divides C.

$$C \div_{RNS} a_i = \hat{c}_j, \dots for \ j \in 0, \dots, n-1 \tag{6.6}$$

where $\hat{c}_j$ is computed as:

$$\hat{c}_j = |c_j \times (a_i)^{-1}_{a_j}|a_j, \ for \ j \neq i,$$

Here $(a_i)^{-1}_{a_j}$ represents the modulo inverse of a_i modulo a_j where a_i and a_j are relatively prime and $i, j \in 0, \dots, n-1 \ and \ i \neq j$. *Note* that at last 1 residue $\hat{c}_j$ will be left obscure and required some alternate ways to recover.

Mixed Radix System (MRS):

To modify the representation of RNS for Montgomery multiplication, the Montgomery algorithm such that it can perform even division. Let modulus's base for MRS is identical for RNS. For integer C the MRS representation is:

Algorithm 6 Montgomery Modular Multiplication Algorithm

Input: X, Y, μ, P $\triangleright$ X,Y and μ is of k bit length
Output: $X \times Y \times P^{-k} \pmod{\mu}$

1: *Initialization* $R = 0; i = 0$
2: **while** $i < k$ **do**
3:      $q_i = ((r_0 + x_i \times y_0) \times (P - \mu_0)_P^{-1}) \pmod{P} \ldots$ $\triangleright \because \mu_0 = \mu \pmod{P}$
4:      $R = R + x_i \times Y + q_i \times \mu$
5:      $R = R \div P$
6:      $i = i + 1$
7: **end while**

Fig. 6.6 Montgomery multiplication algorithm

$$C = c_1' + c_2' a_1 + c_3' a_2 a_1 + \cdots + c_n' a_1 \ldots a_{n-1} \tag{6.7}$$

Where $0 \leq c' < a_i$ $C < A$ and $A = \prod_{i=1}^{n} a_i$. The c' is MRS corresponding representation of RNS's c. This conversion of MRS from RNS is useful for comparison and division operations.

RNS Montgomery Multiplication:

Again visiting Montgomery multiplication algorithm which performs the repetitive reduction operation for multiplication at each loop. The key benefit of this algorithm and RNS integration is that the complexity of division is reduced by shifting-operation of this algorithm at the reduction process.

The Algorithm 6 shown in Fig. 6.6 calculates $R = X \times Y \times P^{-k} \pmod{\mu}$ using standard radix P arithmetic. Few things needs to be known prior to the algorithm definition: $\mu < P^k$; $GCD(\mu, P) = 1$; $X < \mu$ and $Y < \mu$ such that $X = \sum_{i=0}^{k-1} x_i P^i$.

The Algorithm 6 shown in Fig. 6.6 produce the output as an integer R such that $R < \mu$ and $R \cong X \times Y \times P^{-k} \pmod{\mu}$ Inside the loop, the calculation of q_i is performed in such a way that it ensures the intermediate result R is evenly divisible by P. Which in-turn enables the algorithm to perform the division by shifting operation. In concern of memory space for Algorithm 6 shown in Fig. 6.6, $R < 3\mu$ for $Y < 2\mu$ or even less memory is sufficient if $x_k < \frac{P}{2}$ then R is less than 2μ.

It is known that RNS is not a positional based number system, which means the calculation of q_i is a challenging task because it involves the use of the least significant digits of operands. The task is completed using the conceptual benefit of association of the set of modulus with MRS. The analysis made regarding this is:

- An integer has its residue in RNS and MRS representation. There is at least one MRS representation that exists which has the corresponding residue in RNS such that, its corresponding modulus is the first modulus of the mixed-radix system.
- The operand X has its MRS representation.

The Montgomery algorithm accommodated the RNS, calculating $R \cong XYm^{-1}$ (mod μ). Whereas, The MRS is a positional number system which means the integer

---

Algorithm 7 RNS Montgomery Modular Multiplication

Input: X given in MRS from equation 1.5 $X = \sum_{i=1}^{n} x_i' \prod_{j=1}^{i-1} a_j$ and Y given in RNS.
Output: $R \equiv X \times Y \times A^{-1} \pmod{\mu}$ where the integer $R < 2\mu$ expressed in RNS.

1: *Initialization:* $R = 0; i = 0$
2: **while** $i < n$ **do**
3:     $q_i' = (r_i + x_i' \times Y_i) \times (a_i - \mu_i)_i^{-1} \pmod{a_i}$
4:     $R = R +_{RNS} x_i' \times_{RNS} Y +_{RNS} q_i' \times_{RNS} \mu$
5:     $R = R \div_{RNS} x_i$
6:     $i = i + 1$
7: **end while**

Fig. 6.7 RNS Montgomery multiplication

is a product of base with weight associated with a position and the product of the previous weight with a new base (refer Eq. 6.7).

The next Algorithm 7 shown in Fig. 6.7 is simplifying the challenging task of the calculation of q_i by representing it in the MRS system as q_i', using the radix a_i. And the residue y_i represents the least significant digit of operand Y.

From the Eq. 6.3 a residue base $a_1, a_2, \ldots, a_n$ where $A = \prod_{i=1}^{n} a_i$ where GCD $(\mu, A) = 1$.

The Algorithm 7 shown in Fig. 6.7 produces the output as an integer R such that $R < 2\mu$ and $R \cong XYA^{-1} \pmod{\mu}$. The algorithm performs n iterations, such that every-time inside the loop an MRS digit q_i' is calculated and the final value of R is obtained in RNS, with the help of q_i' and x_i'.

6.3 Pipelining Architectures for Modular Multiplication

Quick multiplication is crucial for several applications. Including the situation where the series of multiplication is required to be calculated in order to get the exponential value. The calculation of modular exponentiation is a fundamental and key operation for many PKC. Out of numerous attempts to make modular multiplication efficient Montgomery multiplication approach is an effective technique. That is the reason for being its leading choice for PKC algorithm using modular exponentiation. Mentens and Nele et al. has implemented pipelined architecture over FPGA to perform efficient modular multiplication using Montgomery multiplication technique (Mentens et al. 2007). They considerably minimize the length of the critical path by offering multiple levels (4-level) of pipeline in hardware design.

An increase in pipelining levels enables the PKC system to execute in higher frequency. A higher frequency can be applied where the cycle-time is short and multi-level pipelined architecture is available. Increased frequency provides speed-up in the computation process. If one can attain 10% of speed-up even then the security of a PKC can be doubled. The foremost benefit of the pipelined hardware design is its fewer clock-cycles. Which allows it to produce a better throughput despite the slow clock frequency (Asif and Kong 2017). If multilevel pipelined architecture is implemented for modular multiplication then one can significantly increase the throughput. Using this phenomenon a parallel hardware design has been given by Asif et al. which was is implemented on VHDL (Asif and Kong 2017). In order to achieve parallelism, they have used RNS, as the addition of large integers can be performed in parallel. They analyzed that the sum of residues procedure is suitable for designing a parallel modular multiplication algorithm, which supports long-range operands and modulus. The main feature of RNS is that one can perform addition, subtraction & multiplication using different data paths in parallel for residues $(R_i)_n$. This feature provides speed-up in a parallel environment and attracts many researchers.

To speed up the modular multiplication with a large modulus can be achieved by partitioning the operand (multiplier) into several equal-sized segments. Thereafter, performing the multiplication and residue calculation of each segment in a pipelined fashion. Sheu, Jia-Lin, et al. has given a fast and improved performing algorithm with its corresponding VLSI architecture (Sheu et al. 1998).

6.4 Parallel Modular Multiplication on Multi-core Processors

An alternate way of parallelizing the modular multiplication by avoiding so much processing complexity is based on a quadratic scheme. The logic is simple first partitioned the operand into two parts (possibly equal) let say operand is θ and the two partition is θ_1 and θ_2 chunks and then perform modular multiplications for θ_1 and θ_2 simultaneously (Giorgi et al. 2013; Doliskani et al. 2018). It means the designing of an algorithm for performing modular multiplication of two n-digit integers is not so complex. The complexity of the parallel running algorithm will be in order of $(n/\theta_1, n/\theta_2)$.

Here, the algorithm will run on T = $\theta_1\theta_2$ cores. After processing the two parts in parallel using different threads, requires synchronizing the partial results. In this scenario complexity of the parallel algorithm is based on the quadratic scheme. In order to avoid extra synchronization overhead, summation process is performed sequentially as parallel execution will increase the synchronization overhead.

References

Asif S, Kong Y (2017) Highly parallel modular multiplier for elliptic curve cryptography in residue number system. Circuits Syst Signal Process 36(3):1027–1051

Bajard JC, Didier LS, Kornerup P (1998) An RNS Montgomery modular multiplication algorithm. IEEE Trans Comput 47(7):766–776

Doliskani J, Giorgi P, Lebreton R, Schost E (2018) Simultaneous conversions with the residue number system using linear algebra. ACM Trans Math Softw (TOMS) 44(3):1–21

Giorgi P, Imbert L, Izard T (2013) Parallel modular multiplication on multi-core processors. In: 2013 IEEE 21st symposium on computer arithmetic. IEEE, pp 135–142

Großschädl J, Posch KC, Tillich S (2004) Architectural enhancements to support digital signal processing and public-key cryptography. In: WISES, pp 129–143

Koc CK, Acar T, Kaliski BS (1996) Analyzing and comparing Montgomery multiplication algorithms. IEEE Micro 16(3):26–33

Kwon T, Lee MK, Kwon D (2013) Information security and cryptology-ICISC 2012: 15th international conference, Seoul, Korea, November 28–30, 2012, Revised selected papers, vol 7839. Springer

McIvor C, McLoone M, McCanny JV (2004) FPGA Montgomery multiplier architectures-a comparison. In: 12th annual IEEE symposium on field-programmable custom computing machines. IEEE, pp 279–282

Mentens N, Sakiyama K, Preneel B, Verbauwhede I (2007) Efficient pipelining for modular multiplication architectures in prime fields. In: Proceedings of the 17th ACM Great Lakes symposium on VLSI, pp 534–539

Omondi AR (2020) Cryptography arithmetic. Springer, Berlin

Sheu JL, Shieh MD, Wu CH, Sheu MH (1998) A pipelined architecture of fast modular multiplication for RSA cryptography. In: 1998 IEEE international symposium on circuits and systems (ISCAS), vol 2. IEEE, pp 121–124

Chapter 7
Hardware Realization of Montgomery Multiplication with Radix-2

7.1 Simple Radix-2 Montgomery Multiplication

Well-known PKCs like DHM key-exchange, DSS, RSA, ECC algorithms perform all their mathematical operations in either of the two finite fields:

1. F_p Prime Field or
2. F_{2^m} Binary Field

While the binary field (F_{2^m}) is prominently used by ECC (refer Sect. 2.5) the prime field (F_p) is used by most of the other PKCs. The main operation in PKC is modular multiplication (MM), it has different modulus in both fields. Modulus with prime p for F_p and modulus of an irreducible polynomial $f(x)$ of order n for F_{2^m}. In F_p the addition is done bit wise i.e., it act as *X-OR* operation (without carry propagation).

Algorithm 1 shown in Fig. 7.1 represents a version of Radix-2 modular multiplication ($R = X \times Y \pmod{m}$). Where the length of the operands is k and range of modulus m is $2^{k-1} < m < 2^k$.

7.2 The Tenca–Koc Algorithm

The drawback of the Algorithm 1 (refer Fig. 7.1) is that it comes with a fixed size adder ($k - bit$ adder), therefore scaling the same hardware for varying length operands is not possible. To remove this drawback Tenca and Koc (2003) proposed a technique which works for a fixed word length (w) radix-2 but can be used multiple times to support a multiple word Montgomery multiplication algorithms. The technique is illustrated in Algorithm 2 is shown in Fig. 7.2. Before going for the algorithm we need to consider some assumptions:

- $k = nw$ For an operand of size k the Algorithm 2 (refer Fig. 7.2) can be used n times.
- $m = m^{n-1}, \ldots, m^1, m^0$ 'n' number of words of w size for modular 'm'

© The Author(s), under exclusive license to Springer Nature Switzerland AG 2021
S. Vollala et al., *Energy-Efficient Modular Exponential Techniques for Public-Key Cryptography*, https://doi.org/10.1007/978-3-030-74524-0_7

Algorithm 1 Simple Radix-2 Modular Multiplication

Input: X,Y and m
Output: $R = X \times Y \pmod{m}$

1: *Initialization $R = 0, i = 0$*
2: **while** $i < k$ **do**
3:     $R = R + x_i \times Y$ $\triangleright \because X = Sum_{i=0}^{k-1} x_i \times 2^i$
4:     **if** R is odd **then**
5:         $R = R + m$
6:     **end if**
7:     $R = R \div 2$
8: **end while**
9: **if** $R \geq m$ **then**
10:     $R = R - m$
11: **end if**

Fig. 7.1 Simple radix-2 modular multiplication

- $R = R^{n-1}, \ldots, R^1, R^0$ 'n' number of words of w size for Result 'R'
- $Y = Y^{n-1}, \ldots, Y^1, Y^0$ 'n' number of words of w size for operand 'Y'
- $X = x_{k-1}, \ldots, x_1, x_0$ binary representation of k-bit operand 'X'

Here, the parameters m, R and Y are given with superscript to represent words and these words are padded with zero to $(n + 1)$th word to handle the case of overflow. Whereas X is represented in its binary string form using subscript (Harris et al. 2005).

If we observe the Algorithm 2 shown in Fig. 7.2, there are two loops, one for iterating the k-bits of X and another for iterating n-words of m, Y and Z. The loop for words is overlapped by the loop for bits. We check for the LSB of R, and if $LSB = 1$ then we can say that R is odd. We perform the right shifting operation on R as we want to divide R by 2. The single right shift performed in the jth loop can cause the changes in bits of words i.e., the LSB of $R^j - word$ becomes the MSB of $R^{j-1} - word$. Therefore we need to calculate the LSB prior to the shifting operation in the Algorithm 2 shown in Fig. 7.2.

For the consideration of hardware implementation, we need to find that if there is any dependency present in the algorithm or not. There is a single dependency present which is that we need to have a value of R^j for ith loop before the computation of R^j for $(i + 1)$th loop.

For hardware implementation of Algorithm 2 (refer Fig. 7.2 t number of $w - bit$ processing elements (PEs) are used. These t number of PEs are arranged in pipelined manner to achieve better throughput. The inner configuration of each PE has:

- Two adders of w-bit word length.
- Two banks of w AND gates

The addition of $x_i \times Y^j$ and $odd \times m^j$ is done by an AND gate which is further stored to R^j and Register which holds the result. There is a stall of 2 unit of the clock cycle is needed by PE in order to get the R^j value, as R^{j+1} needs to be calculated and shifted first.

Algorithm 2 Tenca-Koc Multiple Word Radix-2 Montgomery Multiplication

Input: X,Y and m
Output: $R = X \times Y \pmod{m}$

1: *Initialization:* $R = 0, i = 0, j = 0, T_a = 0, T_b = 0$
2: **while** $i \ll$ **do**
3:     **while** $j < n$ **do**
4:         $(T_a, R^j) = T_a + R^j + x_i \times Y^j$
5:         **if** $j = 0$ **then**
6:             $odd = R_0$
7:             **if** (odd) **then**
8:                 $(T_b, R^j) = T_b + m^j + R^j$
9:             **end if**
10:        **end if**
11:        $R^{j-1} = (R_0^j, R_{w-1:1}^{j-1})$
12:    **end while**
13: **end while**

Fig. 7.2   Tenca–Koc multiple word radix-2 Montgomery multiplication

In a single cycle of the kernel, execution of t bits of X can be done. This means for the complete execution of X total c cycles of the kernel will be needed, where $c = k/p$. Unfolding of the outer loop is done based on the divisibility of k by t and w which is usually divisible as their values are in power of 2.

Basic hardware architecture of Montgomery multiplier is shown in Fig. 7.3. With capacity executing wt bit cells at a time the kernel has t $w - bit$ PEs. R is saved in the carry-save redundant form. As per dependency the result R must be kept hold in the **Queue** until $PE - 1$ finishes its execution with R^{n-1} even if $PE - t$ has finished its execution with R^0.

The architecture is shown in Fig. 7.3 holds the result in the queue in redundant form. Holding the result is an overhead as it needs $2w - bits$ per entry. To resolve this, a technique has been given by Harris et al. (2005) where if the queue is not required we can avoid the holding of R' in the queue this saves the carry-propagation latency and also gives the R in non-redundant form.

The basic working idea of Processing Element (PE) is given in Fig. 7.4. The given PE is comprises of

- Two CSA (Carry Save Adder) of size $2w$ is used
- Two AND gates of 2-input
- One multiplexer of size: 2 : 1 and
- $4w + 5$ register bits.

The addition of modulus m is decided by the odd parity which is the least significant word of R. The shifting mechanism is also taken care by PEs.

Fast Radix-2 Montgomery Multiplication Using CSA:
Most of the PKC techniques uses the complexity of IFP and DLP with modular exponentiation to achieve robust cryptosystems such as RSA, ElGamal, ECC, etc.

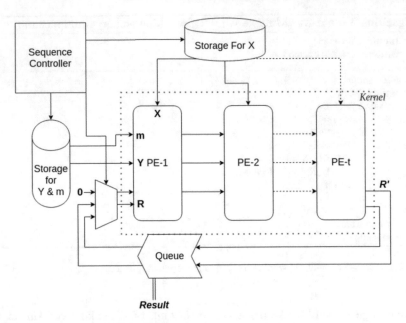

Fig. 7.3 Montgomery multiplier architecture

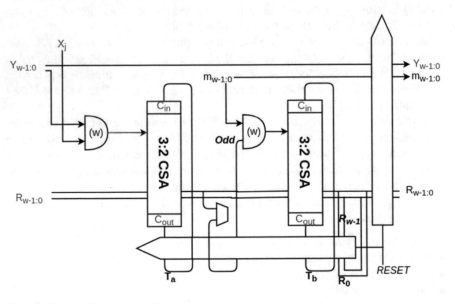

Fig. 7.4 Design of processing element

The process involves modular exponentiation as a key step during encryption and decryption. Montgomery multiplication (MMM) is capable of minimizing the running time and hardware overhead of modular exponentiation. Few techniques that were developed in the process of minimization of complexity are:

- Zhengbing et al. presented the new architecture of an RSA cryptoprocessor (Zhengbing et al. 2007). This architecture was capable of handling 1024-bits with the help of a single *CSA*. The architecture supports the Algorithm 2 shown in Fig. 7.2 as well as minimizes the running time and hardware resource required i.e., it increases the overall performance of MMM.
- Nikumbh and Vandana implemented two advanced hardware architectures to enhance the performance of MMM (Nikumbh and Shah 2018). The key idea is to have some parameters pre-computed based on various operand sizes (composed by the Xilinx project manager). This approach uses *CSA* and minimizes the running time and hardware resource required.
- Grégory and Nelson et al. tested a technique to incorporate the enhancement approach of hardware and software both. They incorporated both the approaches in order to obtain 11 times faster-executing RSA (Marchesan et al. 2018). Their architecture supports the 4096-bit RSA cryptosystem with an overhead of 45K gates. For testing they have used general-purpose lightweight Tensilica® processor and baseline Xtensa® processor and enhance the underlying procedure of MMM.

7.3 Hardware Optimization for Multiple Word Radix-2 Montgomery Multiplication

Huang et al. analysed the algorithm given by Tenca–Koc for multiple word radix-2 Montgomery multiplication (refer Algorithm 2 shown in Fig. 7.2). They found that, parallelism in the inner loop (j-loop) is not possible, because of the data dependencies present in between calculation of result R and right-shift operation. Whereas, the unfolding of outer loop (i-loop) was possible to achieve parallelism (Harris et al. 2005). Therefore, Huang et al. tries to customize the inner loop (j-loop) in order to optimize the hardware for multiple word Radix-2 Montgomery multiplication (MWR2MM) (Huang et al. 2008).

Huang et al. observed that there is a stall of 2 clock cycles is needed by PE in order to get the R^j value as R^{j+1} need to be calculated and shifted first. This stall increases the running time of the Algorithm 2 (refer Fig. 7.2) which has been seen as an opportunity by Huang et al. and they try to minimize the delay of 2 clock cycle between the subsequent iterations of the outer loop (i-loop). If we observe the dependency between the values of result R shown in the Fig. 7.5, the stall of 2 clock-cycles is because of the right-shift ($\div 2$) operation present in both the Algorithms 1 & 2 (refer Figs. 7.1 and 7.2). For the dependency between PEs given in Fig. 7.5, the PEs compute the word R in their first two clock-cycles. PE-2 has to wait for the two

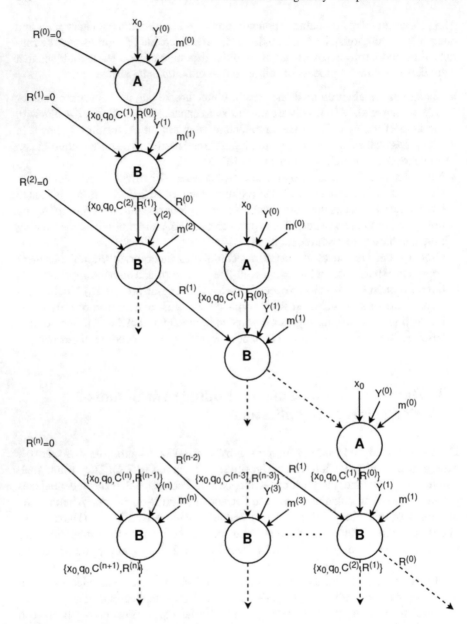

Fig. 7.5 Data dependency of algorithm proposed by Tenca and Koc

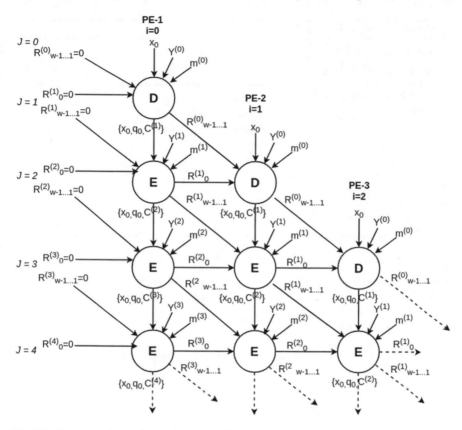

Fig. 7.6 Data dependency of optimized algorithm proposed by Miaoqing Huang

clock cycles before it can proceed with the computation of the word R^0 in the third clock cycle.

Huang et al. has modified the block 'A' and 'B' termed as *atomic operation* codes and optimized the data dependency (Huang et al. 2010). The optimized data dependency graph is shown in Fig. 7.6. The new modified *atomic operation* code blocks are denoted as 'D' and 'E'.

Task D:

Basically, this atomic operation is a sequential execution of three sub-operations:

1. The computation of q_i,
2. The computation of pair of possible results,
3. The selection of one out of the pair of results with the help of extra parameter $R_0^{(1)}$

The extra parameter $R_0^{(1)}$ is accessible at the end of execution of Algorithm 3 Task D (refer Fig. 7.7).

Algorithm 3 Algorithm for Task D

Input: $x_i, Y^{(0)}, m^{(0)}, R_0^{(1)}, R_{w-1...1}^{(0)}$

Output: $q_i, C^{(1)}, R_{w-1...1}^{(0)}$

1: *Initialization* $Q_i = (x_i, Y_0^{(0)}) \oplus R_1^{(0)}$
2: $(CO^{(1)}, RO_{w-1}^{(0)}, R_{w-2...0}^{(0)}) = (1, R_{w-1...1}^{(0)}) + x_i \times Y^{(0)} + q_i \times m^{(0)}$
3: $(CE^{(1)}, RE_{w-1}^{(0)}, R_{w-2...0}^{(0)}) = (0, R_{w-1...1}^{(0)}) + x_i \times Y^{(0)} + q_i \times m^{(0)}$
4: **if** $R_0^{(1)} = 1$ **then**
5:      $C^{(1)} = CO^{(1)}$
6:      $R_{w-1...1}^{(0)} = (RO_{w-1}^{(0)}, R_{w-2...1}^{(0)})$
7: **else**
8:      $C^{(1)} = CE^{(1)}$
9:      $R_{w-1...1}^{(0)} = (RE_{w-1}^{(0)}, R_{w-2...1}^{(0)})$
10: **end if**

Fig. 7.7 Algorithm for task D

Algorithm 4 Algorithm for Task E

Input: $x_i, q_i, C^{(j)}, Y^{(j)}, m^{(j)}, R_0^{(j+1)}, R_{w-1...1}^{(j)}$

Output: $C^{(j+1)}, R_{w-1...1}^{(j)}, R_0^{(j)}$

1: $(CO^{(j+1)}, RO_{w-1}^{(j)}, R_{w-2...0}^{(j)}) = (1, R_{w-1...1}^{(0)}) + C^{(j)} + x_i \times Y^{(0)} + q_i \times m^{(0)}$
2: $(CE^{(j+1)}, RE_{w-1}^{(j)}, R_{w-2...0}^{(j)}) = (0, R_{w-1...1}^{(j)}) + C^{(j)} + x_i \times Y^{(0)} + q_i \times m^{(0)}$
3: **if** $R_0^{(j+1)} = 1$ **then**
4:      $C^{(j+1)} = CO^{(j+1)}$
5:      $R_{w-1...1}^{(j)} = (RO_{w-1}^{(j)}, R_{w-2...1}^{(j)})$
6: **else**
7:      $C^{(j+1)} = CE^{(j+1)}$
8:      $R_{w-1...1}^{(j)} = (RE_{w-1}^{(j)}, R_{w-2...1}^{(j)})$
9: **end if**

Fig. 7.8 Algorithm for task E

Task E:
Basically this atomic operation is a sequential execution of two sub-operations:

1. The data forwarding of $R_0^{(j)}$
2. The data forwarding of $R_{w-1...1}^{(j)}$

Both the sub-operations executed in the same clock cycle in order to forward the data from one atomic operation block 'E' to the two atomic operation blocks in the right column. further these two forwarded parameters $R_0^{(j)}$ and $R_{w-1...1}^{(j)}$ helped in choosing the one in the pair of partial results of $R^{(j-1)}$, and for producing the pair of partial results of $R^{(j)}$ respectively (refer Algorithm 4 shown in Fig. 7.8).

Stealing Clock Cycle:
Task E is an ideal approach for stealing one clock cycle in between the operation of shifting right. Initially two separate value of $C^{(j+1)}$ and $R_{w-1}^{(j)}$ is computed by all PEs in parallel (refer Algorithm 4 Fig. 7.8). Based on the bit value of $R_0^{(j)}$ i.e., 0 or 1, the value of $C^{(j+1)}$ and $R_{w-1\cdots1}^{(j)}$ is computed and saved in registers. As soon as the desired value of $R_0^{(j+1)}$ is obtained, immediately PE forward the selected $C^{(j+1)}$ and $R^{(j)}$. Whereas, the algorithm of Task D computes the value of q_i, $C^{(1)}$ and $R^{(0)}$.

Hardware implementation on FPGA devices:
In the case of FPGA, the designer has an option to allow synthesis tools to take care of actual implementation in order to get better performance with the proper balance of running time and hardware space. If we want to implement two statements (step 1 & 2) of the Algorithm 4 for Task E (refer Fig. 7.8) directly, then 2 ripple-carry adders will be needed. The ripple-carry adder is comprised of 3 $w - bit$ input-parameters besides a carry. It is observed that the addition performed is having the only difference that in MSB of the R-word and other leftover bits are shared. Thus, it is favorable to accumulate the shared bits of the two additions in Algorithm 4 shown in Fig. 7.8, and perform them with another ripple-carry adder having three $(w - 1) - bit$ input-parameters and a carry. The leftover bits are added using 2 basic adders. This approach of implementing the algorithm slightly raise the requirement of hardware resource especially at the time of computing 2 separate cases. If R is presented in redundant form, then the 2 possible cases of $R_{w-1}^{(j)}$ can be handled with only one extra Full-Adder (Huang et al. 2010).

Massolino et al. proposed the pioneer area in optimized MMM architecture on re-configurable FPGAs which consume lesser power (Massolino et al. 2017). They have given two separate FPGA architectures, in order to optimize the area while calculating the Montgomery multiplication procedure for the F_p prime field. The key logic of saving the area with keeping the high performance is the use of Math blocks and embedded storage along with a sophisticated scheduling algorithm. This approach assures the full exploitation of the pipelining approach and minimization of clock-cycles.

7.4 VLSI Based Montgomery Multiplication

As we have discussed earlier that in various PKC, the main operation is modular multiplication (MM), which is more favorable with long length integer parameters. But this MM operation takes maximum running time and complex to perform. In the research of minimizing the running time and complexity of MM, various software and hardware approaches have been presented. Out of those presented algorithms, the MMM algorithm emerges as the most prominent one. It examines the LSB of operands only to resolve the quotient and by-pass the complex division process by a sequence of shifting and addition. In order to compute $R = X \times Y \times T^{-1}$ (mod m),

---

Algorithm 5 Montgomery Modular Multiplication for Radix-2

Input: X, Y, m
Output: $R = X \times Y \pmod{m}$

1: *Initialization:* $R[0] = 0; i = 0$
2: **while** $i < k$ **do**
3:　　$q_i = (R[i]_0 + X_i \times Y_0) \pmod{2}$
4:　　$R[i+1] = (R[i] + X_i \times Y + q_i \times m)/2$
5: **end while**
6: **if** $(R[k] \geq m)$ **then**
7:　　$R[k] = R[k] - m$
8: **end if**
9: **Return** $R[k]$

Fig. 7.9 Montgomery multiplication for radix-2

where length of modulus m is $k - bit$, and T^{-1} represents the modulo m inverse of T i.e., $T = 2^k \pmod{m}$. VLSI circuits are compatible with the implementation and minimize the running time of the encryption and decryption process.

Kuang et al. have given an algorithm and also its hardware implementation and claimed it to be energy-efficient. The technique consumes less energy as well as improves the performance of MMM. This technique avoids redundant CSA and memory-write operation, which saves power consumption and enhances the throughput (Kuang et al. 2012).

It is observed in the Algorithm 5 shown in Fig. 7.9, that the *Addition* step i.e., step 4, requires long carry propagation as the 3 operands are having long length binary strings (Kuang et al. 2015). In order to resolve this issue number of solutions based on CSA are presented. All the presented solutions can be partitioned into two approaches based on the representation of input and output operands. The strategies are: *semi carry-save (SCS) approach and full carry-save (FCS) approach.*

7.4.1　SCS-Based Montgomery Multiplication

In the semi carry-save (SCS) approach, representation of parameters is in a binary format where operands X, Y and modulus m is provided as input-parameter and $R = X \times Y \pmod{m}$ is output. Whereas the input and output parameters are in the binary string. The input and output operands (i.e., X, Y, N, and R) of the Montgomery MM are represented in binary. But, the result in-between the calculation (shifting modular additions) are stored in the carry-save format, which helps to avert the carry propagation. The final result (R) is required in the binary representation which requires the help of an additional carry propagation adder (CPA) or one of the available CSA repeatedly to transform it from the carry-save format.

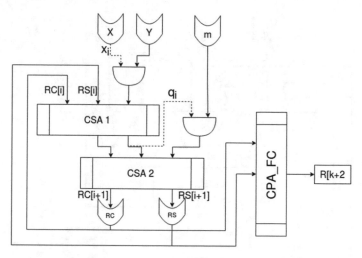

Fig. 7.10 Basic semi carry save MM

Algorithm 6 Semi Carry Save based MM

Input: X, Y, m
Output: $R = X \times Y \pmod{m}$

1: *Initialization:* $RS[0] = 0; RC[0] = 0; i = 0$
2: **while** $i \leq k+1$ **do**
3:     $q_i = (RS[i]_0 + RC[i]_0 + X_i \times Y_0) \pmod{2}$
4:     $(RS[i+1], RC[i+1]) = (RS[i] + RC[i] + X_i \times Y + q_i \times m)/2$
5: **end while**
6: $R[k+2] = RS[k+2] - RC[k+2]$
7: **Return** $R[k+2]$

Fig. 7.11 Semi carry save based MM

The result R in-between the calculation (shifting modular additions) is stored in the carry-save format (RS, RC) which helps to avert the carry propagation as can be observed in Algorithm 6 shown in Fig. 7.11, and its corresponding architecture is given in Fig. 7.10. Here the loop runs $k + 2$ times instead of k times this helps in removing extra steps of comparison and subtraction. Even though there is still one task left, that is the conversion of the final result from carry-save format to binary representation. The transmission of the 1-bit value is represented by the dashed line. Figure 7.10 has a two-level CSA with a format converter that collectively gives the hardware design of the SCS-based modular multiplier. Whereas, Fig. 7.12 has only one level of CSA with 3 additional multiplexers.

Format conversion:
A 32-bit CPA is capable of adding two inputs of 32-bit size and produce an output of 32-bit size. A CPA is consists of multiplexers & registers also termed as *CPA-FC*.

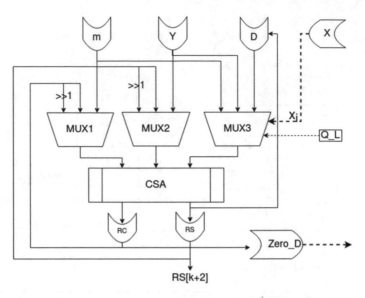

Fig. 7.12 New semi carry save MM-multiplier

This format converter is incorporated with SCS modular multiplier architecture. This CPA-FC is capable of producing an output of 1024 bits per 32 clock cycle. Additional CPA-FC may increase the space overhead and complexity of SCS modular multiplier.

Kuang et al. presented an Algorithm 7 shown in Fig. 7.13, based on a semi carry-save modular multiplier (SCS-MM). The key features in this algorithm are minimization of the stall caused by critical path, required clock-cycles and pre-computation of parameters. It has only one-level CSA architecture (Kuang et al. 2015) and considerably minimizes the needed clock cycles for finishing 1-MM. As we can observe that the SCS-MM-New Algorithm 7, begins with computing the value of $\hat{Y}$ and $\hat{D}$. It is obvious that we have to start the loop from $i = -1$ in order to calculate q_{i+1} and q_{i+2}. Moreover, zero-initialization of other parameters $\hat{q}$ and $\hat{X}$ needs to be done. In the next step for iteration, we select *While* loop instead of *For* loop so that we can skip an iteration if that is avoidable. For passing up we perform $i = i + 1$ or $i = i + 2$. The vector representation of a parameter e.g. $\hat{Y}$ needs 3 extra clock cycles for the exact calculation of division by 2. Therefore number of iterations in SCS-MM-New algorithm are increased by 3 i.e., $(k + 4)$, which was $k + 1$ in previous Algorithm 6 (refer Fig. 7.11). To achieve parallelism the whole algorithm is logically divided into two parts. The first part is executed over one-level CCSA architecture having a 4-to-1 multiplexer. In algorithm step 8 to step 19 inside the while loop is corresponding to this multiplexer. In the second part step 21 to step 27 is executed in parallel with part 1 which is responsible for computation of q_{i+1}, q_{i+2}, and $skip_{i+1}$ in step 21 & the calculation of $\hat{X}$, $\hat{q}$ and i in steps 22–27. Two statements are having the right-shift operation in steps 20 & 23. This right-shift operation cause stall till the next clock cycle to minimize the critical path delay.

Algorithm 7 New Semi Carry Save based Montgomery Multiplication Algorithm

---

Input: X, Y, m
Output: $R = X \times Y \pmod{m}$

1: *Initialization:* $\hat{Y} = Y << 3, \hat{q} = 0, \hat{X} = 0, skip_{i+1} = 0$ & $\hat{m}$ is a new Modulus.
2: $(RS, RC) = 1F - CSA(\hat{Y}, \hat{m}, 0)$
3: **while** $RC \neq 0$ **do**
4: $\quad (RS, RC) = 2H - CSA(RS, RC)$
5: **end while**
6: *Initialization:* $\hat{D} = RS; i = -1; RS[-1] = 0; RC[-1] = 0$
7: **while** $i \leq k + 4$ **do**
8: $\quad$ **if** $\hat{X} = 0 and \hat{q} = 0$ **then**
9: $\quad\quad x = 0$
10: $\quad$ **end if**
11: $\quad$ **if** $\hat{X} = 0 and \hat{q} = 1$ **then**
12: $\quad\quad x = \hat{m}$
13: $\quad$ **end if**
14: $\quad$ **if** $\hat{X} = 1 and \hat{q} = 0$ **then**
15: $\quad\quad x = \hat{Y}$
16: $\quad$ **end if**
17: $\quad$ **if** $\hat{X} = 1 and \hat{q} = 1$ **then**
18: $\quad\quad x = \hat{D}$
19: $\quad$ **end if**
20: $\quad (RS[i+1], RC[i+1]) = 1F - CSA(RS[i], RC[i], x) >> 1$
21: $\quad$ compute q_{i+1}, q_{i+2}, and $skip_{i+1}$
22: $\quad$ **if** $skip_{i+1} = 1$ **then**
23: $\quad\quad RS[i+2] = RS[i+1] >> 1, RC[i+2] = RC[i+1] >> 1$
24: $\quad\quad \hat{q} = q_{i+2}, \hat{X} = X_{i+2}, i = i+2$
25: $\quad$ **else**
26: $\quad\quad \hat{q} = q_{i+1}, \hat{X} = X_{i+1}, i = i+1$
27: $\quad$ **end if**
28: **end while**
29: $\hat{q} = 0, \hat{X} = 0$
30: **while** $RC[k+5] \neq 0$ **do**
31: $\quad (RS[k+5], RC[k+5]) = 1H - CSA(RS[k+5], RC[k+5])$
32: **end while**
33: **Return** $RS[k+5]$

Fig. 7.13 New semi carry save based Montgomery multiplication algorithm

Hardware design for SCS-MM-New Algorithm, termed as SCS-MM-New Multiplier, is given in Fig. 7.14, which comprises of following hardware components:

- A one-level CCSA architecture
- 2 multiplexers of size 4-to-1 denoted as $M1$ and $M2$,
- 1 simplified multiplier denoted as $SM3$,
- 2 smaller $3 - bit$ multiplexers of size 2-to-1 denoted as $M4$ and $M5$,
- 6 registers for holding various parameters.
- 1 zero-detector denoted as *Zero-D* has task in ith iteration to calculate $skip_{i+1}$, $\hat{X}$ & $\hat{q}$ and
- 1 skip detector denoted as *Skip-D*, it acquire insignificant space.

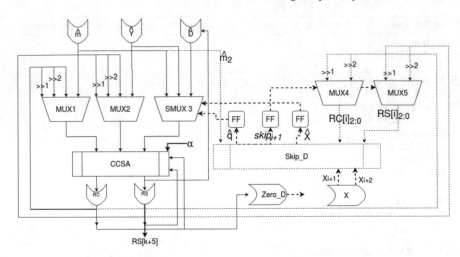

Fig. 7.14 Modified semi carry save MM

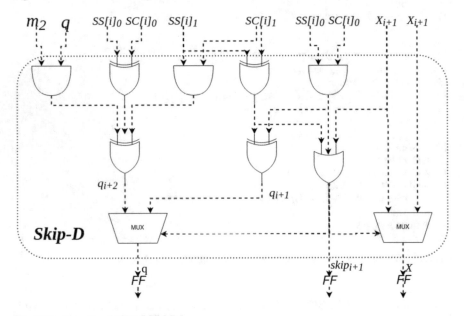

Fig. 7.15 Skip decoder for SCS MM

For the purpose of clear and understandable architecture, the control block is not shown in the Fig. 7.14, control block is responsible of generating signals for multiplexers M1 and M2.

Initially $skip_{i+1}$, $\hat{X}$, $\hat{q}$ are initialized with 0 and saved in FFs as shown in SCS-MM-New Algorithm 7 (refer Fig. 7.13). Using these initialized value, the *CCSA* computes the value of $\hat{D}$ as $\hat{D} = \hat{Y} + \hat{m}$. This computation is done using the one-

---

Algorithm 8 FSC-Montgomery Multiplicatoin

Input: XS, XC, YS, YC, m(modulus)
Output: $RS[k+2], RC[K+2]$

1: *Initialization*: $RS[0] = 0, RC[0] = 0, i = 0$
2: **while** $i \leq k+1$ **do**
3:     $q_i = (RS[i]_0 + RC[i]_0 + X_i \times (YS_0 + YC_0)) \pmod 2$
4:     $(RS[i+1], RC[i+1]) = (RS[i] + RC[i] + X_i \times (YS + YC) + q_i \times m)/2$
5: **end while**
6: **Return** $RS[k+2], RC[K+2]$

Fig. 7.16 FSC-MM

level CCSA architecture. Once we have initialized the values of $skip_{i+1}$, $\hat{X}, \hat{q}$, then later in the loop, the calculation of their next values are performed with the help of skip detector *Skip-D*. The *Skip-D* shown Fig. 7.15 comprises of these hardware components:

- 1 NOR gate,
- 4 XOR gates,
- 2 multiplexers of size 2-to-1 and
- 3 Nos. of AND gates.

According to step 21 in Algorithm 7 shown in Fig. 7.13, skip decoder first compute the q_{i+1}, q_{i+2} and $skip_{i+1}$ values in the ith iteration. Based on $skip_{i+1}$ value the accurate value of $\hat{q}$ and $\hat{X}$ are computed. After completion of ith loop, $\hat{q}$, $\hat{X}$ and $skip_{i+1}$ needs to be saved in respective FFs. For upcoming cycle, it is the responsibility of *SM3* to produce accurate value of x for the ith iteration. *SM3* takes 2 select parameters i.e., $\hat{q}$ and $\hat{X}$ produced by skip-decoder in the ith iteration, as shown in steps 8–19. The multiplexers *M1* and *M2* produce the accurate *RC* & *RS* based on the value of $skip_{i+1}$ which was calculated in the ith iteration. Whether to shift the result once or twice is decided by the value of $skip_{i+1}$ i.e., if $skip_{i+1} = 0$, *RC* & *RS* are simultaneously right shifted by factor of 1, else right shifted by factor of 2. The same is depicted in Algorithm 7 (SCS-MM-New) as step 20 & 23. Both the steps (i.e., 20 & 23) can be performed simultaneously in the next clock cycle of iteration i. The same $skip_{i+1}$ of ith iteration is also responsible for accurate calculation of $RC[i]_{2:0}$ & $RS[i]_{2:0}$ using components *M4* & *M5*. The multiplexers *M4* & *M5* are chosen over *M1* & *M2* to avoid extra clock cycle delay because of their size i.e., they are 4-to-1 multiplexers. The value of $\hat{q}$ & $\hat{X}$ further saved in *FFs* are changed to zero in step 29, that is just the next step after the completion of while loop which runs from step 7 to step 28. Thereafter from step 30 to step 32 the change in format is done with the help of the SCS-MM-New multiplier Fig. 7.14. This format conversion step is very much similar to the initialization step 6 i.e., $\hat{D} = \hat{Y} + \hat{m}$. Finally, if $SC[k+5]$ has the zero value, the result in the binary string is held by $RS[k+5]$.

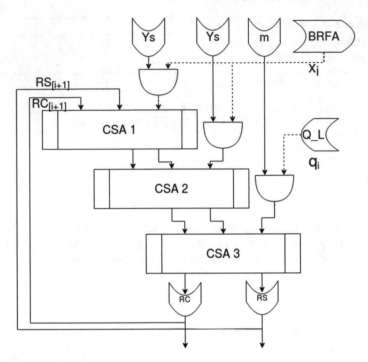

Fig. 7.17 FCS-MM-1

7.4.2 FCS-Based Montgomery Multiplication

Changing the format to and from binary was an overhead in SCS-based MMM to avert the overhead McIvor et al. proposed a Full-carry-save based MMM (FCS). In the FCS-based method, it keeps X, Y and R in the carry-save representations (XS, XC), (YS, YC) and (SS, SC) respectively (McIvor et al. 2004). Basically, McIvor et al. gave 2 FCS-based Montgomery multipliers, termed as FCS-MM-1 and FCS-MM-2. Out of these two, we are going to discuss only one multiplier that is FCS-MM-1. The Algorithm 8 shown in Fig. 7.16 gives the steps for the FCS-MM-1 multiplier. Whereas, the hardware architecture for the same is given in Fig. 7.17. The architecture of FCS-MM-1 is comprised of the following hardware components:

- 1 CSA of five-to-two (three-level)
- 1 CSA of four-to-two (two-level)
- 1 Barrel register full adder (BRFA)
- 3 Shift registers for saving YS, YC and m
- 1 Full adder
- 1 Flip-flop (FF).

7.5 Bit-Serial and Bit-Parallel Montgomery Multiplication and Squaring

All the PKC algorithms execute all arithmetic operations over well-defined finite fields. For PKC, two decisive operations: multiplication and squaring are performed in finite fields. Moreover, to perform operations such as inversion and exponentiation, we can use square and multiply. These two operations are crucial in MMM. Moreover, MMM can be used to implement an Elliptic Curve Cryptography (ECC) based cryptoprocessor (Hariri and Reyhani-Masoleh 2009) and RSA based cryptoprocessor. This section discusses three different algorithms and their architecture for improving and executing MMM in bit by bit manner:

1. MSB-First Bit-Serial Modular Multiplication
2. LSB-First Bit-Serial Modular Multiplication
3. Bit-Parallel Montgomery Multiplication

Finite Fields:

F_{2^m} is a type of finite field (refer Sect. 2.5.1) which has 2^m unique elements. Mrabet and Amine et al. gave a hardware design, to compute the multiplication over F_{2^m} in the power extension field arithmetic for pairing. In PKC, finite field arithmetic is important for elliptic curve cryptography and for pairing (Mrabet and Darmon 2019). Leelavathi et al. tried various keys of dissimilar size over a finite field F_{2^m} and experimented on diverse FPGAs in order to find the most appropriate design for Wireless Sensor Networks (WSNs) applications (Leelavathi et al. 2016). The extended finite field F_{2^m} is an extended version of the binary field F_2 which has 0 and 1. Whereas, finite field F_{2^m} is combined with an irreducible polynomial of degree m over F_2.

$$F(z) = f_m z^m + f_{m-1} z^{m-1} + f_{m-2} z^{m-2} + \cdots + f_1 z + f_0 \cdots f_i \in F_2 \quad (7.1)$$

Here we re-represent the Montgomery Algorithm 9 shown in Fig. 7.18 for finite field F_{2^m}. The polynomial p has main participation for the calculation of modular multiplication in the algorithm. The polynomial p is used to perform modulus operation and also the final result R is divided by p. The value of this important polynomial

---

Algorithm 9 Montgomery Modular Multiplication Over F_{2^m}

Input: $X, Y \in F_{2^m}, p, F(n), F'(n)$
Output: $R = X \times Y \times p^{-1} \ (\text{mod } F(n))$

1: $t = X \times Y$
2: $u = t.F'(n) \ (\text{mod } p)$
3: $R = (t + u \times F(n)) \div p$

Fig. 7.18 Montgomery multiplication over F_{2^m}

Algorithm 10 Bit-Level Montgomery Modular Multiplication Over F_{2^m}

Input: $X, Y \in F_{2^m}, F(n)$
Output: $R = X \times Y \times n^{-m} \pmod{F(n)}$
 1: $R = 0$
 2: **for** $i = 0 \, to \, m - 1$ **do**
 3:     $R = R + y_i \times X$
 4:     $R = R + R_0 F(n)$ $\triangleright R_0 \, is \, LSB \, of \, Result \, R$
 5:     $R = R \div n$
 6: **end for**

Fig. 7.19 The bit-level Montgomery multiplication over F_{2^m}

p is selected as $p = n^m$. The reason behind this type of selection is that we can avoid the modular operation of the terms, whose powers of n are greater than or equal to m. The Algorithm 10 shown in Fig. 7.19 illustrate the advantage of polynomial p. The division by polynomial p can be performed by m times execution of the right shift operation.

Selecting $p = n^u$ such that $1 \le u \le m$, which is termed as a Montgomery reduction element, using this we can formulate the MMM over finite field F_{2^m} as:

$$R = X \times Y \times n^{-u} \pmod{F(n)} \tag{7.2}$$

Knowing the bit representation of operand Y, one can rewrite Eq. 7.2 as

$$R = y_0 X n^{-u} + y_1 X n^{-u+1} + \cdots + y_{m-1} X n^{-u+m-1} \pmod{F(n)}. \tag{7.3}$$

The root of the polynomial $F(z)$ for $F(n) = 0$ is n, and from Eq. 7.1, we can reformulate the Equation as:

$$f_m n^m + f_{m-1} n^{m-1} + f_{m-2} n^{m-2} + \cdots + f_1 x + f_0 = 0 \tag{7.4}$$

For a polynomial which is known to be irreducible, we know that $f_0 = 1$ & $f_m = 1$. Therefore, with the known information we can multiply x^{-1} to both sides of Eq. 7.4, and re-formulate the Equation as:

$$n^{-1} \pmod{F(n)} = n^{m-1} + n^{m-2} + \cdots + f_2 n + f_1. \tag{7.5}$$

Using Eq. 7.5, two different bit-serial multiplication algorithms are discussed:

1. MSB-First Bit-Serial Modular Multiplication
2. LSB-First Bit-Serial Modular Multiplication.

Algorithm 11 MSB-First Bit-serial Montgomery Multiplication Over F_{2^m}

Input: $X, Y \in F_{2^m}, F(n)$
Output: $R = X \times Y \times n^{-u} \pmod{F(n)}$

1: *Initialization* $X^{(0)} = Xn^{-u+m-1} \pmod{F(n)}; R^{(0)} = 0; i = 0$
2: **while** $i < m$ **do**
3:     $R^{i+1} = R^{(i)} + y_{-i+m-1} X^{(i)}$
4:     $X^{(i+1)} = X^{(i)} \times n^{-1} \pmod{F(n)}$
5:     $i = i + 1$
6: **end while**
7: $R = R^{(m)}$
8: **Return** R

Fig. 7.20 MSB-first bit-serial Montgomery multiplication over F_{2^m}

7.5.1 MSB-First Bit-Serial Modular Multiplication

The multiplicand Y is first represented in it's binary form i.e., $Y = y_{m-1}, \ldots, y_1, y_0$ where y_0 is LSB and y_{m-1} is MSB. As the name of the method suggest we start the execution from MSB of the multiplicand Y i.e., from y_{m-1} and proceed bit by bit. In order to formulate the Eq. 7.3 to tune according to MSB-first bit-serial modular multiplication, we change the sequence of addition a re-formulate the Eq. 7.3 into the Eq. 7.6.

$$R = y_{m-1} Xn^{-u+m-1} + \cdots + y_1 Xn^{-u+1} + y_0 Xn^{-u} \pmod{F(n)}. \qquad (7.6)$$

Based on the Eq. 7.6, the Algorithm for MSB-first bit-serial modular multiplication is deduced. The Algorithm 11 shown in Fig. 7.20 have the Montgomery reduction element $p = n^u$. Intermediate value of result at ith iteration is stored in $X^{(i)}$ and $R^{(i)}$. The Equation 7.6 has a pre-requisite $X^{(0)} = Xn^{-u+m-1} \pmod{F(n)}$, Which is calculated as initialization step 1 in the Algorithm 11 shown in Fig. 7.20. Therefore overall complexity of the algorithm is mainly contributed by this initialization step and the loop statements, specially the statements performing multiplication step.

$$X^{(i+1)} = X^{(i)} \times n^{-1} \pmod{F(x)}$$
$$= (x_{m-1}^{(i)} n^{m-2} + \cdots + x_1^{(i)} + x_0^{(i)} n^{-1}) \pmod{F(n)} \qquad (7.7)$$

Now from Eqs. 7.5 and 7.7:

$$X^{(i+1)} = x_0^{(i)} n^{m-1} (x_{m-1}^{(i)} + x_0^{(i)} f_{m-1}) n^{m-2} + \cdots + (x_2^{(i)} + x_0^{(i)} f_2) n^1 + (x_1^{(i)} + x_0^{(i)} f_1) \quad (7.8)$$

The Algorithm 11 and Architecture for MSB-first bit-serial MM is given in Figs. 7.20 and 7.21 respectively. In the architecture, X' & R' are registers of size

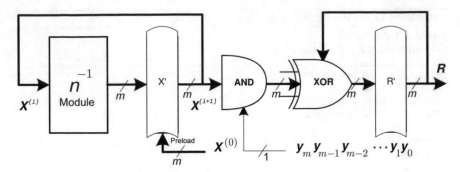

Fig. 7.21 Architecture for MSB-first bit-serial Montgomery multiplication

m-bit, whose responsibility is to keep the value of $X^{(i)}$ and $R^{(i)}$, respectively. As per algorithm 11 the pre-requisite is that, the register X' should have the value of $X^{(0)}$, as $X^{(0)} = Xn^{-u+m-1} \pmod{F(n)}$. Corresponding to the step-3 and step-4 inside the loop of Algorithm 11, the architecture (refer Fig. 7.21) also has circuit to execute those steps. For step 3 execution, right circuit in the architecture compute the $R^{(i+1)}$ for ith iteration and the circuit also has m two-input XOR gates. Whereas for step 4 execution, the left circuit in the architecture compute the value of $X^{(i+1)}$ with the help of $n^{-1}module$. The $n^{-1}module$ is capable of multiplying $X^{(i)}$ by n^{-1} and reducing the results by $F(n)$.

The arrangement of the hardware components in the architecture (refer to Fig. 7.21) is such that, both the circuit (i.e., left & right) can be executed simultaneously and provide parallelism. There are only two types of time delays present in the Algorithm 11.

1. T_X time consumed by a two-input AND gate
2. T_n time consumed by a two-input XOR gate

Apart from these two types of time delays, the latency of the MSB-first bit-serial MM is m clock-cycles.

Note: If we reconfigure the Architecture shown in Fig. 7.21 with padding of a 0 to the MSB of the operand Y $(y_{m-1} \cdots y_1 y_0)$, then we can get the MSB-first bit-serial MM with Montgomery reduction element $p = n^m$. Which in turn raise the latency by one i.e., $m + 1$ clock cycles.

7.5.2   LSB-First Bit-Serial Modular Multiplication

Similar to MSB-First Bit-Serial MM, in LSB-First Bit-Serial MM first we need to represent the multiplicand Y in it's binary form i.e., $Y = y_0, y_1, \ldots, y_{m-1}$ where y_0 is LSB and y_{m-1} is MSB. As the name suggests, we start the execution from LSB of the multiplicand Y i.e., from y_0 and proceed bit by bit. To formulate the Eq. 7.3 to be

---

Algorithm 12 LSB-First Bit-Serial Montgomery Multiplication Over F_{2^m}

Input: $X, Y \in F_{2^m}, F(n)$
Output: $R = X \times Y \times n^{-u} \pmod{F(n)}$

1: *Initialization:* $X^{(0)} = Xn^{-u+m-1} \pmod{F(n)}; T^{(0)} = 0$
2: **for** $i = 0 \, to \, m - 1$ **do**
3:     $T^{i+1} = T^{(i)} \times n^{-1} \pmod{F(n)} + y_i X^{(0)}$
4: **end for**
5: $C = T^m$

Fig. 7.22 LSB-first bit-serial Montgomery multiplication over F_{2^m}

according to LSB-first bit serial modular multiplication, we change the sequence of addition using *Horner's rule* and $X^{(0)} = Xn^{-u+m-1} \pmod{F(n)}$ and re-formulate the Eq. 7.3 into:

$$R = (\cdots (y_0 X^{(0)} n^{-1} \quad (\mathrm{mod} \ F(n)) + y_1 X^{(0)}) n^{-1} \quad (\mathrm{mod} \ F(n)) + \cdots + \quad (7.9)$$

$$y_{m-2} X^{(0)}) n^{-1} \pmod{F(n)} + y_{m-1} X^{(0)}.$$

The Algorithm 12 shown in Fig. 7.22 for LSB-First Bit-Serial MM is deduce from Eq. 7.9. The operations performed in algorithm is performed over finite field F_{2^m}. For LSB-First Bit-Serial MM the key change lies in $X^{(0)} = Xn^{-u+m-1} \pmod{F(n)} = X$ which used to reduce the multiplication step. This gives us $u = m - 1$ i.e., $p = n^{m-1}$ as the new efficient Montgomery reduction element.

Based on Algorithm 12 (refer Fig. 7.22), we design the hardware architecture for it shown in Fig. 7.23. The $n^{-1} module$ is the same as MSB-first Bit-Serial MM, the difference in requirement of hardware is that it has two registers for storing $T^{(i)}$ and X of size m-bit. Apart from the register, the architecture has m two-input AND gates and m two-input XOR gates.

7.5.3 Bit-Parallel Montgomery Multiplication

We have discussed MSB-first bit-serial modular multiplication and LSB-first bit-serial modular multiplication, along with the various formulas and equations. This subsection discusses about a bit-parallel Montgomery multiplier defined over finite field F_{2^m}. As we know that in general modular multiplication, can be given as $R = X \times Y \times p^{-1} \pmod{F(n)}$, where selection of p is: $p = n^u$, and u is in range $[0 < u \leq m]$.

Selection of parameter u is done such that $[1 \leq u \leq m - 1]$, so that we re-formulate the Equation for MMM as

$$R = y_0 Xn^{-u} + \cdots + y_{u-1} Xn^{-1} + y_u X + y_{u+1} Xn + \cdots + y_{m-1} Xn^{-u+m-1} \pmod{F(n)}.$$
$$(7.10)$$

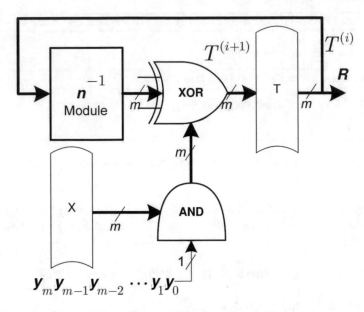

Fig. 7.23   Architecture for LSB-first bit-serial Montgomery multiplication

The important modification for parallel approach is that, X is multiplied with positive exponent of n as well as with negative exponent of n in order to compute the residues of the Eq. 7.10. We can re-formulate the Eq. 7.10 as $R = R_1 + R_2$ where $R_1 = y_0 X n^{-u} + y_1 X n^{-u+1} + \cdots + y_{u-1} X n^{-1}$ (mod $F(n)$). and $R_2 = y_u X + y_{u+1} X n + \cdots + y_{m-1} X n^{-u+m-1}$ (mod $F(n)$). This re-formulation of equation enables to configure the advanced architecture for the common type of MMM. Where Montgomery reduction element is $p = n^u$, as given given in Algorithm 13 shown in Fig. 7.24. We need $m - 1$ number of $n - module$ & $n^{-1} module$ because u lies in the range $[1 \leq u \leq m - 1]$ and $y_u . X$ can be computed from X.

Algorithm 13 Parallel Montgomery Multiplication Over F_{2^m}

Input: $X, Y \in F_{2^m}, F(n)$
Output: $R = X \times Y \times n^{-u}$ (mod $F(n)$)

1: Construct the matrix M for the given irreducible polynomial $F(n)$ using general u.
2: Compute an efficient u to minimize the number of terms summed up in the entities of the matrix.
3: Using computed u re-construct matrix M.
4: Implement $[r_0, r_1, \ldots, r_{m-1}]^T = M.[y_0, y_1, \ldots y_{m-1}]^T$.

Fig. 7.24   Parallel Montgomery multiplication over F_{2^m}

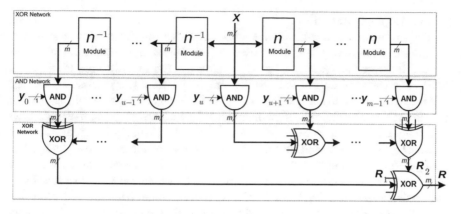

Fig. 7.25 Architecture for bit-level parallel MM

Based on the circuitry Architecture shown in Fig. 7.25, for bit-parallel MM approach, The execution starts with the calculation of the residue Xn^i (mod $F(n)$), where $i \in [-u, -u + m - 1]$. The $X'_{(i)}$ represents the value of Xn_i (mod $F(n)$). This computation is carried out with the help of the matrix M. For matrix M of size $m \times m$:

- Rows are consist of value of i where $i \in [-u, -u + m - 1]$, and
- Columns has the corresponding polynomial basis representation of $X'_{(i)}$

Based on the discussion, parallelization and matrix M, the MMM Equation which is similar to the Mastrovito multiplication (Mastrovito 1991), can be re-formulated over finite field F_{2^m}:

$$[r_0, r_1, \ldots, r_{m-1}]^T = M \times [y_0, y_1, \ldots, y_{m-1}]^T \tag{7.11}$$

Steps to construct the bit-parallel Montgomery multiplier in Algorithm 13 for corresponding architecture is shown in Fig. 7.24.

7.6 Parallelization of Radix-2 Montgomery Multiplication

To implement parallelism in Montgomery multiplication (MMM), we must find a way to execute two inter-reliant multiplication steps simultaneously. One of the ways given by Orup is based on reordering these steps so that they can be executed simultaneously (Orup 1995). This section discusses the enhancement done in the Montgomery algorithm such that it can efficiently perform the scalable and parallel radix-2 modular multiplication (Harris et al. 2005).

Systolic Implementation:

For the purpose of improved implementation of PKCs on hardware, many researchers and organizations have given MMM over FPGAs. However, the main aim of designing a PKC over the systolic array is to minimize the running time (Perin et al. 2010). The essential unit of the systolic array is its processing element (PE). The PEs are arranged in an array fashioned such that each PE or group of PE together executes addition or multiplication operations. As we know there are five basic ways of executing MMM (refer Sect. 6.1). Out of them, the Coarsely Integrated Operand Scanning (CIOS) based well-performing architecture and algorithm over finite fields of large prime F_p is given by Mrabet et al. (2017). The implementation was done on a systolic array as it is portable for various PKCs which use MMM such as ECC, RSA and other Key-pairing based PKCs. Apart from minimizing the time and using PEs efficiently, the hardware designed by Mrabet et al. competes with all the other characteristics of the FPGA. For high-radix MMM, it shows good performance considering *latency × area efficiency*. The given architecture of the systolic array is capable of implementing the CIOS algorithm. This is also scalable for high-radix (refer Chap. 8).

In the process of parallelizing the MMM algorithm, the help of a new precomputed parameter $\hat{m}$ is taken. The purpose of using this $\hat{m}$ is to rearrange the multiplication and result steps of the Montgomery algorithm in such a way that it can be executed simultaneously. The use of $\hat{m}$ for parallel processing Algorithm 14 is shown in Fig. 7.26. Before describing the algorithm some notations to be considered given as follows:

- X: Multiplier
- Y: Multiplicand
- m: Prime modulus
- k: Bit-length of binary representation of X, Y and m
- p: Montgomery Reduction Element where $p = 2^k$
- p^{-1}: Modular multiplicative inverse of p such that: $p \times p^{-1} \pmod{m} = 1$
- m': Such that $p \times p^{-1} = 1 + m \times m'$
- Q = Quotient where $Q = X \times Y \times m' \pmod{p}$
- R: result $R = X \times Y + Q \times m \div p$

Notations are given here to enable us to understand the parallelization process i.e., how we disjoint the multiply and result process to execute independently.

This approach brings two overheads on to the hardware architecture

1. As a result, R is not divided by 2 it will consume one extra bit for storing R. The normalization of the result can be performed at the end of the calculation.
2. For reordering the loop one extra kernel cycle is required.

The Montgomery algorithm discussed here is a combination of Tenca–Koc Multiple Word radix-2 Montgomery multiplication Algorithm 2 shown in Fig. 7.2 and the basic parallel Algorithm 14 shown in Fig. 7.26. The characteristics of the modified radix-2 parallel algorithm are brought in by left shift operation on $\hat{m}$ and Y over each PE. Therefore, the algorithm design is enhanced by taking the advantage of one extra

---

Algorithm 14 Basic Montgomery Modular Parallel Algorithm

Input: X, Y, m, m', Q and p.
Output: $R = X \times Y + Q \times m \div p$

1: *initialization:* $R = 0; i = 0; \hat{m} = ((m' \ (\text{mod } 2))m + 1) \div 2$
2: **while** $i < n$ **do**
3:     $Q = R \ (\text{mod } 2)$
4:     $R = \frac{R}{2} + Q + \hat{m} + X^i \times Y$
5:     $i = i + 1$
6: **end while**

Fig. 7.26 Basic Montgomery parallel algorithm

Algorithm 15 Parallel Radix-2 Algorithm

Input: X, Y, m, m', Q and p.
    w: multiplicand word length
    e: $\lceil \frac{k}{w} \rceil + 2PE$ iterations per kernel
    C: 1-bit carry digit
Output: $R = X \times Y + Q \times m \div p$

1: *Initialization:* $R = 0; Q = 0; i = 0$
2: **while** $i \leq k$ **do**
3:     $C = 0$
4:     $Q = R^0 \ (\text{mod } 2)$
5:     $j = 0$
6:     **while** $j < e$ **do**
7:         $(C, R^{i+1}) = R^i + Q \times \hat{m}^j + X^i \times Y^j + C$
8:     **end while**
9: **end while**

Fig. 7.27 Parallel radix-2 algorithm

cycle latency present between PEs, as well as a parallelized approach of multiplying operands (Jiang and Harris 2007).

We can reconfigure the Algorithm 15 given in Fig. 7.27 for higher radix, this makes it scalable. We can go for a higher radix algorithm by partitioning $\hat{m}$ & Y into $w - bit$ words. Here each *PE* executes e number of times for multiplication in order to perform multiplication of complete binary string of $\hat{m}$ and Y. Here the inner loop is iterate for e times, where $e = \frac{k}{w}$ for $\hat{m}$ and Y. If we observe the outer loop condition $i \leq n$, it is executing one extra iteration in order to process the left-shifted bits of $\hat{m}$ and Y. Also to handle another overhead i.e., the result R is not divided by 2 it will consume one extra bit for storing R. Therefore the inner loop iteration is executed one extra time to normalize the result.

Hardware realization

The hardware design corresponding to Algorithm 15 is given in Fig. 7.28. This architecture is scalable i.e., high radix MMM can also be executed for a variable length of operands and module. There are s number of PEs. The input parameters for a PE

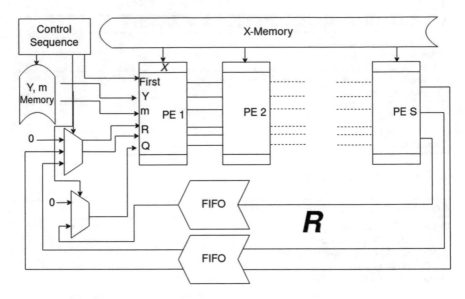

Fig. 7.28 Hardware architecture for parallel radix-2 design

is a single bit of X, Q a word of $\hat{m}$ having length w, Y and R. This input is provided in each step to PEs. In order to execute complete k bits of X, we need to run the kernel t times, where $t = \lceil k/s \rceil + 1$. As per the hardware configuration, s bits of X can be executed in one kernel cycle. The one extra execution of the kernel cycle is reordering the loop for parallel execution of the Algorithm. There are two options after getting the result from the Sth PE of the kernel, either queued in a FIFO unit and wait for the 1st PE to complete its execution, or avoid the FIFO unit and provide the result straight to the 1st PE as an input.

Processing Element (PE):
From the discussion over hardware realization, it is clear that the core part of a kernel cycle is a processing element (PE). For the parallel radix-2 algorithm, the corresponding PE is shown in Fig. 7.29. The basic difference in basic PE presented by Harris et al. and the PE for parallel execution is that, it has two AND-multipliers which is arranged in a parallel manner (refer Fig. 7.29), whereas in the PE given by Harris et al. the multiplexers are excluded (refer Fig. 7.4). The two delay registers given in the architecture is responsible for performing the left-shift operation over modulus $\hat{m}$ and multiplicand Y. Left shifting of s-bit of the modulus and multiplicand is done by a collaborative delay caused by all s number of PEs. This left shifting is done in such a way that the MSB of a word of modulus and multiplicand is shifted to turn into the LSB of the next word of modulus and multiplicand. There is no overhead of hardware space in modifying the PE from radix-2 design to parallel radix-2 design.

   Han et al. (2013) introduced parallelization on the multi-core architecture. A multi-core architecture can contribute more excellent execution and energy-saving in comparison to a single-core architecture. This multi-core parallelized architecture

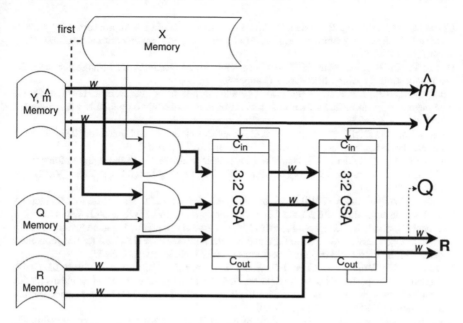

Fig. 7.29 Processing element for parallel radix-2 design

is attracting serious notice in both organizations and academia. By parallelizing the end program or algorithm, we can enhance the performance of a multi-core architecture. Nevertheless, designing a parallel algorithm is challenging, because the mechanisms to parallelize an inherently sequential algorithm and obtain better performance including good atomicity are still not known. Particularly concerning algorithms having eminent data dependency e.g. MMM.

The foremost time consuming operation of modular multiplication techniques rests in a series of a couple of lengthy calculations. One of them requires the addition of the multiplicand operand. The other requires the addition of the modulus, in order to provide the modular reduction. The method proposed by Neto et al. (2011) has a divide-and-conquer approach for partitioning the calculation and acclimatization of partial results. An adequate result is achieved while the calculation of the product of the multiplicand is done by partitioning the multiplier's bits into k parts that can be processed by PEs simultaneously.

References

Han J, Wang S, Huang W, Yu Z, Zeng X (2013) Parallelization of radix-2 Montgomery multiplication on multicore platform. IEEE Trans Very Large Scale Integr (VLSI) Syst 21(12):2325–2330
Hariri A, Reyhani-Masoleh A (2009) Bit-serial and bit-parallel Montgomery multiplication and squaring over GF (2m). IEEE Trans Comput 58(10):1332–1345

Harris D, Krishnamurthy R, Anders M, Mathew S, Hsu S (2005) An improved unified scalable radix-2 Montgomery multiplier. In: 17th IEEE symposium on computer arithmetic (ARITH'05). IEEE, pp 172–178

Huang M, Gaj K, El-Ghazawi T (2010) New hardware architectures for Montgomery modular multiplication algorithm. IEEE Trans Comput 60(7):923–936

Huang M, Gaj K, Kwon S, El-Ghazawi T (2008) An optimized hardware architecture for the Montgomery multiplication algorithm. In: International workshop on public key cryptography. Springer, pp 214–228

Jiang N, Harris D (2007) Parallelized radix-2 scalable Montgomery multiplier. In: 2007 IFIP international conference on very large scale integration. IEEE, pp 146–150

Kuang SR, Wang JP, Chang KC, Hsu HW (2012) Energy-efficient high-throughput Montgomery modular multipliers for RSA cryptosystems. IEEE Trans Very Large Scale Integr (VLSI) Syst 21(11):1999–2009

Kuang SR, Wu KY, Lu RY (2015) Low-cost high-performance VLSI architecture for Montgomery modular multiplication. IEEE Trans Very Large Scale Integr (VLSI) Syst 24(2):434–443

Leelavathi G, Shaila K, Venugopal K (2016) Elliptic curve cryptography implementation on FPGA using Montgomery multiplication for equal key and data size over GF (2 m) for wireless sensor networks. In: 2016 IEEE region 10 conference (TENCON). IEEE, pp 468–471

Marchesan GC, Weirich NR, Culau EC, Weber II, Moraes FG, Carara E, de Oliveira LL (2018) Exploring RSA performance up to 4096-bit for fast security processing on a flexible instruction set architecture processor. In: 2018 25th IEEE international conference on electronics, circuits and systems (ICECS). IEEE, pp 757–760

Massolino PMC, Batina L, Chaves R, Mentens N (2017) Area-optimized Montgomery multiplication on IGLOO 2 FPGAS. In: 2017 27th international conference on field programmable logic and applications (FPL). IEEE, pp 1–4

Mastrovito ED (1991) VLSI architectures for computation in Galois fields. PhD thesis, Linkoping University, Department of Electrical Engineering

McIvor C, McLoone M, McCanny JV (2004) Modified Montgomery modular multiplication and RSA exponentiation techniques. IEE Proc-Comput Digit Tech 151(6):402–408

Mrabet A, El-Mrabet N, Lashermes R, Rigaud JB, Bouallegue B, Mesnager S, Machhout M (2017) A scalable and systolic architectures of Montgomery modular multiplication for public key cryptosystems based on DSPS. J Hardw Syst Secur 1(3):219–236

Mrabet A, Darmon P (2019) High-performance of the multiplication over the quadratic extension in Montgomery domain for the pairing cryptosystems. In: 2019 19th international conference on sciences and techniques of automatic control and computer engineering (STA). IEEE, pp 79–83

Néto JC, Tenca AF, Ruggiero WV (2011) A parallel k-partition method to perform Montgomery multiplication. In: ASAP 2011–22nd IEEE international conference on application-specific systems, architectures and processors. IEEE, pp 251–254

Nikumbh H, Shah V (2018) Hardware implementation of modular multiplication. In: 2018 3rd IEEE international conference on recent trends in electronics, information & communication technology (RTEICT). IEEE, pp 376–380

Orup H (1995) Simplifying quotient determination in high-radix modular multiplication. In: Proceedings of the 12th symposium on computer arithmetic. IEEE, pp 193–199

Perin G, Mesquita DG, Herrmann FL, Martins JB (2010) Montgomery modular multiplication on reconfigurable hardware: fully systolic array vs parallel implementation. In: 2010 VI southern programmable logic conference (SPL). IEEE, pp 61–66

Tenca AF, Koç ÇK (2003) A scalable architecture for modular multiplication based on Montgomery's algorithm. IEEE Trans Comput 52(9):1215–1221

Zhengbing H, Moh'd Al Shboul R, Shirochin V (2007) An efficient architecture of 1024-bits cryptoprocessor for RSA cryptosystem based on modified Montgomery's algorithm. In: 2007 4th IEEE workshop on intelligent data acquisition and advanced computing systems: technology and applications. IEEE, pp 643–646

Chapter 8
High Radix Montgomery Multiplication

High Radix Implementation of Montgomery Multiplication:

We have seen Radix-2 based modular multiplication in the previous chapter (refer to Chap. 7). This chapter explores the various techniques for high-radix modular multiplication. If we talk about the use of these PKC, then many PKC techniques are now installed on various embedded-systems e.g., sensors, electronic cards. It also assures the security of transmission of private and confidential information over a public channel. High radix Montgomery multiplication has its own importance in PKC, as Montgomery multiplication (MMM) is a key operation in most of the PKC like RSA, ECC, etc. The basic mathematical expression of MMM can be given as:

$$R = X \times Y \times 2^{-k} \quad (\text{mod } m) \cdots \quad \because GCD(2^k, m = 1) \tag{8.1}$$

Here modulus m is a k-bit prime integer, X and Y are multiplier and multiplicand. Various implementations of the Montgomery multiplier can be categorized into the following three categories: Morales-Sandoval and Diaz-Perez (2016).

- **Full Parallel Multiplier:** This type of multiplier produces a result R in minimum clock-cycles (single iteration). Having a minimum clock-cycles gives the highest throughput but also acquires maximum hardware resource and area.
- **Bit-Serial Multiplier:** This type of multiplier has the least complex hardware design and the procedure requires exactly k iterations for calculation of result R. From Eq. 8.1, the multiplier X is processed bit-wise whereas multiplicand Y and modulus m are processed in parallel. The hardware design for this type of multiplier is not reconfigurable, it is fixed for $k - bit$ operands.
- **Digit-based multiplier:**

  1. *Type 1*: Here the multiplier X is processed w-bit word wise whereas the multiplicand Y and modulus m are processed as a whole. This approach is known as the high-Radix (2^r) Montgomery multiplication procedure $(R2^r MM)$.

© The Author(s), under exclusive license to Springer Nature Switzerland AG 2021
S. Vollala et al., *Energy-Efficient Modular Exponential Techniques
for Public-Key Cryptography*, https://doi.org/10.1007/978-3-030-74524-0_8

2. *Type 2*: Here the multiplier X is processed bit-wise, whereas the multiplicand Y and modulus m are processed as w-bit word-wise. This approach is known as the multiple-word Radix-2 Montgomery multiplication procedure (MWR2MM).

3. *Type 3:* Here the multiplier X is processed $r - bit$ at once, whereas the multiplicand Y and modulus m are processed word-wise. This approach is known as the multiple-word high-Radix (2^r) Montgomery multiplication procedure $(MWR2^rMM)$.

8.1 High Radix Montgomery Multiplication by Miyamoto

To increase the complexity for intruders more complex mathematical operations are used in encryption & decryption steps with long length operands. Especially, the RSA cryptography scheme (Rivest et al. 1978). The RSA cryptography scheme uses very long length operands for modular exponentiation. Evaluation of modular exponentiation is nothing but a series of modular multiplications. This encourages minimizing the modular multiplication execution time such that RSA and other PKC can achieve higher throughput. In this approach, a well-known modular multiplication (MM) method i.e., Montgomery multiplication (MMM) (Montgomery 1985) plays a vital role as it by-pass the trial division and makes the hardware and software implementation task smooth and faster.

Miyamoto et al. gave a well-organized scheme of RSA execution and its architecture design. The Algorithms 1 shown in Fig. 8.1 presents a version of MMM which has compatible execution and protection against intruder's attack.

8.2 Multiple—Word Montgomery Multiplication

A system includes an integrated circuit configured to receive three inputs a multiplicand, a multiplier and a modulus at once. The multiplicand is partitioned into chunks of words. Each multiplicand word has a fixed word width. The multiplier is also partitioned into an equal length of chunks of words. Each multiplier's word has a word width different from the multiplicand's word width. An outer loop is performed to iterate through the chunks of the multiplicand words. Each outer loop iteration includes iterations of an inner loop, performed to iterate through the chunks of the multiplier words. A Montgomery product of the multiplicand and the multiplier number with respect to the modulus is determined.

In order to perform multiple-word Montgomery multiplication according to some embodiments. As illustrated the process of the Algorithm 2 shown in Fig. 8.2, receives inputs including a first operand X (also referred to as the multiplicand number X), a second operand Y (also referred to as the multiplier number Y), a modulus M, a first-word width w1 (also referred to as the multiplicand word width w1), and a second-word width w2 (also referred to as the multiplier word width w2). In some

---

Algorithm 1 Algorithm High-Radix Montgomery Multiplication by Miyamoto

Input: $X = (x_{k-1}; \ldots x_1, x_0)2^h, Y = (y_{k-1}; \ldots y_1, y_0)2^h, m = (m_{k-1}, \ldots m_1, m_0)2^h; m' = -m^{-1}$
(mod 2^h)
Output: $R = X \times Y \times 2^{-h \cdot k}$ (mod m)

1: *Initialization* $R = 0, i = 0$
2: **while** $i \leq k - 1$ **do**
3:     *In-loop Initialization* $c = 0, j = 0$
4:     $q_i = (r_0 + x_i y_0) m'$ (mod 2^h)
5:     **while** $j \leq k - 1$ **do**
6:         $S = r_j + x_i y_i + q_i m_j + C$
7:         **if** $j \neq 0$ **then**
8:             $r_{j-1} = S$ (mod 2^h)
9:         **end if**
10:         $C = S \div 2^h$
11:     **end while**
12:     $r_{k-1} = C$
13: **end while**
14: **if** $R > m$ **then**
15:     $R = R - m$
16: **end if**

Fig. 8.1 Algorithm high-radix Montgomery multiplication by Miyamoto

embodiments, w1 is equal to w2. In some embodiments, w1 is less than w2. The process may also receive integers R1 and R2, where R1 is equal to 2^{w1} and R2 equal to 2^{w2}. The steps of the Algorithm 2 shown in Fig. 8.2 provide an output S for the MMM equal to $X \times Y \times R1^{L_x}$ (mod M). In some embodiments, the first operand X, the second operand Y and the modulus M are partitioned into multiple words. Specifically, the first operand X is partitioned into L_x words, and each word $x[i]$ of the L_x words has w1 bits, where L_x is an integer, and i is an integer between 0 and $L_x - 1$. Similarly, the operand Y is partitioned into L_y words, and each word $y[i]$ of the L_y words has w2 bits, where L_y is an integer and j is an integer between 0 and $L_y - 1$. The modulus M is partitioned into L_y words, and each word $m[j]$ of the L_y words has w2 bits. For X, Y and M having particular widths. By increasing the word widths w1 and w2, value of L_x, and L_y decrease respectively. The first operand X, the second operand Y, and the modulus M can be expressed as follows:

$$X = \sum_{i=0}^{Lx-1} x[i](R1)^i$$

$$Y = \sum_{j=0}^{Ly-1} y[j](R2)^j$$

$$M = \sum_{j=0}^{Ly-1} m[j](R2)^j$$

Algorithm 2 Multiple - Word Montgomery Multiplication

Input : $X, Y, M, W1, W2, R1,$ *and* $R2$
Assumptions: $w1 \leq w2$; $R1 = 2^{w1}$; $R2 = 2^{w2}$
$X = \sum_{i=0}^{Lx-1} x[i](R1)^i$
$Y = \sum_{j=0}^{Ly-1} y[j](R2)^j$
$M = \sum_{j=0}^{Ly-1} m[j](R2)^j$
Output : $S = X \times Y \times R1^{-Lx} \pmod{M}$

1: Intialize $s[0] = 0, i = 0$ and $j = 1$
2: Choose m' such that $m' \times m[0] \pmod{R1} = -1$
3: **while** $i \leq L_x - 1$ **do** $\triangleright L_x$ is bit length of multiplicand X
4:      $z1 = x[i] \times y[0] + s[0]$
5:      $q[i] = z1 \times m' \pmod{2}^{w1}$
6:      $z2 = z1 + q[i] \times m[0]$
7:      $r = (z2 \pmod{2^{w1}}) >> W1$
8:      $c = z2 >> w2$
9:      **while** $j \leq L_y - 1$ **do** $\triangleright L_y$ is bit length of multiplier Y
10:         $z1 = x[i] \times Y[i] + s[j]$
11:         $z2 = z1 + q[i] \times m[i] + C$
12:         $s[j-1] = ((z2 \pmod{2^{w1}}) << (w2-w1))|r;$
13:         $r = (z2 \pmod{2^{w2}}) >> w1$
14:         $c = z2 >> w2$
15:     **end while**
16:     $z = s[L_y] + c$
17:     $S[Ly-1] = ((z \pmod{2^{w1}}) << (w2-w1))|r$
18:     $S[Ly] = z >> w1$
19: **end while**

Fig. 8.2 Multiple—word Montgomery multiplication

In some embodiment, the Algorithm 2 shown in Fig. 8.2 scans through $x[0 : L_x - 1]$ in an outer while loop (also referred to as the main loop), which corresponds to lines 3 to 19 of the Algorithm 2. During the outer loop processing of $x[i]$ is done after processing $y[0]$ and $m[0]$. The Algorithm 2 scans through $y[1 : L_y - 1]$ and $m[1 : L_y - 1]$ in inner while loop, which corresponds to lines 9 to 15 of the Algorithm 2. During an inner loop processing $y[j]$ and $m[j]$, a result $s[j - 1]$ is calculated using $x[i]$, $y[j]$, $m[j]$ and $s[j]$, where $s[j]$ is calculated during the last outer loop processing $x[i - 1]$. After the algorithm finishes processing $x[L_x - 1]$ of the outer loop, the output S may be computed as follows:

$$S = \sum_{j=0}^{Ly} s[j](R2)^j$$

As illustrated in the formula, in some embodiments, there is a need to expand S by one bit (e.g. where M is greater than $\frac{1}{2} \times (R2)^{L_y}$). As such S may be represented by $L_y + 1$ words, including $s[0]$ to $s[L_y]$.

In some embodiments for the Algorithm 2, each of the $x[i]$, m' and $q[i]$ has a width of w1 bits, and each of the $y[j]$, $s[j]$ and $m[j]$ has a width of w2 bits. The first-word width w1 and the second-word width w2 may be the same or may be different from each other. In some examples, the first-word width w1 and the second-word width w2 may be determined based on the precision of the multipliers used to implement the Algorithm 2 to fully utilize the calculation capability of the multipliers.

Less Switching Operand Scanning Method (LSOS):

We have discussed a comparative study of five MMM derivatives (refer Sect. 6.1.2 from Chap. 6). Out of which, the Less Switching Operand scanning Method (LSOS) commonly known as coarsely integrated operand scanning (CIOS) method was used by most of the researchers for application-oriented purposes with minimum running time and space demands. The LSOS method use high-radix multiple words and smartly performs the minimum switching in the loop for calculation of partial products and routine reduction procedure. Few well known LSOS implementations on FPGAs have been given by Mrabet and Darmon (2019), McIvor et al. (2004), McLoone et al. (2004), Gallin and Tisserand (2019). LSOS method significantly improves the MMM as it allows methods to alter speed between the calculation of partial products and reduction procedures in different iterating loops.

8.3 Hardware Implementation of Radix-4 Montgomery Multiplication

This section discusses a higher radix i.e., radix-4 Montgomery multiplication (R4MMM) method which processes the multiplicand word-wise to obtain fast and extensible architecture. We can categorize the hardware implementation of high-radix MMM methods into two categories (Wang et al. 2012).

1. First category is designed for processing multiplier X as w-bit word wise whereas the multiplicand Y and modulus m are processed as a whole. The parameters provided as input have fixed-precision. This approach process an operand at a time and the precision length of the operand can be very long which can cause high fan-out signals. The word's bit-length for the radix-4 MMM method is $2 - bits$ (Kuang et al. 2016).
2. In the second category the multiplier X is processed $r - bits$ once, whereas the multiplicand Y and modulus m are processed word-wise. This approach is known as The multiple-word high-Radix (2^r) Montgomery multiplication procedure ($MWR2^rMM$) for radix 4 the $r = 2$, and this architecture is extensible (Wang et al. 2012). This approach does not process the full precision length operand at a time instead, divide the input operand into many words and then process them word-wise. Therefore, it averts the possible issue of high fan-out signals (Kuang et al. 2016).

Algorithm 3 Montgomery Modular Multiplication for Radix-4

Input: $\hat{m}, X, Y$
Output: $R = X \times Y \times p^{-1} \pmod{\hat{m}}; \ldots where 0 \leq R \leq 2\tilde{m}; R = 2^{k'} \pmod{\hat{m}}$

1: **for** $i = 0 \, to \, d - 1$ **do**
2:     $q_{-d+i} = 0$ $\triangleright$ Initialization of q_d
3: **end for**
4: *Initialization:* $R = 0, i = 0$
5: **while** $i \leq f - 1$ **do**
6:     $q_i = R \pmod 4$
7:     $R = R/4 + q_{i-d} \times \hat{m} + Y[2i+1:2i] \times X$ $\triangleright$ dependency equation
8: **end while**
9: $R = R \times 4^d + \sum_{j=0}^{d-1} q_{f+j-2} 4^j$
10: **Return** R

Fig. 8.3 Montgomery multiplication for radix-4

Radix-4 Montgomery Multiplication:

For radix-4 we consider the following notations:

- m $\leftarrow$ modulus an odd integer
- X $\leftarrow$ multiplicand $< m$
- Y $\leftarrow$ multiplier $< m$
- k $\leftarrow$ length of binary string of X, Y and m
- p $\leftarrow 2^k \pmod m$
- $X \times p \pmod m$ $\leftarrow$ m residue of X with respect to p
- $X \times Y \times p^{-1} \pmod m$ $\leftarrow$ Montgomery multiplication
- $q_i \leftarrow 2 - bit$ quotient in ith iteration of algorithm R4MMM, The value of q_i is essential for the $(i + d)$th iteration

$\hat{m}$ is defined using the following equations:

$$m' : satisfies(-mm') \pmod 4 = 1$$
$$\tilde{m} = (m' \pmod{4^{(d+1)}})m \tag{8.2}$$
$$\hat{m} = (\tilde{m} + 1)/4(d + 1)$$

The Algorithm 3 for radix-4 Montgomery multiplication (R4MMM) given in Fig. 8.3 and can be understood as follows:

For algorithm 3, let us consider $Y = \sum_{i=0}^{k'-1} Y_i \cdot 2^i$ where $k' = k + 2(d + 1)$ and $f \leftarrow \lceil k'/2 \rceil$ is number of iterations needed for completion of a multiplication.

$X[i : j]$ represents a portion of X starting from the ith bit and end at jth bit since $i > j$ i.e., $X[i : j] = \sum_{l=j}^{i} X_l 2^{l-j}$ where X_l gives the binary-bit value of X.

For simplification of the dependency equation in Algorithm 3 shown in Fig. 8.3 we can use booth encoding for quotient q and multiplier Y by replacing the 0, 1, 2, 3 with $-1, 0, 1, 2$ for radix-4 implementation.

8.4 Hardware Implementation of Radix-16 Montgomery Multiplication

This section discusses high-radix Montgomery multiplication where radix $= 16$. This modular multiplication uses the concept of modified Booth-16 encoding (Nguyen and Pham 2019). The modified Booth-16 encoding concept helps to minimize the computation overhead and critical path-delay for computing the intermediate results. The higher radix implementation reduces the number of iterations required by the factor of h (refer Algorithm 1 shown in Fig. 8.1) and increases the performance by producing the result fast. But, the necessary computation which needs to be performed sequentially and carefully, causes delay. Step-6 of Algorithm 1 shown in Fig. 8.1 requires complex calculation of $x_i Y$ and $q_i m$. The complexity of this step is proportional to the radix i.e., if we increase the radix it sharply increases the complexity of the calculation of this step. This is the main threat for high-radix MMM.

The Radix-16 based MMM Algorithm 4 is shown in Fig. 8.4 is using the well-known modified Booth-16 encoding scheme. It is used for reducing the computation overhead of the step-6 of the Algorithm 1, where the calculation of $x_i Y$ and $q_i m$ is simplified. Usually, the booth's representation has a set of digits for a high-radix h from $-\frac{h}{2}$ to $+\frac{h}{2}$ where h is even. Therefore, the academic booth digit set for $radix - 16$ is $(\pm 8Y, \pm 7Y, \ldots, \pm 1Y, 0)$. Out of these, $radix - 16$ digit set for calculating the intermediate result of odd ones i.e., $(\pm 7Y, \pm 5Y, \pm 3Y)$ totals $3k$ Full-Adders will be needed. To succeed in this disadvantage, this section suggests a revised version of Booth-16 encoding. The intermediate result for suggested Booth-16 encoding is calculated by addition of the two intermediate results of Booth-4 encoding scheme, where $B16_i = 2^2 B4_{2i+1} + B4_{2i}$, where $B16 \leftarrow$ Booth-16 and $B4 \leftarrow$ Booth-4 encoding. The calculation of the Booth-16 encoding scheme is suggested by Nguyen and Pham (2019). The suggested Booth-16 algorithm minimizes the requirement of hardware resources (from $3k$ Full Adders to k Full Adders) and saves the extra clock cycle required for critical path calculation of $x_i Y$ and two $(k + 4) - bit$ 2's-complement conversions. The suggested booth's encoding scheme is used for calculating $x_i Y$ at step 3 and step 7 of the Algorithm 4 shown in Fig. 8.4.

For efficient computation of $q_i \times m$ the Booth's-16 representation is used. The calculation of q_i is obtain after modulus operation of product of result R and modulo m with 2^4 is performed. Thereupon, the digit set of $q^i \in \{0, 1, \ldots, 14, 15\}$ raises the requirement of $3k$ full adders to calculate the term $q_i \times m$. Here the Booth's-16 representation plays a key role in reducing the computation overhead of term $q_i \times m$, the digit set of $q_i \in \{+8, \pm 7, \pm 6, \ldots, \pm 1, 0\}$ and the full adders required are reduced to only $3k$. But, for odd digits i.e., $(\pm 3m, \pm 5m, \pm 7m)$ there yet some difficulties are there for which, the term q_i is partitioned into $B4_1$ and $B4_0$, along side $q_{enc} = ENC(q_i) = 2^2 B4_1 + B4_0$, where $B4_1, B4_0 \in (+2, \pm 1, 0)$. The suggested encoding minimizes the calculation overhead for $q_i \times m$ as the requirement of full adders is decreased to k from $3k$. The use of suggested q_i encoding can be observed in step-5 & step-6 of the Algorithm 4 shown in Fig. 8.4.

Algorithm 4 Radix-16 Montgomery multiplication

Input: Let X, Y, are $k+1-bits$ 2's-complement numbers,
m; $k+1-bits$ odd integer, $-m \leq X,Y < m$
$h = 16^{\lfloor \frac{(k+5)}{4} \rfloor}; m^* = -m^{-1} \pmod{2^4}$
Output: $R_{\lceil \frac{(k+5)}{4} \rceil} = X \times Y \times h^{-1} \pmod{m}$

1: **Intialization:** $R_0 = 0, x_{-1} = 0, x_{k+2} : x_{k+5} \leftarrow x_{k+1}, i = 0$
2: **while** $i \leq \lfloor \frac{(k+5)}{4} \rfloor$ **do**
3:      $B_i = 2^2 B_4(x_{4i+3}, x_{4i+2}, x_{4i+1}) + B_4(x_{4i+1}, x_{4i}, x_{4i-1})$
4:      $q_i = R_i m^* \pmod{2^4}$ ▷ where B_4 is Booth-4
5:      $q_{enc} = ENC(q_i)$
6:      $R_i^* = signext(R_i + q_{enc}m) \div 2^4$
7:      $R_{i+1} = R_i^* + B_i Y$
8: **end while**
9: **if** $R_{\lceil \frac{(k+5)}{4} \rceil} < 0$ **then**
10:     $R_{\lceil \frac{(k+5)}{4} \rceil} = R_{\lceil \frac{(k+5)}{4} \rceil} + m$
11: **end if**
12: **Return** $R_{\lceil \frac{(k+5)}{4} \rceil}$

Fig. 8.4 Radix-16 Montgomery multiplication

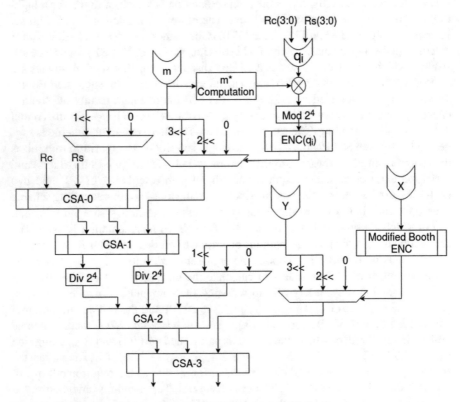

Fig. 8.5 Hardware architecture for radix-16 Montgomery multiplication

A simple hardware architecture to support the Algorithm 4 is given in Fig. 8.5. The intermediate result of $q_{enc} \times m$ and proposed $B_i \times Y$ are easily performed using left shift operation by 3-bit, 2-bit or 1-bit. The 2's complementing method is used for obtaining and processing the negative digits. Carry save adder (CSA) is used for averting long carry propagation. CSA might face some problems because of the sign extension in it. For correcting this sign problem the 4-bit sign extension is used. As we can observe in Fig. 8.5 4 *CSA* and 4 *2's-complementing* device is incorporated for the calculation of the critical path of the Algorithm 4.

8.5 High-Radix Systolic Architectures of Montgomery Multiplication

A systolic device is a special organization of Processing Elements (PE) termed as Unit. The organization is done in such a way that they are connected in a pipelined fashion. This arrangement gives a specific kind of parallel processing, the PE calculates the input parameters and saves them individually. Another way of understanding systolic architecture is to consider a 2-dimensional array comprised of PEs arranged in row and column order. PEs are capable of taking input parameters from sharing the processed information directly to their next connected PEs. A cell at each step takes input data from one or more neighbors.

Many researchers have proposed various systolic architectures implemented on FPGA. Most of which used Montgomery multiplication (MMM) to increase efficiency. Tenca and Koc (2003) gave a version of MMM, which can operate for variable bit-length of modulus and re-configurable for different hardware space. Harris et al. (2005) enhanced the performance of MMM version given by Tenca and Koc (2003) implemented on systolic architecture.

In most systolic architecture, the number of PE used is dependents on the number of words processed. The arrangement of PEs is done in a $1 - D$ array. For the s number of words, the architecture will have s number of PEs arranged in a $1 - D$ array. Steps involved in each iteration of the MMM procedures begin with a word being fetched from RAM and stored in local memory within their architecture. This fetching time of s words from RAM requires s number of clock cycles which needs to be added while estimating the number of clock cycles required for a MMM implemented on a systolic architecture. The initial cycle of the loop in the procedure may require an additional s clock cycles. Eventually, the leftover cycles of the loop of the procedure require $4 \times s$ clock cycles to complete the process.

8.5.1 Systolic Architecture Based on DSP

The design discussed in this section blends the LSOS method of the MMM approach (refer Sect. 6.1.2 of Chap. 6) (Mrabet et al. 2017) with a $2 - D$ systolic design (Vucha and Rajawat 2011). The concept of the LSOS algorithm is switching between the processing of the loops should be minimum. The idea of the $2 - D$ systolic design blends the equivalent PEs (performing a similar task) along with the connection with neighbors. They receive input parameters and process them with the predefined task assigned to them and they are arranged in a pipelined manner. Given the modern design, it is straight forward related to mathematical procedures of the LSOS approach of the MMM algorithm. The calculation is executed in a radix-h (High-Radix) i.e., radix (2^h). Input parameters are partitioned into s number of words. The $h - bit$ words as input parameters are executed. Many variants of this architecture for supporting different word sizes termed as $NW - s$ has been designed. Where s is in the power of 2 such as $s \in \{8, 16, 32 \text{ and } 64\}$, also termed as $NW - 16$, $NW - 32$ and $NW - 64$ (Mrabet et al. 2017). Prior to the discussion of the hardware design and approach for NW-8 and NW-16 architectures, understanding of the minimization of states in the final state machine (FSM) is essential. For which, partitioning of the algorithm of Montgomery, into 5-types of processing elements is done:

1. Unit alpha $\rightarrow \alpha$
2. Unit beta $\rightarrow \beta$
3. Unit gamma $\rightarrow \gamma$
4. Unit alpha final $\rightarrow \alpha_f$
5. Unit gamma final $\rightarrow \gamma_f$

Figure 8.6 shows the dependence of the distinct units. The distinct Units will be discussed one by one. During representation in the Fig. 8.6, the identifier MSB represents the Most Significant Bit of the results and the identifier LSB represents the Least Significant Bit.

Unit α presented by lines 4 and 5 of the Algorithm 5 shown in Fig. 8.7. The PE α is extensible according to the NW in the design. We use this unit to perform the multiplication step. The input of the unit alpha is LSB_{in} and MSB_{in} provided by the previous step (Fig. 8.6).

– x_i: denotes the words of the operand X, and
– y_i: denotes the words of the operand Y.

The output produced by α unit is LSB_alpha_out and MSB_alpha_out which is given as the input to next unit. The Fig. 8.8 illustrate the input and output of the PE recognized as unit-α

Unit β presented by lines 10 to 12 of Algorithm 5 shown in Fig. 8.7. Unit β receives the input as LSB_beta_in which is an output of by the preceding unit.

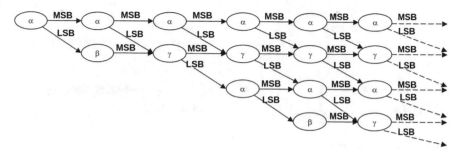

Fig. 8.6 Two-dimensional representation of units of systolic architecture

---

Algorithm 5 Modified LSOS Algorithm for DSP Slices

Input: m, m', h, s, k, p, X, Y
Where: $k = s \cdot h : bit - length, p = r^k, m < 2^k, m' = -m^{-1} \pmod{2^h}, X, Y < m$
Output: $X \times Y \times p^{-1} \pmod{m}$

1: *Initialization:* $R = NULL, i = 0$
2: **while** $i < s$ **do**
3:     $C = 0, j = 0$ ▷ In loop initialization
4:     **while** $j \leq s - 1$ **do**
5:         $(C, S) = R_j + x_i \times y_j + C$
6:         $R_j = S; \ j = j + 1$
7:     **end while**
8:     $(C, S) = R_s + C$
9:     $R_s = S$
10:     $R_{s+1} = C$
11:     $C = 0, j = 0$ ▷ Resetting the value of C and j
12:     $u = R_0 \times m' \pmod{2^h}$
13:     $(C, S) = R_0 + u \times m_0$
14:     **while** $j < s$ **do**
15:         $(C, S) = R_j + u \times m_j + C$
16:         $R_j = S; \ j = j + 1$
17:     **end while**
18:     $(C, S) = T_s + C$
19:     $R_{s-1} = S$
20:     $R_s = R_{s+1} + C$
21:     $i = i + 1$
22: **end while**
23: **Return** R

Fig. 8.7 Modified LSOS algorithm for DSP slices

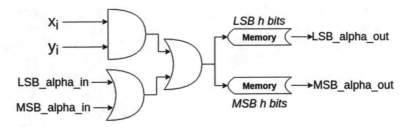

Fig. 8.8 Architecture of unit α's PE

   – m_0: represents the starting word of the modulus m.
   – m': is calculated before the beginning of the algorithm.

The Beta unit provides the output as u and MSB_beta_out to its succeeding unit. Figure 8.9 illustrates the input and output of the PE recognized as unit-β.

Unit γ presented by lines 14 and 15 of Algorithm 5 shown in Fig. 8.7. The unit-gamma is extensible as per the requirement of the architecture of NW. This unit is responsible for performing the reduction procedure. This unit takes LSB_gamma_in, u, and MSB_gamma_in as an input which is given by preceding units.

   – m_i: represents the iterating words of the modulus m.
   – u: given as input by unit beta.

Unit gamma provide the output as *LSB_gamma_out* and *MSB_gamma_out* to its succeeding unit. The Fig. 8.10 illustrate the input and output of the PE recognized as unit-γ.

Unit α_f presented by lines 6 to 9 of Algorithm 5 shown in Fig. 8.7. The unit alpha final gets the input from preceding as *LSB_alpha_f_in* and *MSB_alpha_f_in* which is given by the succeeding unit.

Unit α_f provide the output as *LSB1_alpha_f_out* and *LSB2_alpha_f_out* to its succeeding unit. The Fig. 8.11 illustrate the input and output of the PE recognized as unit-$\alpha - final$.

Unit γ_f presented by lines 16 to 19 of Algorithm 5 shown in Fig. 8.7. The unit gamma final gets the input as *MSB_gamma_f_in*, *LSB1_gamma_f_in* and *LSB2_gamma_f_in* from its preceding unit.
       Unit γ_f provide the output as *LSB1_gamma_f_out* and *LSB2_gamma_f_out* to its succeeding unit. The Fig. 8.12 illustrate the input and output of the PE recognized as unit-$\gamma - final$.

Figure 8.6 shows the input and output of the units with the flow. More details of these DSP slices can be found from a paper published by Mrabet et al. (2017).

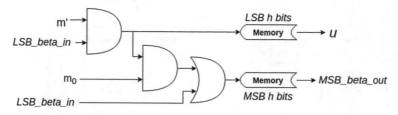

Fig. 8.9   Architecture of unit β's PE

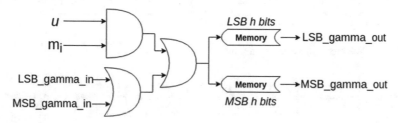

Fig. 8.10   Architecture of unit γ's PE

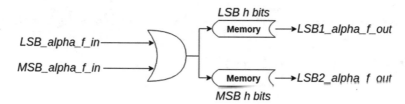

Fig. 8.11   Architecture of unit $\alpha final$'s PE

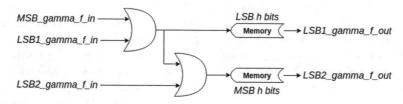

Fig. 8.12   Architecture of unit $\gamma final$'s PE

8.5.1.1   NW-8, NW16 and NW32 Architecture

Till now, the hardware implementation of the algorithm and various DSPs has been discussed. The multiplicand, multiplier & modulus is divided into 8, 16 and 32 bit words. Where NW-8 architecture is comprised of 9 PEs (3 alpha units, 1 alpha-final unit, 1 beta unit, 3 gamma units and 1 gamma-final unit) are arranged in a $2 - D$ array formation, shown in Fig. 8.13. Similarly, the NW-16 and NW-32 architectures

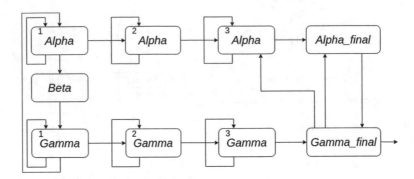

Fig. 8.13 NW8 architecture based on LSOS

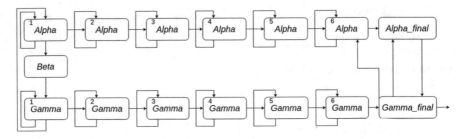

Fig. 8.14 NW16 architecture based on LSOS

are designed shown in Fig. 8.14. This subsection explains the scalability of the architecture given by Mrabet et al. (2017).

The NW-16 architecture is comprised of 15 PEs (6 α units, 1 $\alpha - final$ unit, 1 β unit, 6 γ units and 1 $\gamma - final$ unit) distributed in a two-dimensional array as shown in Fig. 8.14. Similarly NW-32 architecture is comprised of 27 PEs distributed in a two-dimensional array (12 α units, 1 $\alpha - final$ unit, 1 β unit, 12 γ units and 1 $\gamma - final$ unit). By inducing the architecture, the input-parameters which include the modulus are partitioned into s-words. The NW-s architecture is comprised of PEs. The PEs are arranged like a matrix i.e., $2 - D$ array, For all architectures, each PE is responsible for the computation which includes parameters provided as inputs of h-bit words. The required number of PEs are $(s - s/4) + 3$ units. The running time is measured by clock-cycles which is $3 \times (s + max)$, where $max = $ max(number of the alpha unit, number of the gamma unit) $= \frac{(s - s/4)}{2}$, signifying that this approach needs the circuit shown for NW-8 (refer Fig. 8.13) and NW-16 (refer Fig. 8.14) to execute $s + max$ times. Using this architecture the multiplication can be achieved in $3 \times (s + max)$ clock-cycles considering the architecture needs only three states.

Algorithm 6 LSOS for Finely Pipelined Montgomery Modular Multiplication

Input: $X = \sum_{i=0}^{s-1} x_i 2^{ih}, Y = \sum_{j=0}^{s-1} y_j 2^{jh}$

$m = \sum_{j=0}^{s-1} m_j 2^{jh}$ such that $0 \leq X, Y, < 2m$

Assumption: $4m < 2^k$ and $m' = -m^{-1} \pmod{2}^h$

Output: $R \equiv X \times Y \times 2^{-k} \pmod{m}, 0 \leq R < 2m$

1: **Initialization:** $r_{0...s-1} = 0, c1 = 0, c2 = 0, i = 0, j = 0$
2: **while** $i < s - 1$ **do**
3:     **while** $j < s - 1$ **do**
4:         $v_j = r_j + x_i \times y_j$
5:         $(c2, u_j) = v_j + c2$
6:     **end while**
7:     $q_i = v_0 \times m' \pmod{2^h}$
8:     $j = 0$ ▷ Initialization
9:     **while** $j < s - 1$ **do**
10:         $(c1, r_{j-1}) = u_j + q_i \times m_j + c1$
11:     **end while**
12:     $r_{s-1} = r_{-1}^{(m)}$
13: **end while**
14: **Return** $R = \sum_{j=0}^{s-1} r_j 2^{jh}$

Fig. 8.15 LSOS for finely pipelined Montgomery multiplication

8.6   Finely Pipelined Modular Multipliers

Gallin and Tisserand et al. modified the LSOS method to minimize the latency caused by final subtraction (Gallin and Tisserand 2019). They use the less complex and consistent property of LSOS to implement a finely-pipelined design into hardware in order to overcome the latencies caused by the previous pipelined architecture of DSP slices (Mrabet et al. 2017).

In Algorithm 6 shown in Fig. 8.15, the result r_{s-1} produced from the 1st logical multiplier (LM) while iterating for the j where $j = 4$ & again while iterating for j where $j = 0$, the output r_{-1} produced from the 2nd LM has same word of $h - bit$ length. We can observe that the value $r_{-1}^{(n)}$ used as a parameter in step-12 of the Algorithm 6 shown in Fig. 8.15 having the same value as least significant word (LSW) r_{-1} which will be calculated at next iteration of i using the LM. This latency minimization is feasible because the result has the LSW r_{-1} value as 0, which is no significant value and ignored by LSOS MMM. The idea is to utilize the space used by this word for saving the partial result obtained by the upcoming LM calculated during the iteration of the outer loop. In the following, $r_{-1}^{(C)} \leftarrow$ value calculated by present (current) LM and $r_{-1}^{(N)} \leftarrow$ value calculated by upcoming (next) LM.

If we use the same memory space for an $h - bit$ word for two consecutive partial results produced by LMs, it will not harm the final result. This assertion needs to demonstrate that $r_{-1}^{(N)} = r_{s-1}^{(C)} < 2^h$ i.e., LSW of $(i + 1)$th (next) iteration is having same h-bit value as Most significant word (MSW) of ith (current) iteration. This

Table 8.1 Latency reduction by finely pipelined algorithm

Before	← LSW									MSW →
	0					0				
	j = 0	j = 1	j = 2	j = 3	j = 4	j = 0	j = 1	j = 2	j = 3	j = 4
After	0				0					
	j = 0	j = 1	j = 2	j = 3	j = 4/j = 0	j = 1	j = 2	j = 3	j = 4	

demonstration can be done by using a property of the MMM algorithm. Another demonstration is that imbricating of these two consecutive and distinct words is not having any "abstract" carries. The Algorithm 6 has two carries $c1$ and $c2$, which are propagated from previous LM to current LM. As in modified LSOS Algorithm 6, 1st inner loop is demonstrated in step 3 to step 6. Then, from step 9 to step 11 after the last iteration of the 2nd inner loop we define $u_s = c2$, & $r_{s-1} = u_s + c1$. In order to compute R_i by the present LM, it requires the LSW of upcoming partial result $r_{-1}^{(n)}$, which is computed by the next LM of 2nd inner loop.

This approach of minimizing latency removes an additional slot with an advanced hardware design that has control over the imbricate caused by step 12 of the Algorithm 6 shown in Fig. 8.15 & demonstrated in the Table 8.1. This approach has more integrated flow without any significant overhead and as a result, minimizes the latency. We know the relationship is such that the number of logical Multipliers (σ) are inversely proportional to the s number of iteration. Therefore this implementation is saving the number of iterations.

8.7 Montgomery Ladder Modular Multiplication

This section discusses the enhanced methods for the Montgomery ladder used for ECC. This approach preserves the properties of NIST primes and partitioned it in 2 parts:

1. Scalable multiplication (SCAM)
2. Modular reduction (MRUC),

Figure 8.16 demonstrates the working of these two parts parallelly with time-slots. This is clear that we selected the multiply-and-reduce approach so that it can be arranged in a better way to obtain better performance. This approach enables us to perform Montgomery ladder modular multiplication in parallel. We get better performance as well as security from side-channel attacks in ECC by implementing the Montgomery ladder as an inner mechanism.

It is observed that the reduction process is one time-slot behind the multiplication process. i.e., at time T_i if multiplication process is executing for ith iteration then reduction process will be executing $(i - 1)$th iteration simultaneously. Here the extensible multiplication Algorithm 7 shown in Fig. 8.17 for high-radix is capable

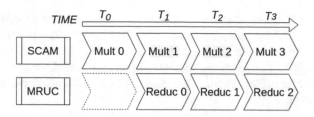

Fig. 8.16 Two-stage pipeline for modular multiplication over NIST prime fields

---

Algorithm 7 Scalable Montgomery Ladder Modular Multiplication

---

Input: $X = \sum_{i=0}^{s-1} x^{(i)} \times 2^{h \times i}, Y = \sum_{i=0}^{s-1} y_i \times 2^{h \times i}$,
Output: $R = X \times Y = \sum_{i=0}^{2s-1} r^{(i)} \times 2^{h \times i}$

1: **Initialization:** $U^{(-1)} = 0, i = 0, j = 0$
2: **while** $i \leq m - 1$ **do**
3:     $T^{(0)} = (U^{(i-1)})^{(0)} + y_j \times x^{(0)}$
4:     $r^{(i)} = T^{(0)} \pmod{2^h}$
5:     **while** $j \leq m - 1$ **do**
6:         $T^{(j)} = (U^{(i-1)}) + y_i x^{(j)} + \lfloor T^{(j-1)} \div 2^h \rfloor$
7:         $(U^{(i)})^{(s-1)} = T^{(j)} \pmod{2^h}$
8:         $j = j + 1$
9:     **end while**
10:     $(U^{(i)})^{(s-1)} = \lfloor T_{s-1} \div 2^h \rfloor$
11:     $i = i + 1$
12: **end while**
13: $(r^{(2s-1)} \ldots U^{(s)}) = U^{(s-1)}$
14: **Return** $(r^{(2s-1)} \ldots r^{(0)})_{2^h}$

Fig. 8.17 Scalable Montgomery ladder modular multiplication

Fig. 8.18 Architecture scalable Montgomery ladder modular multiplier

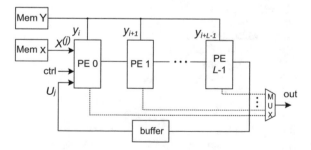

of handling distinct lengths of operands as in turn supports the 5-NIST primes. For the words and high-radix notation the superscripts are used to show the word-wise representation whereas subscripts are used to shown the bit-wise representation.

The architecture of an extensible multiplier corresponding to the algorithm 7 is given in Fig. 8.18. The operands (X & Y) are saved in RAM or Shift register such that it can provide the value bit-wise or word-wise as per requirement. The effort by Wu and Wang (2019), Chung et al. (2012) to develop this Montgomery ladder method for ECC, where it is used for elliptic curve point multiplication. They practiced full-word Montgomery multipliers to minimize the time required. Consider that if we arrange 256-bit multipliers in a pipelined manner to perform MMM, then we can achieve much quicker architecture to complete the work i.e., $22.3K$ clock cycles, instead of $163K$ clock cycles.

8.8 Digit-Digit Computation Approach Scalable Montgomery Multiplier

This section is about extensible hardware design as shown in Fig. 8.20 to perform modular multiplication over the prime fields F_p. An unique iterative digit–digit Montgomery multiplication (IDDMM) Algorithm 8 shown in Fig. 8.19 is discussed & a corresponding architecture for computing that algorithm are described (Morales-Sandoval and Diaz-Perez 2016). The input parameters are denoted as radix 2^h (High-Radix). Multiplication over F_p is achievable by using approximately the same architecture because the hardware designing overhead of PE's kernel is affected by the factor of h and independent of p. Arithmetic in F_p is essential in the current crypto-

---

Algorithm 8 IDDMM Montgomery Modular Multiplication Algorithm

Input: $X = (0, X_{k-1}, \ldots, X_0), Y = (Y_{k-1}, \ldots, Y_0), m = (0, m_{k-1}, \ldots m_0),$
    $Where \ldots 0 < X, Y < 2m, p = \beta^{k+1}$ with $GCD(m, \beta) = 1 and m' = -m^{-1} \pmod{\beta}$
Output: $R = \sum_{i=0}^{m} R_i \beta^i = X \times Y \times p^{-1} \pmod{m}$

1: *Initialisation* $R^{(0)} = 0, i = 0$
2: **while** $i \leq k$ **do**
3:    $C^{(j)} = 0, j = 0$ ▷ In-Loop Initialisation
4:    **while** $j \leq m$ **do**
5:        $S = R_j^{(i)} + X_j \times Y_i$
6:        **if** $j = 0$ **then**
7:            $q^i = S_0 \times m' \pmod{\beta}$
8:        **end if**
9:        $p = q^i \times m_j$
10:       $(C^{(j+1)}, U_j) = S + p + C^{(j)}$
11:       **if** $j > 0$ **then**
12:           $R_{j-1}^{(i+1)} = U_j$
13:       **end if**
14:    **end while**
15: **end while**
16:
17: **Return** $R^{(m+1)}$

Fig. 8.19 IDDMM Montgomery multiplication algorithm

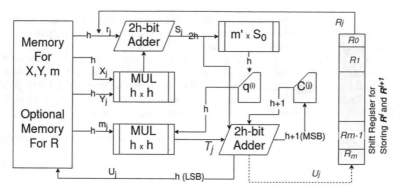

Fig. 8.20 Architecture of IDDMM algorithm

graphic techniques. PKCs like RSA and ECC implement cryptography & DSS using series of MMMs over F_p.

The hardware design shown in Fig. 8.20 is not specifically designed for any particular FPGA-family, i.e., it can be implemented over a number of FPGA-Family and if required it is also configurable for ASIC technology. There is still someplace for enhancement in the architecture by introducing pipeline stages.

References

Chung SC, Lee JW, Chang HC, Lee CY (2012) A high-performance elliptic curve cryptographic processor over GF (p) with spa resistance. In: 2012 IEEE international symposium on circuits and systems. IEEE, pp 1456–1459

Gallin G, Tisserand A (2019) Generation of finely-pipelined gf (p p) multipliers for flexible curve based cryptography on FPGAs. IEEE Trans Comput 68(11):1612–1622

Harris D, Krishnamurthy R, Anders M, Mathew S, Hsu S (2005) An improved unified scalable radix-2 Montgomery multiplier. In: 17th IEEE symposium on computer arithmetic (ARITH'05). IEEE, pp 172–178

Kuang SR, Liang CY, Chen CC (2016) An efficient radix-4 scalable architecture for Montgomery modular multiplication. IEEE Trans Circuits Syst II: Express Briefs 63(6):568–572

McIvor C, McLoone M, McCanny JV (2004) FPGA Montgomery multiplier architectures-a comparison. In: 12th annual IEEE symposium on field-programmable custom computing machines. IEEE, pp 279–282

McLoone M, McIvor C, McCanny JV (2004) Coarsely integrated operand scanning (CIOS) architecture for high-speed Montgomery modular multiplication. In: Proceedings. 2004 IEEE international conference on field-programmable technology (IEEE Cat. No. 04EX921). IEEE, pp 185–191

Montgomery PL (1985) Modular multiplication without trial division. Math Comput 44(170):519–521

Morales-Sandoval M, Diaz-Perez A (2016) Scalable GF (p) Montgomery multiplier based on a digit-digit computation approach. IET Comput Digit Tech 10(3):102–109

Mrabet A, El-Mrabet N, Lashermes R, Rigaud JB, Bouallegue B, Mesnager S, Machhout M (2017) A scalable and systolic architectures of Montgomery modular multiplication for public key cryptosystems based on DSPs. J Hardw Syst Secur 1(3):219–236

Mrabet A, Darmon P (2019) High-performance of the multiplication over the quadratic extension in Montgomery domain for the pairing cryptosystems. In: 2019 19th international conference on sciences and techniques of automatic control and computer engineering (STA). IEEE, pp 79–83

Nguyen BC, Pham CK (2019) An efficient hardware implementation of radix-16 Montgomery multiplication. In: 2019 IEEE 8th global conference on consumer electronics (GCCE). IEEE, pp 1121–1122

Rivest RL, Shamir A, Adleman L (1978) A method for obtaining digital signatures and public-key cryptosystems. Commun ACM 21(2):120–126

Tenca AF, Koç ÇK (2003) A scalable architecture for modular multiplication based on Montgomery's algorithm. IEEE Trans Comput 52(9):1215–1221

Vucha M, Rajawat A (2011) Design and FPGA implementation of systolic array architecture for matrix multiplication. Int J Comput Appl 26(3):18–22

Wang SH, Lin WC, Ye JH, Shieh MD (2012) Fast scalable radix-4 Montgomery modular multiplier. In: 2012 IEEE international symposium on circuits and systems. IEEE, pp 3049–3052

Wu T, Wang R (2019) Fast unified elliptic curve point multiplication for NIST prime curves on FPGAs. J Cryptogr Eng 9(4):401–410

Part IV
Modular Exponentiation Based on Bit Forwarding Techniques

Chapter 9
Bit Forwarding Techniques for Efficient Modular Exponentiation

1. Adaptable Montgomery Multiplication (AMM) for radix-2 implementation.
2. Adaptable High-Radix Montgomery Multiplication (AHRMM) for high-radix implementation.

As per the practicals conducted by Satya et al. Vollala et al. (2016) over ICARUS Verilog simulation and synthesis tool, they found that these methods improve the performance for 1024-bit exponent as shown in the Table 9.1.

This much amount of minimization of required number modular multiplications (MMs) for modular exponentiation (ME) significantly improves the performance of PKC in comparison with currently dominating techniques. This chapter also discusses the mathematical correctness of these bit-forwarding techniques.

9.1 Introduction

Well-known public key cryptography techniques such as RSA, ECC, Rabin's PKC, DSS, ElGamal PKC and Diffie-Hellman Key exchange protocol has its crucial operation involving modular exponentiation (ME) (Diffie and Hellman 1976; Rivest et al. 1978; ElGamal 1984) (Stallings 2003). Therefore the energy-efficient implementation of all these PKCs is strongly affected by the better implementation of ME. In 1984, Montgomery brought in a novel method for calculating the MMs (Montgomery 1985). The key idea was to avoid trial division by replacing it with shift and addition, subtraction operations. The shifting, addition and subtraction are simple operations and less complex for implementing over any device. After this multiplication method, various researchers have proposed a modified and advanced technology to enhance the performance of MM based on this method. Most of the enhancement was centric to enhance *modular multiplication* but for enhancing the *modular exponentiation* insufficient research has been done (Bar-El 2002; Batina et al. 2003). The Bit For-

© The Author(s), under exclusive license to Springer Nature Switzerland AG 2021   185
S. Vollala et al., *Energy-Efficient Modular Exponential Techniques*
for Public-Key Cryptography, https://doi.org/10.1007/978-3-030-74524-0_9

Table 9.1 Performance improved by BFW techniques for 1024-bit exponent

Technique	Improved performance (%)
BFW-1	11.16
BFW-2	15.14
BFW-3	18.20

warding (BFW) techniques work in the direction of enhancing the efficiency of *ME* by minimizing the required number of MMs. Thus, it gives better performance and energy-saving modular exponential technique. These techniques can be efficiently implemented over hardware and don't require altering the clock rate (Vollala and Ramasubramanian 2017).

9.2 Bit Forwarding Techniques for Evaluating Modular Exponentiation

Many cryptographic applications use ME as the main arithmetic operation to provide robust security. Thus, most of the PKC relies on the better performing modular exponential techniques which can be implemented efficiently. Out of various arithmetic operations, the squaring and multiplying operations are more frequently used for the evaluation of ME. Less occurrence of these operations will increase the throughput. The BFW techniques help to reduce the frequency of these operations (Vollala et al. 2014, 2016). BFW techniques discussed in this chapter are based on the special MM properties given below:

$$X \times Y \ (\mathrm{mod}\ m) = (X \ (\mathrm{mod}\ m) \times Y \ (\mathrm{mod}\ m)) \ (\mathrm{mod}\ m)$$

Proof Let $X \ (\mathrm{mod}\ m) = r_1$ and $Y \ (\mathrm{mod}\ m) = r_2$, using quotient remainder theorem:

$$X = m \times q_1 + r_1; \quad \because 0 \le r_1 < m \ and \ q_1 \in Z(integer)$$
$$Y = m \times q_2 + r_2; \quad \because 0 \le r_2 < m \ and \ q_2 \in Z(integer)$$

Now RHS is:

$$(X \ (\mathrm{mod}\ m) \times Y \ (\mathrm{mod}\ m)) \ (\mathrm{mod}\ m) = (r_1 \times r_2) \ (\mathrm{mod}\ m) \qquad (9.1)$$

LHS:

$$X \times Y \ (\mathrm{mod}\ m) = ((m \times q_1 + r_1) \times (m \times q_2 + r2)) \ (\mathrm{mod}\ m)$$
$$= m \times m \times q_1 \times q_2 + m \times q_1 \times r_2 + m \times q_2 \times r_1 + r_1 \times r_2 \ (\mathrm{mod}\ m)$$
$$= m \times (m \times q_1 \times q_2 + q_1 \times r_2 + q_2 \times r_1) + (r_1 \times r_2) \ (\mathrm{mod}\ m)$$

The terms multiplying with modulus m can be ignored when we are performing modulus operation (mod m).

Thus, we get:

$$(X \quad (\text{mod } m) \times Y \quad (\text{mod } m)) \quad (\text{mod } m) = (r_1 \times r_2) \quad (\text{mod } m)$$

This is similar to the Eq. 9.1 and hense $LHS = RHS.$ and we can conclude:

$$X \times Y \quad (\text{mod } m) = (X \quad (\text{mod } m) \times Y \quad (\text{mod } m)) \quad (\text{mod } m) \qquad (9.2)$$

In the Bit Forwarding techniques, traversing from MSB to LSB of the exponent's binary strings is done. The basic approach is to square the partial-result at each iteration irrespective of bit-value and perform multiplication operation only if there is a non-zero bit is encountered. In the BFW techniques if the binary representation is having t successive $1's$ in the exponent's binary string then we can skip $t - 1$ places, following the multiplication of partial-result with g^{2^t-1} (mod m). This requires precomputation of a value $A_{2^t-1} = g^{2^t-1}$ (mod m) and needs to be stored for future use. If we encounter n number of successive 1s in the exponent's binary string then using this technique we can skip $n \times (t - 1)$ number of MMs. Therefore, better throughput by consuming less power can be achieved with a little bit of overhead of extra space.

The ME is comprised of a sequence of MMs (square and multiply). In order to compute MM required for ME, the MMM method (radix-2) is modified to be compatible with the BFW techniques. This modified MMM method is termed as "Adaptable Montgomery Multiplication" (AMM) and is discussed in Sect. 9.2.4. The prefix *Adaptable* means it is suitable for all BFW techniques having k-bit operands for computing g^z (mod m) where exponent $z \leq E$ is a positive integers. When we call the method AMM, it causes one additional multiplication operation for $2^{-\varsigma}$ (mod m). This additional multiplication is replaced by an alternative termed as Proposed Constant $(PC) = 2^{2\varsigma}$ (mod m). First of all the value of A is computed by calling the method $AMM(A, PC, m)$, following this the initial-result is computed by $(A \times PC)$ (mod m) $= A \times 2^{2\varsigma}$ (mod m). Then we proceed with the initial-result to calculate and store the parameters which will be required in the near future in the algorithm. After completion of the loop, the partial-result is again passed as a parameter with 1 to the AMM method to obtain the final result.

The aim of these BFW techniques with modified MMM is to obtain a better performing modular exponential technique by minimizing the clock-cycles (Vollala and Ramasubramanian 2017). We will also discuss the up-gradation of *AMM* method to *AHRMM* (Adaptable high-radix Montgomery multiplication). We need to reformulate the PC for AHRMM as: $PC = 2^{(2wh+2)}$ (mod m) for supporting high-radix.

9.2.1   BFW-1: Bit Forwarding 1-Bit Algorithm

For this we need to compute two pre-computed values:

1. $A_1 = AMM(g, PC, m)$
2. $A_3 = AMM(A_1, A_2, m) \cdots \therefore A_2 = AMM(A_1, A_1, m)$

While traversing from MSB to LSB of exponent's binary string, if two successive $1's$ are encountered then, we can skip one-bit. The partial-result is multiplied with A_3. The BFW-1 Algorithm 1 shown in Fig. 9.1 is reducing the required number of multiplications by $n \times (t - 1) = n \times (2 - 1) = n \because t = 2$ for every two successive $1's$.

9.2.2   BFW-2: Bit Forwarding 2-Bits Algorithm

For this we need to compute three pre-computed values:

1. $A_1 = AMM(g, PC, m)$
2. $A_3 = AMM(A_1, A_2, m) \cdots \therefore A_2 = AMM(A_1, A_1, m)$
3. $A_7 = AMM(A_6, A_1, m) \cdots \therefore A_6 = AMM(A_3, A_3, m)$

While traversing from MSB to LSB of exponent's binary string, if three successive $1's$ are encountered then we can skip 2-bits. The partial-result is multiplied with A_7. The BFW-2 Algorithm 2 shown in Fig. 9.2 is reducing the required number of

---

Algorithm 1 BFW1:Bit forwarding 1-bit algorithm

    Input: $g, E, m \ldots E = (e_{k-1}, \ldots, e_1, e_0)_2$
    And a new constant referred to as the proposed constant $PC = 2^{2\zeta} \pmod{m}$
    Output: $Res = g^E \pmod{m}$

1: *Precompute the value of A_1, A_3*
2: $A_1 = AMM(g, PC, m)$;
3: $A_2 = AMM(A_1, A_1, m)$;
4: $A_3 = AMM(A_2, A_1, m)$;
5: $R[k-1] = A_1$;
6: **for** $i = k - 2$ *Down to* 0 **do** $R[i] = AMM(R[i+1], R[i+1], m)$
7:     **if** $((e_i \neq 0) \, and \, (e_{i-1} \neq 0))$ **then**
8:         $i = i - 1$;   ▷ Forwarding one bit
9:         $R[i] = AMM(R[i+1], R[i+1], m)$;
10:        $R[i] = AMM(R[i], A_3, m)$;
11:     **else if** $(e_i \neq 0)$ **then**
12:        $R[i] = AMM(R[i], A_1, m)$;
13:     **end if**
14: **end for**
15: $Res = AMM(R[0], 1, m)$;
16: **Return** Res.

Fig. 9.1 BFW-1:Bit Forwarding 1-bit Algorithm

Algorithm 2 BFW2:Bit forwarding 2-bit algorithm

Input: $g, E, m \ldots E = (e_{k-1}, \ldots, e_1, e_0)_2$
And a new constant referred to as the proposed constant $PC = 2^{2\zeta} \pmod{m}$
Output: $Res = g^E \pmod{m}$

1: *Precompute the value of A_1, A_3, A_7*
2: $A_1 = AMM(g, PC, m)$;
3: $A_2 = AMM(A_1, A_1, m)$;
4: $A_3 = AMM(A_2, A_1, m)$;
5: $A_6 = AMM(A_3, A_3, m)$;
6: $A_7 = AMM(A_6, A_1, m)$;
7: $R[k-1] = A_1$;
8: **for** $i = k - 2$ *Down to* 0 *do* **do** $R[i] = AMM(R[i+1], R[i+1], m)$
9:    **if** $((e_i \neq 0) \, and \, (e_{i-1} \neq 0) \, and \, (e_{i-2} \neq 0))$ **then**
10:       $i = i - 1$;   ▷ Forwarding one bit
11:       $R[i] = AMM(R[i+1], R[i+1], m)$;
12:       $i = i - 1$;   ▷ Forwarding 1 - bit
13:       $R[i] = AMM(R[i+1], R[i+1], m)$;
14:       $R[i] = AMM(R[i], A_7, m)$;
15:    **else if** $((e_i \neq 0) \, and \, (e_{i-1} \neq 0))$ **then**
16:       $i = i - 1$;   ▷ Forwarding one bit
17:       $R[i] = AMM(R[i+1], R[i+1], m)$;
18:       $R[i] = AMM(R[i], A_3, m)$;
19:    **else if** $(e_i \neq 0)$ **then**
20:       $R[i] = AMM(R[i], A_1, m)$;
21:    **end if**
22: **end for**
23: $Res = AMM(R[0], 1, m)$;
24: **Return** Res.

Fig. 9.2 BFW-2:Bit forwarding 2-bit algorithm

multiplications by $n \times (t - 1) = n \times (3 - 1) = 2n \, \because \, t = 3$ for every three successive 1's. This algorithm also searches for two successive 1s that are not imbricating. If non-imbricating two successive 1s are encountered then we can skip one-bit and the partial-result is multiplied with A_3. Moreover, it also reduces the multiplication required by a factor of 1 as the BFW-1 algorithm does.

9.2.3 BFW-3: Bit Forwarding 3-Bits Algorithm

For this algorithm we need to compute four pre-computed values:

1. $A_1 = AMM(g, PC, m)$
2. $A_3 = AMM(A_1, A_2, m) \cdots \because A_2 = AMM(A_1, A_1, m)$
3. $A_7 = AMM(A_6, A_1, m) \cdots \because A_6 = AMM(A_3, A_3, m)$
4. $A_{15} = AMM(A_{14}, A_1, m) \cdots \because A_{14} = AMM(A_7, A_7, m)$

Algorithm 3 BFW3: Bit forwarding 3-bit algorithm

Input: $g, E, m \ldots E = (e_{k-1}, \ldots, e_1, e_0)_2$
And a new constant referred to as the proposed constant $PC = 2^{2\zeta} \pmod{m}$
Output: $Res = g^E \pmod{m}$

1: *Precompute the value of A_1, A_3, A_7, A_{15}*
2: $A_1 = AMM(g, PC, m)$;
3: $A_2 = AMM(A_1, A_1, m)$;
4: $A_3 = AMM(A_2, A_1, m)$;
5: $A_6 = AMM(A_3, A_3, m)$;
6: $A_7 = AMM(A_6, A_1, m)$;
7: $A_{14} = AMM(A_7, A_7, m)$;
8: $A_{15} = AMM(A_{14}, A_1, m)$;
9: $R[k-1] = A_1$;
10: **for** $i = k - 2 \, Down to \, 0$ **do** $R[i] = AMM(R[i+1], R[i+1], m)$
11:     **if** $((e_i \neq 0) \, and \, (e_{i-1} \neq 0) \, and \, (e_{i-2} \neq 0) \, and \, (e_{i-3} \neq 0))$ **then**
12:         $i = i - 1$;   ▷ Forwarding one bit
13:         $R[i] = AMM(R[i+1], R[i+1], m)$;
14:         $i = i - 1$;   ▷ Forwarding one bit
15:         $R[i] = AMM(R[i+1], R[i+1], m)$;
16:         $i = i - 1$;   ▷ Forwarding one bit
17:         $R[i] = AMM(R[i+1], R[i+1], m)$;
18:         $R[i] = AMM(R[i], A_{15}, m)$;
19:     **else if** $((e_i \neq 0) \, and \, (e_{i-1} \neq 0) \, and \, (e_{i-2} \neq 0))$ **then**
20:         $i = i - 1$;   ▷ Forwarding one bit
21:         $R[i] = AMM(R[i+1], R[i+1], m)$;
22:         $i = i - 1$;   ▷ Forwarding 1 - bit
23:         $R[i] = AMM(R[i+1], R[i+1], m)$;
24:         $R[i] = AMM(R[i], A_7, m)$;
25:     **else if** $((e_i \neq 0) \, and \, (e_{i-1} \neq 0))$ **then**
26:         $i = i - 1$;   ▷ Forwarding one bit
27:         $R[i] = AMM(R[i+1], R[i+1], m)$;
28:         $R[i] = AMM(R[i], A_3, m)$;
29:     **else if** $(e_i \neq 0)$ **then**
30:         $R[i] = AMM(R[i], A_1, m)$;
31:     **end if**
32: **end for**
33: $Res = AMM(R[0], 1, m)$;
34: **Return** Res.

Fig. 9.3 BFW-3: Bit forwarding 3-bit algorithm

While traversing from MSB to LSB of exponent's binary string, if four successive $1's$ are encountered then we can skip 3-bits. The partial-result is multiplied with A_{15}. The BFW-3 Algorithm 3 shown in Fig. 9.3 is reducing the required number of multiplications by $n \times (t - 1) = n \times (4 - 1) = 3n \; \because t = 4$ for every four successive $1's$. This algorithm also searches for three and two successive $1's$ that are not imbricating. If non-imbricating $1's$ are encountered then we can skip 2-bits and 1-bit respectively. The partial-result is multiplied with A_7 and A_3 respectively. Moreover, it also reduces the multiplication required by a factor of 2 and 1 as the BFW-2 algorithm and BFW-1 algorithm respectively do.

The discussed bit-forwarding algorithms are generic for integer $z < E$ i.e., if the desired output is g^z (mod m), then calling AMM method with parameters R[i], 1 and m is required. AMM is called after the last conditional *if* statement, but inside the loop. For ith iteration the BFW algorithms will give $g^{((((2+e_i)^2+e_{i-1})^2+e_{i-2})^2+...+e_0)}$ (mod m) where e_i is the ith digit of the exponent E.

Following a similar approach as discussed for BFW-1, BFW-2 and BFW-3 techniques, we can also design the algorithm for the *Bit Forwarding t-bits (BFW-t)*. Carefully designed BFW-t algorithm can obtain better minimization of the required number of MMs, where $t \geq 1$. Different version of $BFW - t_k$ algorithms can be practiced i.e., $BFW - t_1$, $BFW - t_2$, ..., $BFW - t_i$. If we get equal amount of minimization is required MM, then we select $BFW - t_\alpha$ as an optimum option such that $\alpha = Min(t_1, t_2, \ldots, t_r)$. The selection of minimum value is done in order to save storage space as well as reduces the overhead of precomputation. The minimization of the required number of MMs is inversely proportional to the throughput i.e., minimum the required number of multiplications, more the throughput.

9.2.4 AMM: Adaptable Montgomery Multiplication

MM is executed in a series to obtain ME. The MM requires trial divisions and its hardware implementation is complex and consumes more time. On the other hand, the MMM algorithm is more efficient. This section deals with the modified version of MMM where the algorithm is modified according to the requirements of the BFW algorithms. This new modified Algorithm 4 is termed as the Adaptable Montgomery Method (AMM) and illustrated in Fig. 9.4. In this algorithm, the main complex and

---

Algorithm 4 Adaptable Montgomery Multiplication Algorithm (AMM)

Input: X, Y, m ζ is the length of m
Output: $R = X \times Y \times 2^{-\zeta}$ (mod m)

1: *Initialization:* $C = X \times Y; P = 0;$ ▷ C and P are register
2: **for** $i = 0$ to $\zeta - 1$ **do**
3:     **if** $((C_i \neq 0)\&\&(P_0 \neq 1))$ **then**
4:        $P = (P + m + 1) >> 1;$
5:     **else if** $((C_i \neq 0)\&\&(P_0 \neq 0))$ **then**
6:        $P = (P + 1) >> 1;$
7:     **else if** $((C_i \neq 1)\&\&(P_0 \neq 0))$ **then**
8:        $P = (P + m) >> 1;$
9:     **else**
10:       $P = P >> 1;$
11:     **end if**
12: **end for**
13: $R = P_\zeta + C_{2\zeta-1,\zeta}$
14: **Return** R;

Fig. 9.4 Adaptable Montgomery Multiplication Algorithm (AMM)

time-consuming task of trial divisions are interchanged with shifting and addition operations. Whenever the AMM method is called, it performs multiplication of the partial-result and $2^{-\varsigma}$ (mod m). After completion of the loop, the AMM method is again called with the parameters as partial-result and 1 to obtain the final result.

9.2.5   AHRMM: Adaptable High-Radix Montgomery Multiplication

Another approach for reducing the clock cycle is with high-radix algorithms. In order to support high-radix modular exponentiation algorithms, we use Adaptable High-Radix Montgomery Multiplication (AHRMM). AHRMM is equally compatible with all the BFW algorithm techniques.

For high-radix representation, the integer is partitioned into s words of size of $h - bit$ where the length of the integer is $k - bit$ such that $k = s \times h$. For example, a $k - bit$ integer A having words representation as $A^{(i)}$ where $A^{(i)}$ is a $h - bit$ word, then:

$$A = \sum_{i=0}^{s-1}(2^h)^i.A^{(i)} \dots 0 \le i < s$$

For AHRMM algorithm let us consider some representations:

- $X = (X^{(s-1)}, X^{(s-2)}, \dots, X^{(2)}, X^{(1)}, X^{(0)})_H$
- $Y = (Y^{(s-1)}, Y^{(s-2)}, \dots, Y^{(2)}, Y^{(1)}, Y^{(0)})_H$
- $m = (m^{(s-1)}, m^{(s-2)}, \dots, m^{(2)}, m^{(1)}, m^{(0)})_H$
- Radix $H = 2^h \dots h > 1$
- $C_{hr} \leftarrow$ New proposed high-radix constant $C_{hr} = m^{-1}$ (mod H)
- $k = s \times h$

Using these representations, the evaluation of the MMM result, $R = X.Y.2^{-sh}$ (mod m) can be performed in steps that are illustrated in Algorithm 5 shown in Fig. 9.5.

Initially, the value of MMM result R is kept zero. Then for every digit of the modulus m, the updation of R-value is performed as $R = (R + X^{(i)} \times Y + t_i \times m) >> h$, here t_i is a temporary variable calculated in step-3 of the given algorithm AHRMM. There is one benefit in the calculation of t_i i.e., modulus operation can be performed by shifting, as radix H will be always in the power of 2.

This substitution can be done by expressing the modulus α as an exact power of 2, e.g. $\alpha = 2^\gamma$, after this representation for substitution: β mod α is reduced to β (mod α) = $\beta - ((\beta >> \gamma) << \gamma)$, here the trial division by 2^γ, which is very complex for implementation is substituted by right shift ($>>$) whereas, left shift ($<<$) is used to substitute the multiplication by 2^γ.

Algorithm 5 Adaptable High-Radix Montgomery Multiplication Algorithm (AHRMM)

Input: $X, Y, m, H = 2^h$, and $C_{hr} = -m^{-1} \pmod{H}$
Output: $R = X \times Y \times 2^{-s \times h} \pmod{m}$

1: *Initialization $R = 0$*
  Updation Phase:
2: **for** $i = 0$ to $s - 1$ **do**
3:     $t_i = (R^{(0)} + X^{(i)} \times Y^{(0)}) \times C_{hr} \pmod{H}$
4:     $R = (R + X^{(i)} \times Y + t_i \times m) >> h$ ▷ right shift
5: **end for**
6: **if** $(R \geq m)$ **then**
7:     $R = R - m$;
8: **end if**
9: **Return** R;

Fig. 9.5 Adaptable High-Radix Montgomery Multiplication Algorithm (AHRMM)

Table 9.2 Required # clock-cycles for AMM and AHRMM using different size of modulus

Algorithm	Radix	# Clock-cycles	
		1024-bit	2048-bit
AMM	2	1,027	2,051

Table 9.3 Required # clock-cycles for AHRMM using different size of modulus

Algorithm	Radix	# Clock-cycles	
		1024-bit	2048-bit
AHRMM	2^{32}	323	643
	2^{16}	643	1,283
	2^8	1,283	2,563
	2^4	2,563	5,123
	2^2	5,123	10,243

The constant PC similar to BFW-techniques is modified as $PC = 2^{(2sh+2)}$ (mod m). This modification helps in calling the AHRMM module in place of the AMM module, in order to evaluate MM.

The clock cycles needed for evaluation of a single MM having s-bit modulus using the AHRMM module is $10s + 3$. Table 9.2 gives the required number of clock cycles by AMM algorithm and Table 9.3 gives the required number of clock cycles by AHRMM algorithm for different values of radix. The modulus is having a length of 1024-bits or 2048-bits.

By analyzing the Tables 9.2 and 9.3, it can be observed that for higher-radix, the required clock-cycles are less. On the other hand, it requires more space. Therefore, the best value of radix is decided based on the application requirement. E.g., the organization like banking and others having heavy servers for whom the memory space is not a constraint, the AHRMM module is an optimal choice. Whereas, lightweight devices like embedded systems are having memory space constraints, therefore the AMM module is a better option for them.

9.2.6 Correctness of BFW Techniques

This section illustrates the verification of BFW techniques and their supporting algorithms such as AMM and AHRMM.

Verification 1 *Correctness of AMM Algorithm*

Proof From the computation phase of AMM algorithm, the overall if condition in for loop can be written as

$2.P[i + 1] = (P[i] + (P[i] + 1)m + C[i])$

$\Rightarrow 2.P[i + 1] = (P[i] + \alpha_i.m + C[i])$

By Mathematical induction

$2^\zeta P[\zeta] = \sum_{k=0}^{\zeta-1} 2^k(\alpha_k.m + C[k])$

$\Rightarrow 2^\zeta.P[\zeta] = \sum_{k=0}^{\zeta-1} 2^k(\alpha_k.m) + \sum_{k=0}^{\zeta-1} 2^k.C[k]$

$\Rightarrow 2^\zeta.P[\zeta] = \beta.m + C[\zeta - 1, 0]$

In AMM, the final result is $R = P[\zeta] + C[2\zeta - 1, \zeta]$

$\Rightarrow 2^\zeta.R = 2^\zeta.P[\zeta] + 2^\zeta.C[2\zeta - 1, \zeta]$

Since $2^\zeta.P[\zeta] = \beta.m + C[\zeta - 1, 0]$, Then

$2^\zeta.R = \beta.m + C[\zeta - 1, 0] + 2^\zeta.C[2\zeta - 1, \zeta]$

$C[\zeta - 1, 0]$: Lower Order $\zeta - bits$ of C

$C[2\zeta - 1, \zeta]$: Higher Order $\zeta - bits$ of C

So, $2^\zeta.C[2\zeta - 1, \zeta] + C[\zeta - 1, 0]$ represents C

Hence, $2^\zeta.R = \beta.m + C$

$\Rightarrow R = (2^{-\zeta}.\beta).m + X.Y.2^{-\zeta} \ (\because C = X.Y)$

It is in the form of $D = q.d + r$, Hence, $R = X.Y.2^{-\zeta} \ (\text{mod } m)$

Verification 2 *Correctness of AHRMM Algorithm*

Proof For simplification, let the updated Montgomery value after the kth iteration be: R_k

From the step 4 of Algorithm 5, the updated Montgomery value can be written as:

$\quad R = (R + x_i.Y + t_i.m).2^{-h}$,

where $t_i = (p_0 + x_i.y_0).C \ (\text{mod } H)$

After the first iteration the updated value is:

$R_1 = (R_0 + x_0.Y + t_0.m).2^{-h}$

After the second iteration the updated value is:

$R_2 = (R_1 + x_1.Y + t_1.m).2^{-h}$

$\quad \Rightarrow R_2 = ((R_0 + x_0.Y + t_0.m).2^{-h} + x_1.Y + t_2.m).2^{-h}$

$\quad \Rightarrow R_2 = (R_0 + x_0.Y + t_0.m).2^{-2h} + (x_1.Y + t_2.m).2^{-h}$

After the third iteration the updated value is:

$$R_3 = (R_2 + x_2.Y + t_2.m).2^{-h}$$
$$\Rightarrow R_3 = ((R_0 + x_0.Y + t_0.m).2^{-2h} + (x_1.Y + t_2.m).2^{-h} + x_2.Y + t_2.m).2^{-h}$$

$$\Rightarrow R_3 = (R_0 + x_0.Y + t_0.m).2^{-3h}$$
$$+ (x_1.Y + t_2.m).2^{-2h}$$
$$+ (x_2.Y + t_2.m).2^{-h}$$

Similarly, after the sth iteration, the updated Montgomery Value R is:

$$R = (R_0 + x_0.Y + t_0.m).2^{-sh}$$
$$+ (x_1.Y + t_1.m).2^{-(s-1)h}$$
$$+ (x_2.Y + t_2.m).2^{-(s-2)h}$$
$$+ \cdots$$
$$+ (x_{s-2}.Y + t_{s-2}.m).2^{-2h}$$
$$+ (x_{s-1}.m + t_{s-1}.m).2^{-h}$$

Multiplying this equation with 2^{sh} on both sides, we get

$$2^{sh}.R = R_0 + (x_0.Y + t_0.m)$$
$$+ (x_1.Y + t_1.m).2^{h}$$
$$+ (x_2.Y + t_2.m).2^{2h}$$
$$+ \ldots\ldots\ldots$$
$$+ (x_{s-2}.Y + t_{s-2}.m).2^{(s-2)h}$$
$$+ (x_{s-1}.m + t_{s-1}.m).2^{(s-1)h}$$

$\Rightarrow 2^{sh}.R = R_0 + Y.\sum_{i=0}^{s-1} x_i.(2^h)^i + m.\sum_{i=0}^{s-1} t_i.(2^h)^i$
But initially R is zero, *i.e.*, $R_0 = 0$
$\therefore 2^{sh}.R = Y.\sum_{i=0}^{s-1} x_i.(2^h)^i + m.\sum_{i=0}^{s-1} t_i.(2^h)^i$
Since, $\sum_{i=0}^{s-1} x_i.(2^h)^i$ is high-radix representation of X and $\sum_{i=0}^{s-1} t_i.(2^h)^i$ is high-radix representation of T, where the coefficient $t_i = (p_0 + x_i.y_0)C \pmod{H}$
So, the final equation can be written as:
$2^{sh}.R = XY + Tm$ for some coefficient T
$\Rightarrow R = X.Y.2^{-sh} + (T.2^{-sh}).m$
It is in the form of $C = q.d + r$, which can be written as: $C = r \bmod q$,
Hence, $R = X.Y.2^{-sh} \bmod m$, is the desired output of AHRMM.

Verification of BFW techinques:
In the process of finding ME, a standard algorithm is *Square and Multiply*. If we illustrate that the BFW techniques algorithm is having equivalent results with the Square and Multiply algorithm at any stage then we can verify the process. The

---

Algorithm 6 $MSM(g,E,m,PC)$

Input: g,E,m and $PC(proposed\ constant)$
Output: $R = g^E \pmod{m}$

1: $A_1 = AMM(g,PC,m)$;
2: $R[k-1] = A_1$;
3: **for** $i = K - 2$ Down to 0 **do**
4:     $R[i] = AMM(R[i+1],R[i+1],m)$;
5:     **if** $(e_i \neq 0)$ **then**
6:         $R[i] = AMM(R[i],A_1,N)$;
7:     **end if**
8: **end for**
9: $R = AMM(R[0],1,m)$;
10: **Return** R

Fig. 9.6 Modified Square and Multiply

algorithm is modified according to the Montgomery method and which is listed in Algorithm 6 shown in Fig. 9.6 and referred to as MSM.

Verification 3 Correctness of $BFW - 1$ Algorithm

Proof Consider a scenario for ith iteration where MSM and BFW-1 algorithms are processing for R_i bit of result, at the same moment the exponent has it's $(i - 1)$th, $(i - 2)$th bit value to be $\neq 0$

Status of result R in MSM algorithm after processing for exponent's $(i - 2)$th bit:

From step-4, step-5 and step-6 of algorithm MSM for exponent's $(i - 2)$th bit, the result will be: $R_i^2 \times A_1 = R_i^2.g$

From step-4, step-5 and step-6 of algorithm MSM shown in Fig. 9.6 for exponent's $(i - 2)$th bit, the result will be $(R_i^2.g)^2.A_1 = (R_i^2.g)^2.g = R_i^4.g^3$

Therefore, after processing for $(i - 2)$th bit of the exponent using MSM algorithm, the result is: $R_i^4.g^3$

Now from step-6, step-7 and step-9 of Algorithm 1 BFW-1 shown in Fig. 9.1 and if exponent's $(i - 1)$th and $(i - 2)$th bits are $\neq 0$ then, the result is $((R_i)^2)^2 = R_i^4$.

Whereas step-10 of the BFW-1 algorithm, the result is $R_i^4.A_3$.

$\because A_k = g^k$, then it is clearly observed that after processing for $(i - 2)$th bit of the exponent by BFW-1, the result will be $R_i^4.g^3$, i.e., equal to the result of MSM.

Thus, the BFW-1 algorithm is verified.

Similarly, the correctness of other Bit Forwarding algorithms BFW-2 and BFW-3 can be proved.

9.2.7 Completeness of BFW Algorithms

An algorithm is said to be **sound** $'S'$, if it is not including a wrong answer, but it might miss a few right answers. Here 'S' includes a complete set of right answers of a given algorithm. The soundness of an algorithm means that the algorithm doesn't yield any untrue results. An algorithm is **complete**, if it gets every right answer in S. It might return a wrong answer for a single input. Completeness, on the other hand, means that the algorithm addresses all possible inputs and doesn't miss any input.

The correctness of the BFW algorithms is substantiated with relevant proof in Sect. 9.2.6. For a given pair of keys and messages, the BFW algorithms will always return only one unique solution. This claims the proof of completeness and soundness. For all set of possible valid combinations of key and message, the BFW algorithms are always guaranteed to provide exactly one correct solution which is feasible.

9.3 Analysis of BFW Algorithms

This section describes the efficiency of Bit Forwarding algorithms in terms of operational cycles. For all bit forwarding algorithms, to estimate the efficiency, metric reckon algorithms have been devised. This algorithm will figure out the measures in terms of operational cycles, the required number of MMs, and the percentage of reduction in operational cycles (Vollala et al. 2019).

9.3.1 BFW-1

For every pair of consecutive 1's in the exponent, the BFW-1 algorithm reduces one MM. If there are n bits in the exponent, out of which nz bits are non-zero, with c numbers of pair of consecutive ones, then only $(n + nz - c + 1)$ number of MMs are required to evaluate ME. It minimizes $(c - 1)$ number of MMs in comparison with existing algorithms. On average BFW-1 algorithm is able to reduce 169.57 number of MMs for the 1024-bit exponent and similarly, 343.11 number of multiplications can be reduced for the 2048-bit exponent, as tabulated in the Table 9.4. It will result in increased throughput and reduced power consumption but demands an extra negligible space to store pre-computed values, which are of integer in nature.

Table 9.4 Performance of BFW-1 technique for different exponent's size

Exponent's size	Required # MMs by other methods	Required # MMs by BFW-1 technique	#MMs reduced
2048	3072	2728.89	343.11
1024	1536	1366.43	169.57
512	768	684.60	83.40
256	384	343.46	40.54
128	192	172.79	19.21

Table 9.5 Performance of BFW-2 technique for different exponent's size

Exponent's size	Required # MMs by other methods	Required # MMs by BFW-2 techniques	# MMs reduced
2048	3072	2576.64	495.36
1024	1536	1303.31	232.69
512	768	655.96	112.04
256	384	330.48	53.52
128	192	167.97	24.03

9.3.2 BFW-2

For every three consecutive ones in the exponent, the BFW-2 algorithm reduces two MMs. If there are n bits in the exponent, out of which, nz bits are non-zero, with c pair of consecutive ones, and d is the frequency of three consecutive ones, then only $(n + nz - c - 2 \times d + 4)$ numbers of MMs are required to evaluate ME. As given in Algorithm 2, four values for A_2, A_3, A_6 and A_7 are precomputed as $A_2 = A^2$ (mod m), $A_3 = A^3$ (mod m), $A_6 = A^6$ (mod m), and $A_7 = A^7$ (mod m). These pre-computed values can be used while forwarding the bits. Hence, $(c + 2 \times d - 4)$ numbers of MMs can be reduced in comparison with existing algorithms. On average BFW-2 algorithm is able to cut down 232.69 and 495.36 number of multiplications for 1024-bits and 2048-bits of exponent respectively. The statistics of the BFW-2 algorithm are given in the Table 9.5.

9.3.3 BFW-3

For every four consecutive ones in the exponent, BFW-3 algorithm reduces three MMs. If there are n bits in the exponent, out of which nz bits are non-zero, with c pair of consecutive ones, and d is the frequency of three consecutive ones, and e is the frequency of four consecutive ones, then only $(n + nz - c - 2 \times d - 3 \times e + 6)$ number of MMs are required to evaluate ME. As given in Algorithm 3, six values for A_2, A_3, A_6, A_7, A_{14}, and A_{15} are precomputed as $A_2 = A^2$ (mod m), $A_3 = A^3$ (mod m), $A_6 = A^6$ (mod m), $A_7 = A^7$ (mod m), $A_{14} = A^{14}$ (mod m), and $A_{15} = A^{15}$ (mod m). These precomputed values can be used while forwarding the bits. Hence $(c + 2 \times d - 3 \times e - 6)$ number of MMs can be reduced in comparison with existing algorithms. On an average BFW-3 algorithm is able to cut down 279.66 and 570.73 number of multiplications for 1024-bits and 2048-bits of exponents respectively as tabulated in the Table 9.6.

Figure 9.7 shows the comparison between the existing algorithms and the BFW algorithms BFW-1, BFW-2 and BFW-3 for varying number of bits of the exponent.

Table 9.6 Performance of BFW-3 technique for different exponent's size

Exponent's size	Required # MMs by other methods	Required # MMs by BFW-3 techniques	# MMs reduced
2048	3072	2501.27	570.73
1024	1536	1256.34	279.66
512	768	631.82	136.18
256	384	317.84	66.16
128	192	159.85	32.15

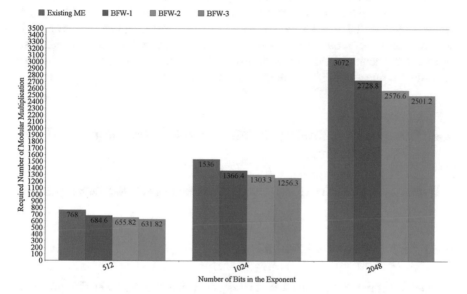

Fig. 9.7 Comparison between BFW and Existing ME Techniques in Terms of Required Number of MMs

The best choice among the BFW algorithms BFW-1, BFW-2, BFW-3, ..., BFW-k algorithms can be selected based on the following criteria:

1. *Higher throughput and no constraint on physical area*: If the frequency of $j + 1$ consecutive ones in the exponent is f_1, frequency of j consecutive ones in the exponent is f_2, frequency of $j - 1$ consecutive ones in the exponent is f_3, and so on, the frequency of 3 consecutive ones in the exponent is f_{j-1}, and the frequency of 2 consecutive ones in the exponent is f_j, then the number of reduction in MMs is given in the Eq. 9.3.

$$NoM = j.f_1 + (j - 1)f_2 + \cdots + 3.f_{j-2} + 2.f_{j-1} + f_j = \sum_{i=1}^{j} \{(j - i + 1).f_i\}$$

(9.3)

If the Eq. 9.3 yields maximum value for j, then $BFW - j$ will be the best choice where $1 \le j \le k$. The optimal value of j minimizes the more number of multiplications that influence the reduction in the clock cycle.

2. *Higher throughput with physical area constraints*: Settle down with an appropriate $time - area$ trade-off that can satisfy the requirements.
3. *For smart card applications that have strict memory constraint*: BFW-1 will be the ultimate choice and sometimes BFW-2 can also provide better performance.

Energy consumption is directly proportional to the product of the number of clock cycles, processor's clock cycle speed and power consumption. In all the mentioned scenarios, without having extra complication an implementation can be realized. As the frequency of MMs has been drastically reduced, resulting in a reduction of the required clock cycle count. An increase in the speed without increasing the processor clock cycle is achieved. Power requirements will also be minimized as the frequency of MMs is reduced, leading to energy-efficient realizations.

9.4 Comparative Study of Sliding Window Techniques and BFW Techniques

This section compares the BFW Techniques and Sliding Window Techniques.

9.4.1 Bit Forwarding Techniques

We start the comparison with BFW techniques, where the exponent E is processed by scanning its bits from MSB to LSB. The algorithm proceeds in such a way that the partial result is squared for every bit, but it also searches for successive ones in the exponent simultaneously. If we encounter $d + 1$ successive ones then, skipping of d bits is possible by multiplying the partial result with the adequate multiplying factor $MF_{2^d} = g^{2^d} \pmod{m}$. It means for every $d + 1$ successive ones of the exponent, BFW algorithms skip d-bits using $(BFW - d)$ algorithm and minimizes the required number of MMs by a factor of d. Along with the d successive ones, the BFW-d algorithm also search for $d - 1$, $d - 2$, $\ldots$, 2, 1 successive ones.

The exponent's binary string has n-*bits* and out of which k bits are non-zero, C_α number of (α) successive ones where α can be from d to 1 for a $BFW - d$ algorithm. Then ME evaluation needs only $n + nk - \sum_{\alpha=1}^{d}(\alpha - 1).C_\alpha$ number of MMs using $BFW - \alpha$ algorithm. It means $BFW - \alpha$ algorithm is reducing $(\alpha.C_{\alpha+1} + (\alpha - 1).C_\alpha + (\alpha - 2).C_{\alpha-1} + (\alpha - 3).C_{\alpha-2} + \ldots + 3.C_4 + 2.C_3 + C_2 - 2.\alpha)$ number of MMs.

This discussion leads us to the requirement of computation of the average number of MMs needed by the BFW techniques for the evaluation of ME. This average can be estimated by recurrence relation with the help of the sequence and series method. One

---

Algorithm 7 Metric Reckon Algorithm for $BFW5$

$Intialization\ C_2 = 28, C_3 = 12, C_4 = 5, C_5 = 2, C_6 = 1;$ ▷ Up to 6 bits
$Intialization\ C_2 = 64, C_3 = 28, C_4 = 12, C_5 = 5, C_6 = 3;$ ▷ Up to 7 bits
$Intialization\ \theta_2 = 8, \theta_3 = 4, \theta_4 = 2, \theta_5 = 1, \theta_6 = 1;$ ▷ Temporary Variables

---

1: **for** $i = 8$ **to** n **do**
2:      $R[i] = AMM(R[i+1], R[i+1], N);$
3:      **if** $(i\%6 == 0)$ **then**
4:          $\theta_2 = 2.\theta_2, \theta_3 = 2.\theta_3, \theta_4 = 2.\theta_4 + 1, \theta_5 = 2.\theta_5 - 2, \theta_6 = 2.\theta_6 + 1;$
5:      **else if** $(i\%6 == 1)$ **then**
6:          $\theta_2 = 2.\theta_2, \theta_3 = 2.\theta_3, \theta_4 = 2.\theta_4, \theta_5 = 2.\theta_5 + 1, \theta_6 = 2.\theta_6 - 1;$
7:      **else if** $(i\%6 == 2)$ **then**
8:          $\theta_2 = 2.\theta_2 + 1, \theta_3 = 2.\theta_3, \theta_4 = 2.\theta_4, \theta_5 = 2.\theta_5 - 2, \theta_6 = 2.\theta_6;$
9:      **else if** $(i\%6 == 3)$ **then**
10:         $\theta_2 = 2.\theta_2 - 2, \theta_3 = 2.\theta_3 + 1, \theta_4 = 2.\theta_4, \theta_5 = 2.\theta_5, \theta_6 = 2.\theta_6;$
11:      **else if** $(i\%6 == 4)$ **then**
12:         $\theta_2 = 2.\theta_2 + 1, \theta_3 = 2.\theta_3 - 2, \theta_4 = 2.\theta_4 + 1, \theta_5 = 2.\theta_5, \theta_6 = 2.\theta_6;$
13:      **else if** $(i\%6 == 5)$ **then**
14:         $\theta_2 = 2.\theta_2, \theta_3 = 2.\theta_3 + 1, \theta_4 = 2.\theta_4 - 2, \theta_5 = 2.\theta_5 + 1, \theta_6 = 2.\theta_6;$
15:      **end if**
16:      $C_j = 2.C_j + \theta_j\ for\ j=2,3,4,5\ and\ 6;$
17: **end for**
18: $E_m = (5.C_6 + 4.C_5 + 3.C_4 + 2.C_3 + C_2) >> n;$
19: $F_{r5} = \frac{2.E_m}{3.n} \times 100;$
20: **Return** E_m, F_{r5}

Fig. 9.8 Metric Reckon Algorithm for $BFW - 5$

example of a reduction in the required number of MMs by the $BFW - 5$ Algorithm 7 is shown in Fig. 9.8 and a Metric Reckon recurrence relation is devised for the same.

In Algorithm 7, C_i denotes the average number of i successive ones where $i = 2, 3, \ldots, 6$ for all 2^n probable combinations of the exponent of $n - bit$ length. Let E_m denote the number of modular-multiplications reduced using the $BFW - 5$ technique and F_{r5} denote the percentage of reductions in operational cycles using the $BFW - 5$ technique. The $BFW - 5$ algorithm consists of steps to estimate the reduction in the expected number of MMs and a reduction in the percentage of operational cycles with the help of the $BFW - 5$ technique.

9.4.2 Sliding Window Techniques

After discussing the BFW techniques, this subsection compares them with the sliding window technique, which is known to be a foremost software technique for evaluation ME. It uses the concept of the *m-ary* method and its motive is to minimize the required number of MMs, with the help of the partitioning approach. Basically, a window (consist of a certain number of bits) slides (traverses) through the exponent's bits and execution is done based on the zero and non-zero value of windows. Execution of this technique can be understood in 3 steps:

1. **Partitioning Step:** Here the partitioning of exponent E is done into zero and non-zero windows. The minimization of the number of MM is proportional to the number of non-zero windows. We can perform the partitioning in both directions i.e., by scanning the exponent's bit from MSB to LSB or from LSB to MSB.
2. **Pre-computation Step:** Here we calculate and store the values of X^i (mod m) where $i = 1, 2, \ldots, 2^q - 1$, and q denotes the maximum size of the non-zero window partitioned.
3. **Exponentiation Step:** Here the actual MM is performed using square and multiply operation, with the help of pre-computed values and partitioned windows.

   C. K. Koc has given the software technique of sliding window and performs the *partitioning step* with the help of the Markov Chain method to estimate the average number of required MMs (Koç, 1995). The authors also analyzed the two separate partitioning approaches known as constant length non-zero windows (CLNZW) and variable-length non-zero windows (VLZW).

9.4.2.1 Constant Length Non-zero Windows

This scheme traverses the binary representation of exponent E and forms the words ZW and NZW on the go. As the name suggests the length of NZW (q) is fixed. Whereas ZW is variable (*however* $\leq q$). Two ZW needs to be concatenated if they are adjacent to each other. But a concatenation of two NZW is optional. We start with ZW and perform the labeling of the windows as follows:

- **Case 1**: For ZW check the next bit, if the bit value is equal to zero then continue labeling as ZW else switches to NZW.
- **Case 2**: For NZW first cover d bits without checking for 1 or 0 then check for the next bit, if it is zero go to ZW labeling or go to NZW labeling.

   The state diagram of the portioning process of the exponent is presented in Fig. 9.9.

Fig. 9.9 State diagram of portioning process of CLNZW

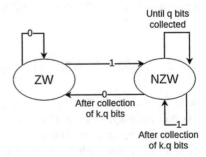

In order to estimate the average number of required MMs the Markov chain method had been illustrated as follows:

Let: $n \leftarrow$ number of bits of the exponent,

$C \leftarrow$ number of Non-zero Windows,

$w \leftarrow$ size of Non-zero Windows, then:

$$M_{avg} = 2^{(w-1)} + n - w + C - 2$$

9.4.2.2 Variable Length Non-zero Windows

The key change is that, in the variable-length NZ window (VLNZW) approach, for partitioning the binary string. It checks for upcoming $q - 1$ bits values, if the value is zero or one. It switches to ZW if the upcoming $q - 1$ bits are having value as zero. This approach decreases the average number of NZ words. Suppose we start with ZW, then to carry on with ZW or NZW the labeling of the windows is performed as follows:

- **ZW:** Examine the upcoming one bit, if it has value as 0 then carry on with ZW or else switch to NZW.
- **NZW:** Examine the upcoming q bits, if all of them are having value as 0 then switch to ZW or else carry on with NZW.

Note:

$d \leftarrow$ maximum length of the NZW.

$q \leftarrow$ minimum number of zeros that ends the current NZW.

k and r $\leftarrow$ positive integers such that $d = kq + r + 1$, where $1 \leq r < q$.

For VLNZW the domain of the possible state is $\{ZW, NW_1, NW_2, NW_3, \ldots, NW_{k+1}, NW_{k+2}\}$, where the state variable is associated with the number of scanned bits in the current non-zero window. The state diagram that generates zero and the non-zero window is outlined in Fig. 9.10.

Starting from ZW and consider current window we will traverse from NZW_1, $NZW_2, NZW_3, \ldots, NZW_{k+1}, NZW_{k+2}$.

- Let the current state be ZW: For every single incoming current bit, remain in the same state for a zero bit, otherwise move to NZW_i, $1 \leq i \leq k + 2$.
- If the current state is NZW_i, for $1 \leq i < k$, read q bits. If all these q-bits are all zero, go to ZW. Else go to NZW_{i+1}.
- If the current state is NZW_i, for $i = k + 1$, then read r bits. If all these bits are zero, then go to ZW. Else go to NZW_{k+2}.
- If the current state is NZW_i, for $i = k + 2$, then read current bit. If it is zero, then go to ZW. Otherwise, start a new non-zero window state at the current bit and move to NZW_1.

The average number of multiplications needed to evaluate exponentiation, can be calculated with the help of Markov chain process. It can be formulated as $M_{avg} =$

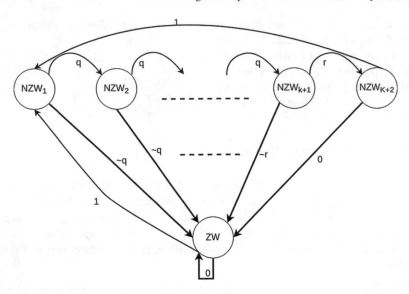

Fig. 9.10 State diagram of portioning process of VLNZW

$2^{(d-1)} + n^{(1)} + C_2 - \frac{C_3}{C_2} - 2$, where $n^{(1)} \leftarrow$ size of window for optimum values of M_{avg}, $d \leftarrow$ maximum window size, $C_2 \leftarrow$ average number of NZW and $C_3 \leftarrow$ average size of the NZW.

9.4.3 Comparison Between Sliding Window Techniques and BFW Techniques

The modern base-2 modular exponential techniques need 1536 number of MMs for calculating the exponent of 1024-bits exponent. The sliding window technique with the size of window $= 2$ and the BFW-1 algorithm both require just 1366 number of MMs. We use tabular representation (refer Table 9.7) for comparing the sliding window technique with window size k+1 and BFW-k algorithm. Table 9.7 lists the number of MMs required to evaluate ME of 1024-bits exponent using BFW and Sliding window techniques. From the Table 9.7 the authors has concluded that BFW algorithms are better than sliding window techniques (Vollala et al. 2016).

Table 9.7 Comparison between Sliding window and BFW techniques

Window size	Required # MMs	BFW techniques	Required # MMs
window-size $= 2$	1366	BFW-1	1366
window-size $= 3$	1332	BFW-2	1303
window- size $= 6$	1195	BFW-5	1168

Moreover, the implementation of the sliding window techniques in hardware are more complex and has much more overhead in comparison to BFW techniques, because:

- The partitioning of ZW and NZW has required a very complex logic circuit and it is the main process to be executed. Whereas the main process in BFW techniques is counting of successive ones that require only uncomplicated AND gates for execution.
- One process is common in both the techniques i.e., Pre-computation. The underlying difference is that the sliding window technique having window-size $= d$ needs $2^d - 1$ number of pre-computations, but BFW-d needed just $2d - 1$ number of pre-computations.
- As more precomputing terms are required the sliding window techniques leads to more memory space requirement for saving the pre-computed terms in comparison to BFW techniques.

It means BFW techniques outperform the sliding window technique in terms of reducing the frequency of required MMs with less memory space and less complex hardware circuits.

Discussed techniques in this chapter i.e., BFW-1, BFW-2, BFW-3 and BFW-k are implementable for applications having PKC using ME. This technique requires a supporting method termed as AMM, which is also illustrated in this chapter. Apart from evaluating ME, this AMM method also calculates the point arithmetic used in other PKC e.g. Elliptic Curve Cryptography. The Higher-radix Montgomery multiplication (AHRMM) method enhances the performance of the BFW techniques. The use of BFW-1 is favorable for small portable devices that make use of smart cards like mobile phones where memory-space is a physical constraint because it requires less memory space. Whereas the BFW-k (k best value of NoM) is favorable for large server-based organizations like banks where the software requires higher throughput irrespective of memory space constraint. If the exponent E is of length 1024-bit then, BFW-1, BFW-2 and BFW-3 algorithms reduce the required number of MM by 11.16%, 15.14%, and 18.20% respectively. It is already known that a reduction in the frequency of MM improves throughput without modifying the processor clock cycle's speed, thus consume less power.

References

Bar-El H (2002) Security implications of hardware vs. software cryptographic modules. Discretix White Paper

Batina L, Örs SB, Preneel B, Vandewalle J (2003) Hardware architectures for public key cryptography. Integr VLSI J 34(1):1–64

Diffie W, Hellman ME (1976) New directions in cryptography. IEEE Trans Inf Theory 22(6):644–654

ElGamal T (1984) A public key cryptosystem and a signature scheme based on discrete logarithms. In: Advances in cryptology. Springer, pp 10–18

Koç ÇK (1995) Analysis of sliding window techniques for exponentiation. Comput Math Appl 30(10):17–24

Montgomery PL (1985) Modular multiplication without trial division. Math Comput 44(170):519–521

Rivest RL, Shamir A, Adleman L (1978) A method for obtaining digital signatures and public-key cryptosystems. Commun ACM 21(2):120–126

Stallings W (2003) Network security essentials: applications and standards, 4/e. Pearson Education India

Vollala S, Ramasubramanian N (2017) Energy efficient modular exponentiation for public-key cryptography based on bit forwarding techniques. Inf Process Lett 119:25–38

Vollala S, Geetha K, Ramasubramanian N (2016) Efficient modular exponential algorithms compatible with hardware implementation of public-key cryptography. Sec Commun Netw 9(16):3105–3115

Vollala S, Tiwari U, Amin R (2019) A metric reckon algorithm for bit forwarding techniques. In: 2019 IEEE international symposium on smart electronic systems (iSES)(Formerly iNiS). IEEE, pp 21–24

Vollala S, Varadhan V, Geetha K, Ramasubramanian N (2014) Efficient modular multiplication algorithms for public key cryptography. In: 2014 IEEE international advance computing conference (IACC). IEEE, pp 74–78

Chapter 10
Hardware Implementation of Bit Forwarding Techniques

10.1 Introduction

Modular Exponentiation (ME) is the main and basic operation used in many PKC techniques, e.g., Diffie-Hellman key exchange algorithm, elliptic curve cryptography, RSA algorithm and ElGamal cryptography (Rivest et al. 1983; Desmedt 2011; Diffie and Hellman 1976; Bernstein 2006). This operation is achieved by a series of repeated modular multiplications (MMs), which are time-consuming for large operands. Hence, the accountable implementation of ME is needed to improve the performance of many public-key systems (William 2006). We have discussed one of the enhanced ME approaches i.e., the BFW technique in Chap. 9, Its simulation is providing assuring outcomes in enhancing the efficiency of ME in software.

In order to prove these algorithms to be energy efficient, hardware realization of bit forwarding techniques has to be done. Therefore, in this chapter, the hardware implementation of BFW techniques which is proposed by Satya et al. has been discussed (Vollala and Ramasubramanian 2017). These hardware realizations minimize the required number of MMs for performing energy-efficient ME. This chapter also illustrates how the BFW technique provides better throughput with less power consumption and the same processor clock speed.

The Hardware approach is better than the software approach because:

- **Memory Access Prevention:** The main problem with software-based solutions was the shared memory, whereas the hardware-based solution has its own memory. This property of hardware having internal memory space makes it more protected. Another advantage is that it prevents illegal access to memory. The hardware approaches are inherently better providers of security than software approaches for the operating system. Even-though the hardware approach for PKC is complex for implementations but, provides better performance than software-based approaches (Bar-El 2002).
- **Integrity Assurance:** The intruder with a high skill set can alter the source code of software-based solutions whereas the hardware-based solutions have their code being burnt onto a dedicated chip. The burning of the source code makes the code read-only, which cannot be altered by any intruder remotely. Even during the power-up stages, the modification of these burnt codes is not possible, this gives integrity to PKC applications.

© The Author(s), under exclusive license to Springer Nature Switzerland AG 2021
S. Vollala et al., *Energy-Efficient Modular Exponential Techniques for Public-Key Cryptography*, https://doi.org/10.1007/978-3-030-74524-0_10

- **Resistance to Power Analysis Attacks:** The intruder can read the power fluctuation and form a particular pattern to guess the secret key but hardware-based solutions can mask the power consumption fluctuation with the help of some special measure. This mask prevents the intruder from gathering the exact information required for guessing the secret key.
- **Key Storage Problems:** The software-based solution doesn't have its own memory that's why they tend to save the secret key in a shared environment. But, the hardware implementations have a better solution, as it can hide internal keys by burning them during the hardware fabrication. Which makes them notably challenging to steal by the intruder. Another way is to store the key in ROM with dedicated space and make that space inaccessible for other applications using hardware methods.
- **Dependence on OS Security:** The security services provided by higher-level applications are not so much reliable as they run over an operating system but, hardware-based solutions are independent of this operating system. Therefore, it is more reliable.

10.2   Hardware Design of Bit Forwarding Algorithms

In this section, the hardware design of Modified Square and Multiply (MSM) method, Bit Forwarding 1-bit (BFW-1), Bit Forwarding 2-bits (BFW-2), Bit Forwarding 3 bits (BFW-3) and Adaptable Montgomery Multiplication (AMM) are discussed Vollala and Ramasubramanian (2017); Vollala et al. (2016, 2014). The algorithms discussed in the previous chapter reduces the number of operational clock cycles required. Thus enhance the performance. Power consumption is reduced as the frequency of MMs is minimized by the BFW techniques. The AMM procedure is called after verification of partial result is done. The AMM procedure is called by a modified square and multiply procedure. The AMM procedure is tuned to satisfy the requirements of the Modified Square and Multiply algorithm (MSM). The practical implementation of the BFW and other supporting algorithms are performed by Satya et al., Vollala and Ramasubramanian (2017) on the Xilinx FPGA Virtex-7 evaluation board and also using Cadence for ASIC. The outcome of these implemented algorithms i.e., throughput, power, operational clock cycles, energy and area are also analyzed. The hardware realization of all the above-discussed algorithms are illustrated in this order: AMM, MSM, BFW-1, BFW-2 and BFW-3. This chapter also explores the additional uses of AMM.

10.3   AMM: Adaptable Montgomery Multiplication

Figure 10.1 illustrate the hardware design of AMM. In this design, the multiplier multiplies X and Y & save the product in the register C. The register C present in

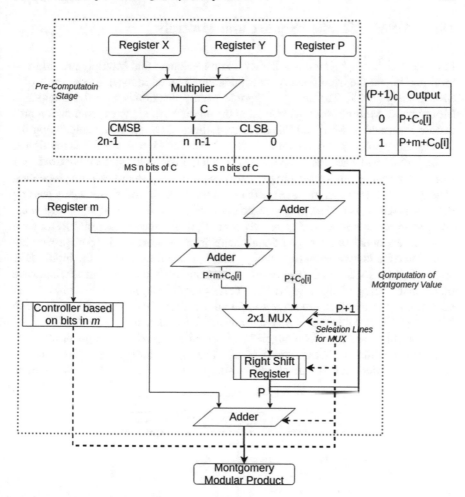

Fig. 10.1 Architecture of AMM for Modular multiplication

pre-computation step is partitioned and termed as $CMSB$ and $CLSB$, having length $n - bits$ each. The Fig. 10.1 illustrate that, $CMSB$ and $CLSB$ denotes the MSBs ranging from n to $2n - 1$ and LSB ranging from 0 to $n - 1$ respectively. Based on the selection line $P + 1$, the multiplexer selects one out of the two input parameters denoted as $P + C_0[i]$ and $P + C_0[i] + m$. The selected parameter from the MUX is given as input to the shift register then the output of this shift register is added with $CMSB$ to calculate the Montgomery product R. It is the responsibility of the controller to provide a control signal to each processing unit and also iterate the complete process for the complete length of m.

10.4 MSM: Modified Square and Multiply

For calculation of g^E (mod m), the well-known Square and Multiply procedure is modified to and the Montgomery multiplication is tuned to meet the demands of it Montgomery (1985). The tuned Montgomery multiplication is termed as Adaptable Montgomery Multiplication (AMM) and the modified modular exponentiation procedure is termed as Modified Square and Multiply (MSM). While calculating the Montgomery product of two numbers using AMM, an extra factor 2^{-n} is multiplied to the partial result each time when AMM is called. In order to extract this extra factor from the partial result, we need to perform pre-processing steps and post-processing steps in the MSM procedure. Start with pre-processing, the information g by passing the parameters g, m and a new proposed constant $PC = 2^{2n}$ (mod m) to AMM for computing $A_1 = AMM(g, PC, m)$. A_1 is multiplied to the partial result R, for each non-zero exponent bit. The additional factor is eliminated by the post-processing step. After the last iteration of *for loop* AMM is called by passing the inputs R, 1 and m. In this procedure, the information g and the modulus m are integers and have their binary string of size $n - bit$. The parameter C is an integer of size $2n - bit$ that secures the result at any stage should not overflow. The Algorithm 6 shown in Fig. 9.6 of Chap. 9 illustrate the MSM procedure to calculate g^E (mod m).

The architecture for MSM algorithm is given in Fig. 10.2. The given architecture illustrates the block diagram of MSM. The input parameter g, m and PC, are stored in registers that is passed while calling AMM to compute A_1. In order to

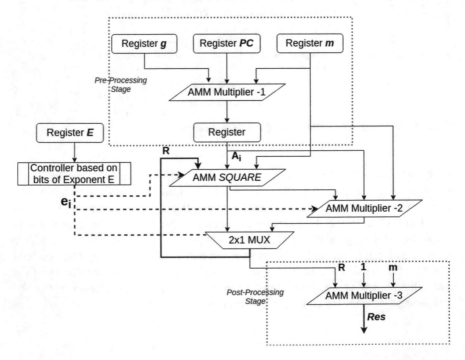

Fig. 10.2 Architectural Diagram of MSM for Modular exponentiation

calculate R^2 (mod m) the $SQUARE\ AMM$ module is used. Whereas to calculate Montgomery product of R and A_1 the $AMM\ Multiplier - 1$ module is used. Based on Exponent's current bit value i.e., e_i provided as a select line to the multiplexer, it selects $AMM\ Multiplier - 2$ or $SQUARE\ AMM$ module. Responsibility of $AMM\ Multiplier - 3$ is to provide the final result as ME and it has three input parameters R, 1 and m. The controller has exponent E's binary bit string and based on this e_i, it iterates the process and controls all the operations.

10.5 BFW-1: Bit Forwarding 1-Bit Algorithm

For BFW-1, the hardware design is illustrated in Fig. 10.3. The process starts with the pre-processing of information g with proposed constant PC and with modulus m by calling AMM Multiplier-1. We use register A_1 to save the result. A_1 is also

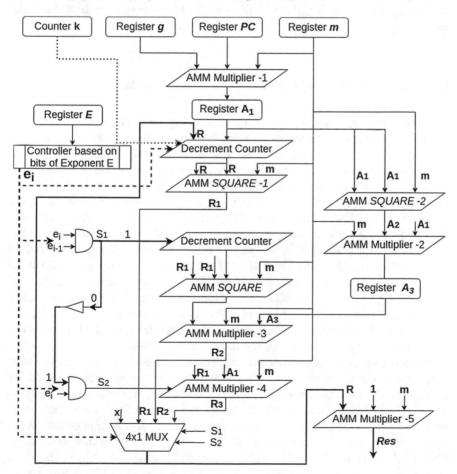

Fig. 10.3 Architecture Diagram of BFW-1

the initial partial result R. For calculation of A_3 we pass A_2 and A_1 as parameter, here the A_2 is computed by passing A_1 to Square AMM multiplier. We start the iteration with $(k - 2)$ where k is the binary string size of the exponent E. For each bit of the exponent, the *Square AMM multiplier* is invoked to get the squared result R_1. Whenever two successive ones are encountered in the exponent's binary string, we skip one bit by decrementing the counter value by 1. R_2 is obtained by squaring the result R_1 with the help of *Square AMM multiplier*, then multiplied with A_3. Whereas, if pair of ones is not found then for a non-zero bit we simply multiply to compute R_3. For computing R_3, AMM Multiplier-4 is invoked with input parameters: R_1, A_1 and m. The process will continue in the loop until the loop condition is satisfied. The partial results R_1, R_2 and R_3 are provided as inputs to a 4x1 MUX and X is an another input. The X has no use as it belongs to ($S_1 = 1$ and $S_2 = 1$), which is a never occurring case. The S_1 and S_2 are two selection lines to the MUX, based on this selection line the MUX decide proper input for the next iteration. As the post-processing step, the AMM Multiplier-5 receives three inputs, the first input is the output of the MUX from the last iteration, the second is 1 and the third is m, then we get the final result of g^E (mod m).

10.6   BFW-2: Bit Forwarding 2-Bits Algorithm

For BFW-2 the hardware design is illustrated in Fig. 10.4. The process starts with the pre-processing of information 'g' with proposed constant PC and with modulus m by calling AMM Multiplier-1. We use register A_1 to save the result and it is also the initial partial result R. For calculation of A_3 we pass A_2 and A_1 as parameter to *AMM Multiplier-2*, here the A_2 is computed by passing A_1 to Square AMM multiplier. Calculation of A_6 is similar to the calculation of A_2, the change is input parameter A_3 instead of A_1. As the final process of the pre-processing step, the A_7 is calculated by passing A_6, A_1 and m as input parameters to *AMM Multiplier-3* module. The stored values of A_1, A_3, and A_7 will play their role, when we skip the bits to reduce the MM. We start the iteration with $(k - 2)$, where k is the binary string size of the exponent E. For each bit of the exponent, the *Square AMM multiplier* is invoked to get the squared result R_1. When-ever three successive ones are encountered in the exponent's binary string, we skip two bits by decrementing the counter value by 2. Square AMM Multiplier is invoked two times. Then the result R_2 is obtained by multiplying A_7 with the partial result. If three successive ones are not found, then the exponent is scanned for two consecutive ones. If two successive ones are encountered in the exponent's binary string, we skip one bit by decrementing the counter value by 1 and *AMM Square* is invoked one time. Then the result R_3 is obtained by multiplying A_3 with the partial result. If these two conditions discussed above are not true, next we process for a non-zero bit. Therefore, the partial result is multiplied with A_1 to get R_4. The process will continue in the loop until the loop condition is satisfied. The partial results R_1, R_2, R_3 and R_4 is provided as inputs to a 4x1 MUX. The MUX has selection lines S_1 and S_2 which is provided by AND gates: $AND1$ and $AND3$

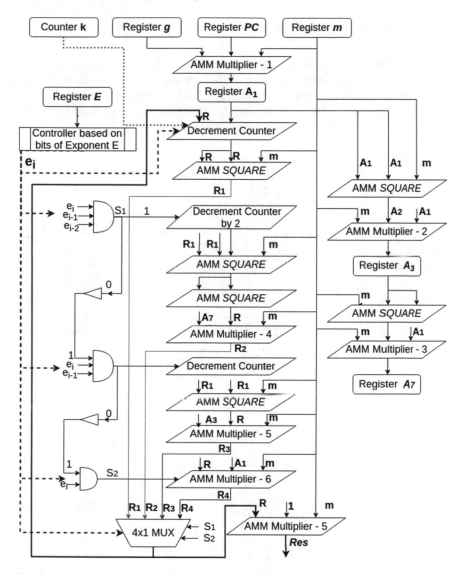

Fig. 10.4 Architecture Diagram of BFW-2

respectively. Based on these selection lines the MUX decides proper input for the next iteration. As the post-processing step, the AMM Multiplier-7 receives three inputs, the first input is the MUX output from the last iteration, the second input is constant 1 and the third input is modulus m. Then, we get the final result of g^E (mod m).

10.7 BFW-3: Bit Forwarding 3-Bits Algorithm

For BFW-3 the hardware design is illustrated in Fig. 10.5. We start the iteration with $(k - 2)$ where k is the binary string size of the exponent E. Proper registers are used to store the information g, proposed constant PC and the modulus m. For calculating A_1 we provide g, PC and m as inputs to AMM Multiplier-1. The value of A_1 is saved in a register which can be used soon by other operations.

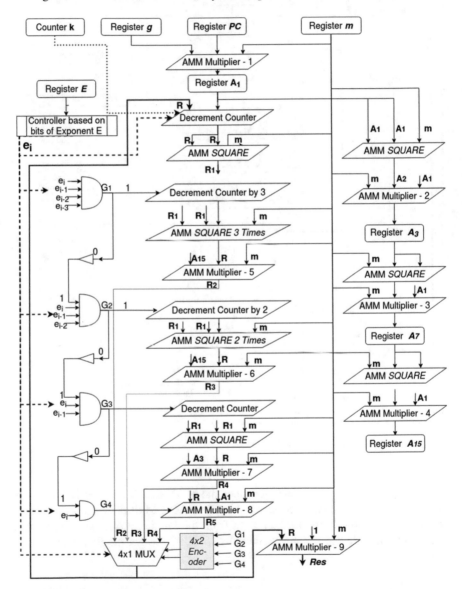

Fig. 10.5 Architecture Diagram of BFW-3

In pre-computation step we calculate $A_i = g^i \pmod{m}$ for $i = 3, 7$ and 15. This operation is performed by modules denoted by the dotted blocks in the Fig. 10.5. The results of the pre-computation steps are saved in the proper registers which can be used soon by other operations.

The G_1, G_2, G_3, G_4 are the outputs of AND gates denoted as $AND1$, $AND2$, $AND3$, $AND4$. These outputs are given as input to an encoder of size 4×2. The encoder's responsibility is to encode this $4 - bit$ code into a $2 - bits$ selection line. This selection line is used by a 4×1 MUX to select anyone out of 4 lines. The MUX has inputs as R_2, R_3, R_4, R_5 provide the output R_6 the decision is taken by the values of the selection lines S_1, S_2 which was provided by encoder. For enabling the multiplexer in the ith iteration e_i bit of the exponent E is used which is stored in the controller block.

The second multiplexer is of size 2×1 this MUX takes R_1 and R_6 as inputs. The bit e_i plays a role as the selection line as well as enables signal. The output of this MUX is provided in two modules first as feedback for the next iteration and second it is provided as input to the AMM Multiplier-8 module for performing the post-processing operation.

For every 4 successive ones encountered in the exponent, the counter k is subtracted by 3, as a result, we skip $3 - bits$ of the exponent. Next, the Square AMM module is called thrice, where R_1, R_1 and m is provided as input after which, the output is provided to AMM Multiplier module along with A_1 & m this module provide R_2 as the output. Similarly, For every 3 and 2 successive ones encountered in the exponent, we subtract the counter k by 2 and 1 respectively, this results in skipping the exponent's bit by $2 - bits$ and $1 - bit$ respectively. Next, the Square AMM module is called twice and once for 3 and 2 successive ones respectively, where R_1, R_1 and m are provided as input to the module. If we are processing for 3 successive ones then the result is multiplied with A_7 using the AMM Multiplier-5 module which gives the result R_3. And if we are processing for 2 successive ones then the AMM Multiplier-6 module is used and provided with A_3 and m as input to get R_4 as the output. In the last case on a non-zero bit instead of successive ones, then we use AMM Multiplier-7 module and R_1, A_1 and m is provided as input to the module and it produces the output R_5. In the last case, if there is a zero-bit in the exponent E, then 2×1 MUX is enabled and R_1 is selected as the output. Further, this R_1 is given back for the next iteration.

10.8 Analysis of Hardware Realization of BFW Algorithms

This section analyse and illustrate the hardware realization of MMM and ME algorithms namely AMM, MSM, $BFW - 1$, $BFW - 2$ and $BFW - 3$.

10.8.1 Adaptable Montgomery Multiplication

For the calculation of the Montgomery product of two numbers, we use the AMM module. Let X, Y and m are the input integers, output of AMM module is $X.Y.\sigma^{-1}$ (mod m), termed as Montgomery value. Here, $\sigma^{-1} \leftarrow$ modular inverse of σ ($= 2^n$ (mod m)) where n is a length of modulus m. The calculation of Montgomery product is done with the help of either of these two formulas:

1. $P = P + C_0[i] + m$
2. $P = P + C_0[i]$

The selection formula is dependent on the LSB of P+1, the parameter C_0 is the lower order $n - bits$ of C. Next step is to shift: $P = P >> 1$. The above-discussed steps need to be performed k times. Then the last value of P is summed with C_1 ($\because$ C_1 is the higher-order $n - bits$ of parameter C). Initial multiplication operation is common in traditional Montgomery multiplication and AMM. But, multiplication done within the loop is bypassed in the AMM module, therefore n number of ($1 - bit$) multiplications are reduced. AMM practices easy mathematical operations e.g., shifting and addition. The expense of this operation is lesser than that of given Montgomery methods (McIvor et al. 2004; Kuang et al. 2013). It is probable to achieve the above specified mathematical procedures in $(n + 3)$ clock cycles for $1 - bit$ in the exponent, rather than $(n + 5)$ clock cycles. The decrements have a positive effect if the exponent's binary string is increased to 1024 bits.

10.8.2 Modified Square and Multiply Algorithm

The responsibility of the MSM module is to calculate the ME with the help of the AMM module. Here we need to call the AMM module $k + r$ times to perform MM where k is the length of the exponent & r is the number of non-zero bits of exponent. Using this approach the number of MMs required for the different case is:

- Worst case: $2k$
- Average case: $1.5k$
- Best case: $(k + 1)$

This AMM module requires $(n + 3)$ clock cycles. The number of clock cycles are less for MSM module than the existing ME techniques, it is more optimal than the already present methods like McIvor et al. (2004); Kuang et al. (2013). The MSM module requires clock cycles for different cases as follows:

1. Worst case : $2k(n + 3)$.
2. Average case : $1.5k(n + 3)$

10.8.3 BFW-1: Bit Forwarding 1-Bit Algorithm

The BFW-1 module is reducing the required number of clock cycles by 11%, which helps in increasing the throughput. The reduction in the frequency of MMs is directly proportional to power consumption, and reduces power consumption by 1.93%. All this benefit requires 0.37% of additional memory space for saving pre-computed parameters.

10.8.4 BFW-2: Bit Forwarding 2-Bits Algorithm

If the number of triplets of ones is more in exponent then the BFW-2 module is preferable. This module saves two MMs for each triplet of ones. In a particular discussed scenario the BFW-2 module will perform better than MSM and BFW-1 modules. This module can achieve 15% more gain in throughput and require 0.74% of additional memory space for saving the pre-computed parameters. It depends on the bit-pattern present in the exponent whether to choose BFW-1 or BFW-2 module.

10.8.5 BFW-3: Bit Forwarding 3-Bit Algorithm

The BFW3 module skips 3 MMs if it encounters 4 successive ones, If the number of successive four ones is more in exponent then the BFW-3 module is preferable. In the particular discussed scenario, the BFW-3 algorithm will perform better than MSM, BFW-1 and BFW-2 modules. This module can achieve 18.11% more gain in throughput, in comparison with MME42_C2 (Kuang et al. 2013) and require 1.09% of additional memory space for saving the pre-computed parameters. The power consumption is reduced by 8.53% and saves the required energy by 10.10%. It depends on the bit-patterns present in the key whether to choose BFW-1, BFW-2, or BFW-3 module.

10.9 Analysis of the BFW Techniques

The Bit Forwarding algorithms(BFW-1, BFW-2 and BFW-3) are offering better performance than the already present methods introduced in McIvor et al. (2004); Kuang et al. (2013) and others Eldridge and Walter (1993); Lin et al. (2014). Table 10.1 illustrates the comparison between different modules in terms of required clock-cycles (Vollala and Ramasubramanian 2017). Let n be the number of bits in modulus m, k be the length of the exponent, N_1 is number of non-zero bits present in the exponent, N_2 is number of 2 separate successive ones and N_3 is number of 3 separate successive

Table 10.1 Complexity of MSM and BFW algorithms

Sl. No.	BFW Algorithms	Avg. No. of MMs	Clock cycles consumed with AMM	Clock cycles consumed with existing modified Montgomery multiplication
1.	BFW-3	$A_1 = (k + N_1 - N_2 - 2.N_3 - 3.N_4 + 6)$	$(n + 3)A_1$	$(n + 5)A_1$
2.	BFW-2	$A_2 = (k + N_1 - N_2 - 2.N_3 + 4)$	$(n + 3)A_2$	$(n + 5)A_2$
3.	BFW-1	$A_3 = (k + N_1 - N_2 + 2)$	$(n + 3)A_3$	$(n + 5)A_3$
4.	MSM	$A_4 = (k + N_1)$	$(n + 3)A_4$	$(n + 5)A_4$

Where
k: Number of bits in the exponent E
n: Number of bits in the modulus m
N_1: Number of ones in the exponent
N_2: Number of two independent consecutive ones
N_3: Number of three independent consecutive ones, which are non-overlapping with N_2
N_4: Number of four independent consecutive ones which are non-overlapping with N_2 and N_3

ones. Separate means they are not overlapping with N_2. N_4 number of 4 separate successive ones. Similarly, here separate means they are not overlapping with N_3 and N_2. The initial plan is to enhance the Montgomery multiplication represented as the AMM module. This module requires $(n + 3)$ clock cycles whereas already present MM modules require $(n + 5)$ clock cycles and the conventional approach requires $2n$ clock cycles for a single MM.

Table 10.1 (Vollala and Ramasubramanian 2017) gives the concluded complexity of the bit forwarding techniques discussed in this chapter. The Table 10.1 also gives the complexity of the bit forwarding techniques using conventional Montgomery multiplication (Vollala and Ramasubramanian 2017). The comparison of performance in terms of throughput, power, area and energy of BFW-1, BFW-2 and BFW-3 techniques with the existing algorithms is given in the rest of this section.

The Table 10.2 illustrate the comparative performance values of other ME approaches like ME42 (McIvor et al. 2004) and MME42_C2 (Kuang et al. 2013) and methods proposed by Satya et al. i.e., MSM and BFW techniques. The comparison is done for 512-bit of exponents. The Table 10.3 [(Vollala and Ramasubramanian, 2017) illustrate the comparative performance values of other ME approaches like ME42 (McIvor et al. 2004) and MME42_C2 (Kuang et al. 2013) and methods proposed by Satya et al. i.e., MSM and BFW techniques. The comparison is done for 1024-bit of exponents. The comparative study is illustrated in Table 10.3. It is observed that $BFW - 1$, $BFW - 2$ and $BFW - 3$ technique requires less number of MMs for calculating ME which provides better throughput.

Figure 10.6 illustrates the count of MMs saved compare to the exponent's bit-length concerning the discussed algorithms $BFW - 1$ $BFW - 2$ and $BFW - 3$ techniques. The relation between the binary string length of the exponent and the number of MMs saved is proportional.

Table 10.2 Performance of other technique, MSM and BFW algorithms for 512-bit exponent length

ME design	Power (μw)	Avg No. of MMs	Area (μm²)	Throughput Rate (kbps)
ME42 (McIvor et al. 2004)	41.10	768	498633	707.42
MME42_C2 (Kuang et al. 2013)	19.30	768	351881	873.09
BFW3	18.24	631	356121	1031.20
BFW2	18.62	657	354488	1000.38
BFW1	19.29	685	353053	967.82
MSM	20.82	768	352021	875.89

Table 10.3 Performance of ther technique, MSM and BFW algorithms for 1024-bit exponent length

ME design	Power (μw)	Avg No. of MMs	Area (μm²)	Throughput Rate (kbps)
ME42 (McIvor et al. 2004)	70.60	1536	852899	354.23
MME42_C2 (Kuang et al. 2013)	40.30	1536	714676	433.04
BFW3	36.86	1256	722524	511.03
BFW2	37.74	1304	720123	498.60
BFW1	39.52	1367	717621	480.80
MSM	43.30	1536	714976	432.71

Computation of throughput:

Let:

1. F_{Hz} : the processor frequency
2. x : number of cycles required by the cryptography algorithm.

$$Time\ Required = \frac{x}{F} \ldots in\ seconds$$

$$Throughput = \frac{F}{x}$$

We can observe that if we do not change the processor's frequency i.e., F, then the relation between throughput and required number of clock cycles i.e., x is inversely proportional to the throughput. It means for a fixed frequency if we reduce the number of clock cycles required for a cryptographic algorithm, then we can achieve better throughput. Figure 10.7 gives the anticipated gain in throughput by the various length of exponents, for the bit forwarding algorithms. The length of the exponent

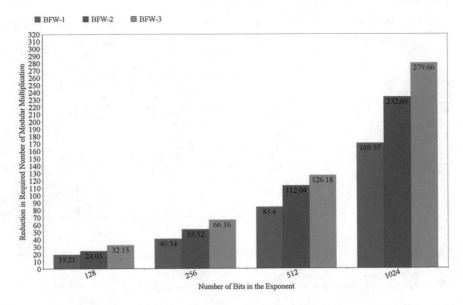

Fig. 10.6 Reduction of Number of MMs by BFW algorithms

can be $32 - bits$ to $1024 - bits$. Whereas Fig. 10.8 shows the comparative study of throughput between already present methods and the bit forwarding techniques.

Power analysis of BFW techniques and existing ME technique: In comparison with MME42_C2 (Kuang et al. 2013) algorithm, the bit forwarding techniques BFW-1, BFW-2 and BFW-3 for 1024 bit exponent consumes less power by 1.93%, 6.35% and 8.53% respectively. Similarly, for the 512-bit exponent, BFW1, BFW2 and BFW3 technique power consumption are less by 0.05%, 3.52% and 5.4% respectively.

Throughput analysis of BFW techniques and existing ME technique: In comparison with MME42_C2 (Kuang et al. 2013) algorithm, the bit forwarding techniques BFW-1, BFW-2 and BFW-3 for 1024-bit exponent gains more throughput by an order of 11.02%, 15.13% and 18.11% respectively. Similarly, for the 512-bit exponent, BFW1, BFW2 and BFW3 technique the throughput gain is 10.84%, 14.57% and 17.54% more for respective BFW technique.

Area analysis of BFW techniques and existing ME technique: In comparison with MME42_C2 (Kuang et al. 2013) algorithm, the bit forwarding techniques BFW-1, BFW-2 and BFW-3 for 1024 bit exponent the throughput is increased and power is saved, this is done with an additional space requirement of 0.41%, 0.76% and 1.09% respectively. Similarly, for the 512-bit exponent, BFW1, BFW2 and BFW3 technique the enhancements were achieved with an additional space of 0.33%, 0.74% and 1.02% for BFW1, BFW2 and BFW3.

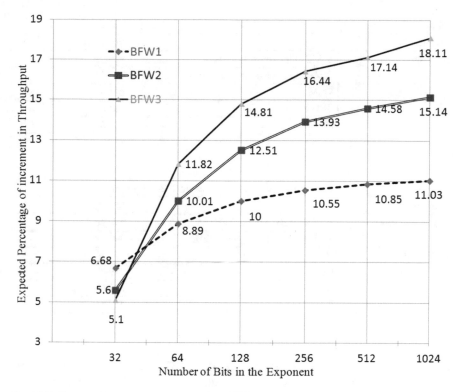

Fig. 10.7 Expected increase in throughput by BFW1, BFW2 and BFW3 techniques

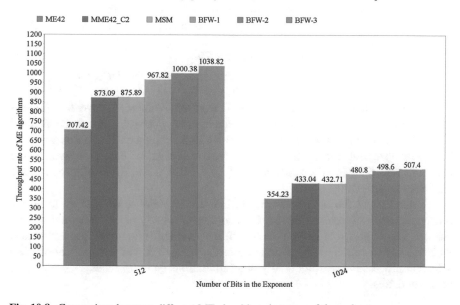

Fig. 10.8 Comparison between different ME algorithms in terms of throughput

Table 10.4 Energy comparison for BFW ME designs using 512-bit exponent

ME design		Energy (μJ)
Existing designs	ME42 (McIvor et al. 2004)	109.38
	MME42_C2 (Kuang et al. 2013)	41.65
BFW designs	MSM	44.93
	BFW3	38.96
	BFW2	40.18
	BFW1	41.62

Table 10.5 Energy comparison for BFW ME designs using 1024-bit exponent

ME design		Energy (μJ)
Existing designs	ME42 (McIvor et al. 2004)	748.26
	MME42_C2 (Kuang et al. 2013)	344.52
BFW designs	MSM	370.16
	BFW3	309.72
	BFW2	322.63
	BFW1	337.85

Energy analysis of BFW techniques and existing ME technique: BFW techniques minimize the consumption of power by minimizing the required number of MMs. The formula for energy consumption is: $E = T.C_t \cdots \therefore$ T time needed by cryptographic module, and C_t amount of power is consumed. It means the relation between energy and power consumption is directly proportional. the formulation is as follows:

$$Energy = Power \times Execution\ Time$$
$$= Power \times Clock\ Period \times No.\ of\ Clock\ Cycles$$

The relation between *clock period* and the *clock frequency* is inversely proportional. Based on the above formula the value of energy consumption by BFW techniques is illustrated in Table 10.4 and in Table 10.5 (Vollala and Ramasubramanian 2017). By observing Tables 10.4 and 10.5, we can say that the energy is saved by the order of 1.9%, 6.37% and 10.10% using BFW-1, BFW-2 and BFW-3 bit forwarding techniques respectively.

We can extend the bit forwarding techniques to BFW-4, BFW-5 up to BFW-k and the hardware realization can be also done similarly as we discussed in this chapter. The selection of BFW-j, from different available bit-forwarding techniques where ($for\ j = 1, 2, 3, ..., k$) is done according to the need of the application. The selection process is also affected by other limitations and properties as throughput, power and area.

If the primary objective of an application is to attain higher throughput then it can select appropriate BFW-j and save a significant number of required clock cycles. As per the discussion in Sect. 10.10 the maximum value of NoM (*Number of Multiplications*) reduced by Bit Forwarding technique providing BFW-j module is selected if there is no area constraint. The smart card application has space limitations, therefore the BFW-1 module will be a more suitable selection. Whereas the web servers that manage several concurrent requests prefer to select the BFW technique with a higher value of j (where $j \in 1 \ldots k$) for cryptographic purposes. In order to minimize the response time at the client-side, higher throughput is desirable. The hardware implementation overhead can be handled by the server-side for better performance. Especially when providing authenticity to multiple entities the increment in throughput gain is significant by these BFW techniques.

10.10 Selection Criteria of $BFW - j$

To simplify the process of selection for optimum $BFW - j$ technique, in order to implement in hardware for ME. The Algorithm 1 is illustrated in Fig. 10.9, termed as $SOBFW$ (*Selection of Optimal BFW*). The objective of SOBFW is to calculate

---

Algorithm 1 Selection of Optimal BFW (SOBFW)

Input: *An k-bit exponent E and j*
Output: *Index : j, that yields maximum NoM*

1: *Intialization: $f_i = 0$; for all $i=2, 3, 4,\ldots, k, k+1$*
2: *Count $= 0, NoM = 0$;*
3: **while** (k) **do**
4:     **if** $(e_0 \neq 0)$ **then**
5:         **if** $(Count < k)$ **then**
6:             $(Count = Count + 1, E = E \div 2)$;
7:         **else**
8:             $(f_{(Count-1)} = f_{(Count-1)} + 1, Count = 0)$;
9:         **end if**
10:     **else**
11:         $(f_{(Count-1)} = f_{(Count-1)} + 1, Count = 0, E = E \div 2)$;
12:     **end if**
13: **end while**
14: **if** $(Count > 0)$ **then**
15:     $f_{(Count-1)} = f_{(Count-1)} + 1$;
16: **end if**
17: **for** $i = 2$ to $k+1$ **do**
18:     $NoM = NoM + f_i.(i-1)$;
19: **end for**
20: Select j such that NoM is maximum, where $1 \leq j \leq k$ **return** j

---

Fig. 10.9 Selection of Optimal BFW (SOBFW)

NoM: *Number of Multiplications reduced*. This algorithm requires input parameters exponent E and j, where j stands for denoting $BFW - j$ it means the algorithm will skip j bits i.e., saving j MMs. Here $f_i \leftarrow$ frequency of i successive ones, for $i = 2, 3, 4, \ldots, k, k + 1$ and $f_i \geq 0$. Then $NoM = \sum_{i=2}^{j+1} f_i.(i-1)$ denotes the count of saved MMs by $BFW - j$ technique. Once the value of NoM is calculated then based on this value, the SOBFW algorithm will choose the optimum value of j. The SOBFW algorithm selects optimum $BFW - j$, here j gives maximum NoM, to reduce the required number of MM.

References

Bar-El H (2002) Security implications of hardware vs. software cryptographic modules. Discretix White Paper

Bernstein DJ (2006) Curve25519: new diffie-hellman speed records. In: Public Key Cryptography-PKC 2006. Springer, pp 207–228

Desmedt Y (2011) Elgamal public key encryption. In: Encyclopedia of cryptography and security. Springer, pp 396–396

Diffie W, Hellman ME (1976) New directions in cryptography. IEEE Trans Inf Theory 22(6):644–654

Eldridge SE, Walter CD (1993) Hardware implementation of montgomery's modular multiplication algorithm. IEEE Trans Comput 42(6):693–699

Kuang SR, Wang JP, Chang KC, Hsu HW (2013) Energy-efficient high-throughput montgomery modular multipliers for rsa cryptosystems. IEEE Trans Very Large Scale Integr (VLSI) Syst 21(11):1999–2009

Lin WC, Ye JH, Shieh MD (2014) Scalable montgomery modular multiplication architecture with low-latency and low-memory bandwidth requirement. IEEE Trans Comput 63(2):475–483

McIvor C, McLoone M, McCanny JV (2004) Modified montgomery modular multiplication and rsa exponentiation techniques. IEE Proc-Comput Digital Tech 151(6):402–408

Montgomery PL (1985) Modular multiplication without trial division. Math Comput 44(170):519–521

Rivest RL, Shamir A, Adleman L (1983) A method for obtaining digital signatures and public-key cryptosystems. Commun ACM 26(1):96–99

Vollala S, Geetha K, Ramasubramanian N (2016) Efficient modular exponential algorithms compatible with hardware implementation of public-key cryptography. Sec Commun Netw 9(16):3105–3115

Vollala S, Ramasubramanian N (2017) Energy efficient modular exponentiation for public-key cryptography based on bit forwarding techniques. Inf Process Lett 119:25–38

Vollala S, Varadhan V, Geetha K, Ramasubramanian N (2014) Efficient modular multiplication algorithms for public key cryptography. In: 2014 IEEE international advance computing conference (IACC). IEEE, pp 74–78

William S (2006) Cryptography and network security: 4/E. Pearson Education India

Part V
Multi-core Environment for Modular Exponentiation

Chapter 11
RSA Processor for Concurrent Cryptographic Transformations

11.1 Introduction

Public key cryptography is playing a tremendously important role in several applications in the modern electronics world, for providing security services (William 2006). In 1977 Rivest, Shamir and Adleman recommended the first applied scheme, which is known as the RSA public-key cryptography (Rivest et al. 1983), based on the idea conceived by Diffie and Hellman (1988). The security of the RSA public-key cryptography depends on the intractability of identifying the factors of the product of two large prime numbers. Any system which handles transactions must provide security and most of the existing systems operate on RSA cryptography (Hu et al. 2011). This can be implemented in software as well as in hardware. However, providing dedicated hardware for processing security can improve the performance of the system. The RSA arithmetic has modular exponentiation (ME) which involves modular multiplication (MM) as prime mathematical processes. The modular multiplication process requires costly division operations. These two operations (ME and MM) strongly affect the RSA performance. Various enhancements have been done on the Montgomery method used by MM for better performance (Montgomery 1985). Whereas, the field of modular exponentiation process is unattended. For addressing the same issue the Bit Forwarding techniques have been discussed in previous chapters (refer Chap. 9), that perform ME (Vollala et al. 2016). The BFW techniques minimize the required number of MMs for calculating ME, therefore gain higher throughput.

For gaining additional throughput by an RSA processor to perform more encryption/decryption operation per unit time, a single-core needs higher clock frequency. Which consumes more power and heat emission is increased. This chapter discusses an approach for performing the RSA technique over a multi-core architecture to execute multiple cryptographic modules simultaneously (Vollala et al. 2019).

The role of a scheduler is to manage multiple cores efficiently. This scheduler can be designed at either of the two different levels, first at the software level or second at the hardware level. The idea of designing more cores and hardware-based schedulers over a single chip gives higher throughput and more reliable security at a low cost. Modular multiplication involved in the RSA processor given by Satya et al. (2019), has been evaluated with the help of Adaptable Montgomery Multiplication.

© The Author(s), under exclusive license to Springer Nature Switzerland AG 2021
S. Vollala et al., *Energy-Efficient Modular Exponential Techniques*
for Public-Key Cryptography, https://doi.org/10.1007/978-3-030-74524-0_11

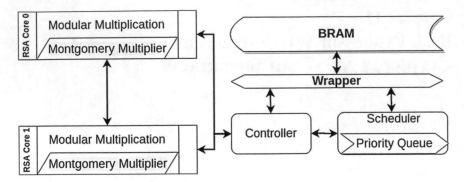

Fig. 11.1 Block Schematic diagram of Dual core RSA Processor (DCRSAP)

11.2   RSA Processor by Vollala et al.

A Dual-core RSA processor *(DCRSAP)* has been illustrated, which is given by Satya et al. (2019). This DCRSAP is capable to execute multiple cryptographic modules simultaneously and achieve higher throughput. This execution is performed while keeping the clock frequency constant. The Fig. 11.1 illustrates the block schematic diagram of DCRSAP. The essential units of the given processors are:

1. **Controller:** Searches for an idle RSA core and assigns the work.
2. **Scheduler:** Responsible for selecting the next work which needs to be assigned.
3. **Block RAM:** Utilized for saving the requests and outputs moreover, a wrapper is utilized for performing read or write requests in Block RAM.
4. **RSA Cores:** Performs cryptographic transformation using different ME methods.

11.2.1   Controller

Whenever the DCRSAP encounters a new request, the controller searches for an idle RSA core and assigns the requested task to it. The requested task is kept in a priority queue, if all RSA cores are performing some tasks. The Fig. 11.2 illustrates the queue's structure which stores the task to be performed. The priority of tasks is decided by parent applications, or else it is decided by the FIFO (first in first out) style. The controller waits for an RSA core to be available, if an RSA core finishes its current task and becomes free, then the controller dequeue a task from the priority queue and assigns a new task to that newly free RSA core. There is another responsibility of the controller to assures a well-balanced load distribution for all the cores. After completion of a task by an RSA core, the output of the task is written by the controller, into the buffer random access memory termed as BRAM. The state diagram of the controller is illustrated in the Fig. 11.4. The Algorithm 1 shown in Fig. 11.3 illustrate the step-by-step process of the controller.

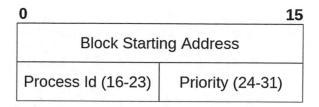

Fig. 11.2 Structure of the task in Hardware Scheduler

Algorithm 1 Controller

1: Initialize the RAM and Scheduler;
2: Initialize RSA core;
3: Create Registers of M,N,E,PC; which will be useful for latching values of particular task;

4: **if** (*Any one of the RSA core is FREE*) **then**
5:   Assign task to that core;

6: **else**

7:   **while** ((*!Scheduler is busy*) & (*!Scheduler is empty*)) **do**
8:     de-queue value from the scheduler(Priority queue);
9:     parse output of scheduler and store into the RAM;
10:     Load values from RAM, pointed by the starting address;
11:     Check if any RSA core is free or not;
12:     **if** (*FREE*) **then**
13:       Take a process from the Scheduler and schedule it;
14:     **else**
15:       wait for any RSA core to become IDLE;
16:       Assign task to RSA core;
17:     **end if**
18:   **end while**

19: **end if**

20: Write the result of RSA to BRAM;

Fig. 11.3 Controller

11.2.2 Hardware Scheduler

The software-based scheduler is common and designed by most of the cryptographer. In this subsection, the hardware-based scheduler is illustrated. This scheduler is capable of executing multiple RSA core simultaneously. The hardware scheduler generates higher throughput and more reliable because:

- Multiple works can be executed simultaneously.
- Absence of inter-dependency evades the requirement of synchronization, thus running the operation smoothly.

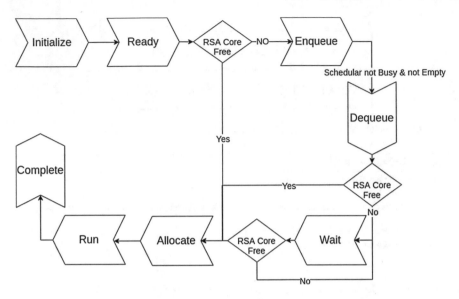

Fig. 11.4 State Diagram of Controller

- Executing RSA procedures over a hardware-based design remain extremely secured, since intruder invasions and tampering with the content at any stage, especially while the system is starting is not attainable.
- Power consumption in the DCRSAP is very less in contrast with conventional processors. The dependency on the operating system's services is not required therefore does not depends on the security measures of these services.
- The keys for cryptographic modules are saved in specified particular hardware components, which makes them remarkably hard to obtain. Moreover, it is unavailable to unauthorized users. The cryptographic modules are burnt on specified particular hardware components, which are kept as a fully secure read-only code.
- It is known that software design is simple for implementation and modification, also vulnerable to intruder attacks. Another disadvantage is the memory sharing mechanism of the operating system that share memory-space between different applications which makes the software-based approach more vulnerable. Whereas, the storage-space is inherently secured in dedicated BRAM. The BRAM is discussed in this chapter. The BRAM is capable of avoiding unauthorized access to the information.

The controller, with the help of a priority queue, balances the load distribution between different cores. This priority queue is heap-based and realized over the hardware scheduler. The heap data structure for the queue has 32 registers, where the size of each register is 32 bits. A binary heap is the common data structure chosen for fulfilling the requirements of implementing a priority queue. The conventional processes like enqueue and dequeue can be performed in $O(log\ n)$ time. The first element of this heap is stored in the root. The root has a linear array structure. Consider a case where i denotes an index of the linear array for binary heap then:

1. $i/2 \leftarrow$ store parent of the element.
2. $2i \leftarrow$ store left child of the element
3. $2i + 1 \leftarrow$ store right child of the element.

The Binary heap is realized over the hardware and does enqueue and seek processes in $O(1)$ time complexity and does the dequeue process in $O(log\ n)$ time. There is a chance that the dequeue process is overlapping with the other process because the dequeue provides the highest priority task which is stored in the root. The root stores the highest prioritized element. The scheduler requires three things, first the process-ID, second priority of the process and third the starting address of the process from BRAM as input. The scheduler practices a binary heap as its data structure, where the binary heap poses the max heap property. Which means it stores the highest priority task in the root, for which it uses a $max - heapify$ function whenever a new task is given as input and store the highest priority task at the root.

11.2.2.1 Queue Operations

Basically there are two main operations for the priority queue:

1. **Enqueue:** The steps is illustrated in Algorithm 2 shown in Fig. 11.5.
2. **Dequeue:** The steps is illustrated in Algorithm 3 shown in Fig. 11.6.

When a task comes as a request in the hardware scheduler it also stores its address in the Process Control Block. The restoration process of heap requires $O(log\ n)$ time. First, the task is assigned to the immediately available space, then the *max heapify* operation rearranges the task and keeps the highest priority task at the root. When an RSA core becomes idle, then using *dequeue* operation a task is loaded to that RSA Core. The dequeue operation requires $O(1)$ time. After dequeue, the rearranging of max-heap is required which arranges the highest priority task in the root. These operations can be simultaneously executed by the hardware scheduler.

Algorithm 2 *Enqueue − Process*

1: *Initialization* number_of_ process = 0   ▷ when circuit is reset
2: All Register file = 0
3: status of scheduler = WORKING
4: Copy the content of the CPU register and Program counter to memory
5: Store the starting address of task segment in first 16 bits of register and store the taks ID in the next 8 bits followed with an 8 bit priority
6: number_of_process = number_of_process +1
7: Use Max-heapify procedure to rearrange the tasks based on the priority of the task
8: Set the status of the scheduler to IDLE;

Fig. 11.5 *Enqueue−Process*

Algorithm 3 *Dequeue − Process*

1: Wait till scheduler status is IDLE
2: Provide the starting address of task Register to Controller
3: Controller loads the Program Counter and Register values in corresponding RSA core
4: Set the status of scheduler to WORKING
5: Copy the contents of the register [*number_of_process*] to register and decrement it
6: Increment the age of all the process   ▷ to avoid starvation
7: Use *Max − heapify* procedure to rearrange down the task inserted at the top
8: Set the status of the scheduler to IDLE

Fig. 11.6 *Dequeue−Process*

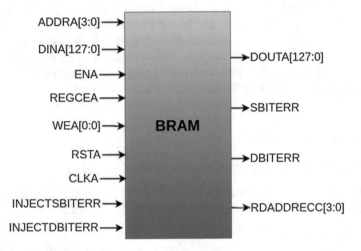

Fig. 11.7 Structure of BRAM

11.2.3 BRAM Controller

The responsibility of the BRAM controller is to give an interface, for the purpose of reading the data and writing the data into BRAM (buffer-RAM). An RSA cryptographic module requires 3 inputs, each of size 1024-bits. This large size data for inputs cannot be handled by the General Purpose Input Output(GPIO) register. Therefore, the inputs are stored and loaded from BRAM. The block diagram of BRAM is shown in Fig. 11.7. This memory is designed using the BRAM Azure IP core in Bluespec. The IP core of Xilinx has a Block RAM generator to generate this. The Cadence doesn't have any IP cores and is therefore implemented as a black box.

11.2.4 RSA Core

We make use of two different RSA cores. One is based on MSM modular exponentiation and another based on BFW-1 modular exponentiation. Both have been discussed in previous Chap. 10 under Sects. 10.4 and 10.5 respectively. MSM and BFW-1 both exponentiation algorithms include calling Adaptable Montgomery Multiplication *(AMM)* algorithm for calculating modular multiplication.

11.2.4.1 Adaptable Montgomery Multiplication

The Montgomery product of two numbers is calculated by Adaptable Montgomery multiplication (AMM), which is proposed by Satya et al. (2016). The AMM Algorithm 4 as shown in Fig. 11.8. This module performs modular multiplication by avoiding trial divisions (Shieh et al. 2008; Cilardo et al. 2004). This algorithm calculates $AMM(X, Y, m) = A.B.2^{-n}$ (mod m), where n is the length of modulus m. This new method eliminates the final subtraction step, which was performed in all conventional approaches, for adjusting the final product. This new approach helps in attaining higher throughput, because while processing each bit of exponent it saves the 2 operational cycles, whenever used by MSM and $BFW-1$ algorithms. The modular product is computed by AMM has 2 steps. The first step is to compute the multiplication of two integers X & Y and store it in a register C, and a temporary variable P is set to zero. In the second step, the partial result is computed using

---

Algorithm 4 *Enhanced Montgomery Multiplication*

Input: X, Y, m
Output: $R = X.Y.2^{-n}$ (mod m)...n is the length of m

1: *Initialization $P = 0$*
2: $C = A.B$
3: **for** $i = 0$ to $n-1$ **do**   ▷ Computation Phase
4:     **if** $((C[i] \neq 0) \&\& (P[0] \neq 1))$ **then**
5:         $P = (P + m + 1) >> 1$;
6:     **else if** $((C[i] \neq 0) \&\& (P[0] \neq 0))$ **then**
7:         $P = (P + 1) >> 1$;
8:     **else if** $((C[i] \neq 1) \&\& (P[0] \neq 0))$ **then**
9:         $P = (P + m) >> 1$;
10:     **else**
11:         $P = P >> 1$;
12:     **end if**
13: **end for**
14: $R = P[n] + C[2n - 1, n]$;
15: **Return** R;

Fig. 11.8 Adaptable *Montgomery Multiplication*

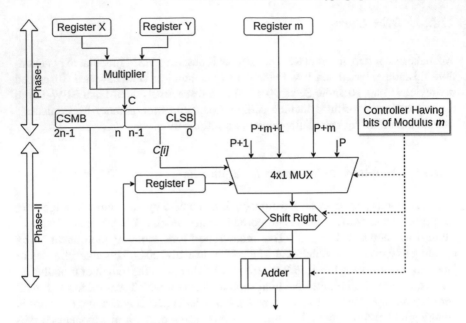

Fig. 11.9 Architecture diagram of AMM

lower-order $n - bits$ of C and a least significant bit (LSB) of P. The final result is achieved by adding higher-order $n - bits$ of C with P.

The hardware design for the AMM module is illustrated in Fig. 11.9. According to the algorithm, $X.Y$ is stored into register C after calculation. The size of register C is $2n - bits$. A 4×1 MUX has 2 selection lines one of which is taken from lower-order $n - bits$ of C and another one is taken as $P[0]$. The calculation of P depends upon these selection lines. The calculation of P is formulated as:

$$P = (P + (LSB(C[i] + P[0])).m + C[i]). \tag{11.1}$$

Right shifting by one bit is done on the result, which is saved in the register P. In order to obtain the final result, the final value of P is added with register C's higher-order $n - bits$. The dotted lines denote the controlled line, based on the size (n) of the binary string of modulus m.

For RSA PKC, the key operation is modular exponentiation g^E (mod m). In order to evaluate g^E (mod m), two methods namely MSM module and $BFW - 1$ technique are illustrated in Chap. 10 Sects. 10.4 and 10.5 respectively.

11.3 Hardware Implementation of the Architecture

This section illustrates the hardware implementation of architectures of *AMM* & *DCRSAP*.

11.3.1 AMM

The AMM module calculates the Montgomery multiplication $(X.Y.\sigma^{-1} \pmod{m})$ of couple of numbers X and Y under modulus m. The Eq. 11.1 gives updated value of P. The value of P is updated again and again for n-times. After the loop execution, the final result is accomplished by adding P to the most significant $n - bits$ of C. While starting the processes the first multiplication is the same in AMM and Montgomery method. But, the improvement in the conventional Montgomery algorithm is achieved by eliminating $1 - bit$ multiplication for each bit in the loop i.e., n-number of 1-bit multiplications. The AMM module requires simply primary operations like additions and shift operations. The expense by AMM is less in comparison to conventional methods. Using these simple primary operations, the AMM module requires just $n - clock$ cycles for $1 - bit$ of the exponent instead of $n + 5$ clock cycles.

11.3.2 Dual Core RSA Processor

Satya et al. have used two kinds of RSA core processors, which was designed either using MSM or using $BFW - 1$ algorithms (Vollala et al. 2016). Both cores are capable of executing multiple cryptographic modules simultaneously. The hardware scheduler used for implementation by Satya et al., needs only two additional clock cycles for scheduling a new task. Using a dual-core processor instead of a single processor, one can achieve double throughput. Therefore, improving the performance of the architecture. Throughput produced by a Dual-core RSA is approximately two times the throughput of the single RSA processor. The *power consumed* and *area required* for the discussed modules, for *512-bit and 1024-bit* keys are illustrated in Table 11.1 and in Table 11.2.

11.4 Comparative Analysis

The discussed RSA in multi-core architecture by Satya et al. is one of a kind and therefore its comparative study is intangible (Vollala et al. 2017). The time-saving parallel processing hardware scheduler is used in this Dual-core RSA processor,

Table 11.1 Power and Area of various ME and modules used in DCRSAP using 512-bit exponent

Module	Power (μw)	Area (μm^2)
MSM based DCRSAP	39.48	702321
BFW-1 based DCRSAP	39.02	706305
Scheduler	0.41	1367
BRAM	0.13	912
MSM based RSA core	19.47	350021
BFW-1 based RSA core	19.29	352013

Table 11.2 Power and Area of various ME and modules used in DCRSAP using 1024-bit exponent

Module	Power (μw)	Area (μm^2)
MSM based DCRSAP	82.33	1431495
BFW-1 based DCRSAP	80.03	1434785
Scheduler	0.76	1367
BRAM	0.23	2176
MSM based RSA core	40.72	713976
BFW-1 based RSA core	39.52	715621

which schedules the RSA cores. This task scheduler saves time as it requires fewer clock cycles for scheduling the cores by using parallel processing environment.

If a ME technique (MME42_C2) which is proposed by Kuang et al. is kept as the base technique for comparison (Kuang et al. 2013), then the MSM based DCRSAP can speed up the execution by 95.85% where the size of the key is 1024-bits. This speed-up comes with a cost of additional space as it performs on a dual-core processor so almost double space is required. The other benefit is that it doesn't require additional power and the clock speed of the processor can be also kept unchanged. Whereas, if the same MME42_C2 technique is compared with BFW-1 based DCRSAP, for key size 1024-bits, then the BFW-1 based DCRSAP can speed up the execution by 117.61%.

The discussed architecture is synthesized by Satya et al. with the help of Xilinx for FPGA and synthesized with the help of Cadence for ASIC (Vollala et al. 2017). Similarly synthesized for the Quad-core. The key size is tested from 32 bits to 1024-bit exponent, though they have given the values for keys of size 512-bit & 1024-bit over a dual-core processor only. Using the induction mechanism one can scale the similar architecture up to 32 cores. If someone still wants to scale the cores more than 32, then he needs to bear the cost of the extended size of BRAM and priority queue. The enhancement in RSA core implementation improves the overall system performance. The Tables 11.3 and 11.4 gives a comparative study of MSM and BFW-1 for single-core and dual-core RSA processors for key size 512-bit and

Table 11.3 Analysis of different modules for DCRSAP WRT 1024-bit key size

Module	Power(μw)		
	MSM	BFW-1	MME42_C2
RSA core	40.72	39.52	40.30
DCRSAP	82.33	80.03	NA

Table 11.4 Analysis of different modules for DCRSAP WRT 1024-bit key size

Module	Area (μm²)			Throughput Rate (kbps)		
		BFW-1	MME42_C2	MSM	BFW-1	MME42_C2
RSA core	713976	715621	714676	432.71	480.80	433.04
DCRSAP	1431495	1434785	NA	848.11	942.36	NA

Table 11.5 Hardware components statistics analysis for DCRSAP using MSM or BFW-1

DCRSAP using HW Component (↓) (→)	MSM	BFW-1
Multipliers—1024 × 1024-bit multiplier	2	2
Adders/Subtractors—All types	20	20
Registers—Flip-Flops	4503	4749
Comparators—All Types	18	18
1-bit 1024-to-1 multiplexer	4	6
32-bit 32-to-1 multiplexer	5	5

1024-bit. The Tables 11.3 and 11.4 gives values of MME42_C2 for single only. The Table 11.5 illustrates the comparison of the macro statistics of MSM-based DCRSAP and BFW-1 based DCRSAP. The BFW-1 based DCRSAP requires two additional 1-bit multiplexers of size 1024-to-1 and additional 246 flip-flops for saving results of precomputations.

The dual-core RSA processor (DCRSAP) claims that it can execute 2 cryptographic modules (encryption/decryption) with only 2 additional clock cycles, in comparison to the required clock cycles by a single RSA core. By keeping the clock frequency constant this DCRSAP gives two times the throughput that in result minimizes the heat emission.

The Table 11.6 illustrates an observation done on time-delay by the architecture of various modules for exponent's size 1024-bit. The comparison is done while executing two cryptographic modules using dual-core. From the Table 11.6, it is deduced that MSM-based RSA Processor requires 2.23 ns for one cryptographic module however, BFW-1 based RSA Processor acquires 2.36ns. In comparison technique given by Kuang et al. (2013) for a 1024-bit size key, this delay is the same level but attain higher throughput.

Table 11.6 Delay time for various modules of DCRSAP (Key Size $=$ 1024-bit)

Delay time module ($\downarrow$)($\rightarrow$) (ns)	MSM	BFW-1
Scheduler	0.79	0.79
BRAM	0.11	0.11
AMM	1.02	1.02
RSA Core 0	1.78	1.91
RSA Core 1	1.78	1.91
DRSAP	4.46	4.72

This technique satisfies the requirements of the heavy servers, running over the internet. Which requires load balancing and manages concurrent requests. This technique is also quite suitable for banking sectors, as they require highly secured transactions. It means that any device that claims or requires more secure communication and executes robust cryptographic modules, can use this technique and achieve better performance.

11.5   Quad-Core RSA Processor

The RSA processor with four cores is illustrated in this section. Here each RSA cores has an inbuild $BFW-1$ module with it. Each RSA core is able to execute cryptographic modules simultaneously. The hardware scheduler is used in this architecture. This scheduler can schedule a new request, if one of the four cores is not busy, by using two additional clock cycles only. The throughput is increased 4 times if the architecture is shifted from the uni-core processor to the Quad-core processor and enhances the overall performance. Figure 11.10 shows the architecture of the Quad-core RSA Processor (QCRSAP).

Without consuming more power and keeping the processor clock cycle speed unchanged, a BFW-1 based QCRSAP for a key (exponent) size $=$ 1024-bits, is capable of improving the execution speed by 331.76%. Whereas, it can improve the execution speed by 322.84%, for a 512-bit key (exponent). Where Satya et al. consider the MME42_C2 technique as the base for comparison. The power consumption is saved by the factor of 0.86% when the key size is 1024-bits using BFW-1 based QCRSAP. All this benefit comes with a little cost of extra space as the implementation was done over multiple cores by Satya et al. (2017).

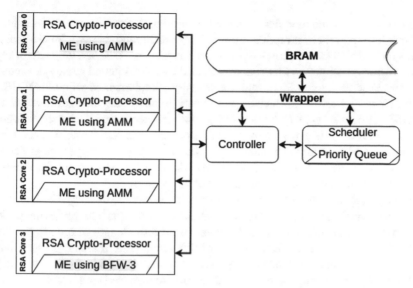

Fig. 11.10 Block Schematic diagram of Quad-core RSA Processor

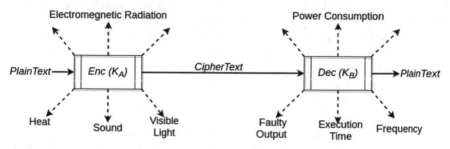

Fig. 11.11 A cryptosystem with side channel attacks

11.6 Security Analysis

For securing the data, the hardware techniques are comparatively more securer than software techniques due to its inherent property of having personal memory space. Even though the side-channel attacks make them susceptible, because their targets are protocols and modules. The Fig. 11.11 also illustrates this fact. An intruder who wants to extract secret information specially the *key* tries to read Electromagnetic Radiation, Visible Light, Sound, Power consumption, Heat, Frequency, Execution Time and other useful information. The RSA processor discussed in this chapter prevents the attacks through Electromagnetic radiation, Sound, Visible Light. The rest of the parameters like execution time, heat and power consumption only requires proper security measures.

The techniques and modules discussed are aiming to optimize the execution time and minimize power consumption. Moreover, this technique also avoids side-channel attacks using the above-mentioned parameters by keeping fixed and long length keys. This is assured as improvements accomplished by the discussed techniques require the same execution time. Therefore, the technique implemented with the DCRSAP processor is secured from distinct power consumption side-channel attacks. The DCRSAP processor is placed in a safe region. The selection of RSA core is done in run-time therefore, they are random and thus prevents the side-channel attack based on monitoring heat and power parameters. The assurance of storage area protection is addressed by the use of the dedicated BRAM which comes as an inbuilt part of the DCRSAP and also secure from unauthorized access.

Intruder targeting the software implementation part of the discussed techniques is infeasible. Consider a scenario, where a mathematical approach for retrieving the key is attempted. This approach is not feasible, because the length of the keys is fixed i.e., 1024-bits and integer factorization of this much large number are very hard. Research states that RSA is naturally protected from decryption attacks. The attacks performed by monitoring the time-based pattern are managed by a selection of RSA cores in run time thus, providing a timing attack-proof architecture. The dynamic selection of the core of DCRSAP improves the safety of the complete device and also stops the intruders from commencing differential side-channel attacks. Moreover, for addressing the power analysis attack, which can be performed by the intruders for stealing the private key. The hardware-based solutions that can mask the power-fluctuations is used.

The discussed DCRSAP (Dual-core RSA processor) is capable of executing simultaneous cryptographic modules. A DCRSAP can attain higher throughput while keeping the clock frequency unchanged. As the clock frequency is unchanged, it results in keeping the heat emission under the limit. This chapter discussed the implementation and characteristics of two processors first is MSM based DCRSAP and the second is BFW-1 based DCRSAP. Both of them have an inbuilt hardware scheduler and the MSM-based DCRSA is capable to attain 95.85% more throughput whereas the BFW-1 based DCRSAP is capable of attaining 117.61% more throughput, this verification is done for a 1024-bit key, and the MME42_C2 technique has been kept as a base technique for comparison. The architecture discussed does consume additional power, as the architecture is based on two cores therefore, it requires a double area for its implementation. The outcomes achieved have shown a notable influence on cryptographic modules. It is verified that the hardware scheduler is better than the software scheduler in terms of attaining higher throughput, minimal overhead and security level. The scalability of these architectures is flexible because the scheduler's implementation is based on the priority queue data structure. For scheduling the RSA cores, the hardware scheduler requires just a single additional clock-cycle. The hardware scheduler is customizable, as a selection of scheduling algorithms done from a vast range of available algorithms thus, providing a flexible and customizable architecture. This flexibility and customizability make this architecture more suitable for embedded systems. Satya et al. have verified this architecture up to 32-cores and by increasing the size of BRAM and priority queue more than 32-cores can be implemented.

References

Cilardo A, Mazzeo A, Romano L, Saggese GP (2004) Exploring the design-space for fpga-based implementation of rsa. Microprocess Microsyst 28(4):183–191

Diffie W (1988) The first ten years of public-key cryptography. Proc IEEE 76(5):560–577

Hu J, Guo W, Wei J, Chang Y, Sun D (2011) (2011) A novel architecture for fast rsa key generation based on rns. In: Fourth international symposium on parallel architectures, algorithms and programming (PAAP). IEEE, pp 345–349

Kuang SR, Wang JP, Chang KC, Hsu HW (2013) Energy-efficient high-throughput montgomery modular multipliers for rsa cryptosystems. Very Large Scale Integration (VLSI) Systems. IEEE Trans 21(11):1999–2009

Montgomery PL (1985) Modular multiplication without trial division. Math Comput 44(170):519–521

Rivest RL, Shamir A, Adleman L (1983) A method for obtaining digital signatures and public-key cryptosystems. Commun ACM 26(1):96–99

Shieh MD, Chen JH, Wu HH, Lin WC (2008) A new modular exponentiation architecture for efficient design of rsa cryptosystem. Very Large Scale Integration (VLSI) Systems. IEEE Trans 16(9):1151–1161

Vollala S, Geetha K, Ramasubramanian N (2016) Efficient modular exponential algorithms compatible with hardware implementation of public-key cryptography. Sec Commun Netw 9(16):3105–3115

Vollala S, Varadhan V, Geetha K, Ramasubramanian N (2017) Design of rsa processor for concurrent cryptographic transformations. Microelectron J 63:112–122

Vollala S, Ramasubramanian N, Begum BS, Joshi AD (2019) Dual-core implementation of right-to-left modular exponentiation. In: Recent findings in intelligent computing techniques. Springer, pp 43–53

William S (2006) Cryptography and Network Security: 4/E. Pearson Education India

Chapter 12
Implementation of Modular Exponentiation in Dual-Core

12.1 Introduction

An efficient implementation of ME and MM provides enhanced performance of
RSA (Rivest et al. 1983; Galindo et al. 2003). In order to enhance the performance
of ME computation there are two approaches. The first is to reduce the required
number of modular multiplications, which will save the number of clock cycles,
and the second approach is increasing the processor clock cycle speed. Montgomery
presented a method to improve the evaluation of MM procedure in hardware. Since
then, many algorithmic techniques have been modified and implemented using a Left-
to-right modular exponentiation algorithm, but only a few works have been carried
out through the Right-to-left modular exponentiation. This gave good inspiration
to choose the right-to-left method, where the square and multiply procedures can
be executed in parallel. In order to improve the throughput of the MM process, a
high-radix Montgomery multiplication has been adopted (Vollala et al. 2019, 2016,
2017; Vollala and Ramasubramanian 2017; Kuang et al. 2016; Shieh et al. 2009).
This takes less number of operational cycles, so that the frequency will be increased
and the number of clock-cycles will be less.

12.2 High-Radix Montgomery Multiplication

For minimizing the number of instructions per one modular multiplication, a high-
radix approach is employed in Montgomery multiplication (Miyamoto et al. 2011;
Yao et al. 2014). Particularly in high-radix representation, in order to use normal
$\theta - bit \times \theta - bit$ multipliers, a $k - bit$ integer needs to be divided into η number
of $\theta - bit$ blocks (i.e., $k = \eta.\theta$). An integer X can be expressed using $\theta - bit$ words
$x_i (0 \le i \le \eta - 1)$ as follows:
$$X = \sum_{i=0}^{\eta-1}\{x_i.2^{i.\theta}\} = x_{\eta-1}.2^{\theta(\eta-1)} + x_{\eta-2}.2^{\theta(\eta-2)} + \ldots + x_1.2^h + x_0$$

© The Author(s), under exclusive license to Springer Nature Switzerland AG 2021
S. Vollala et al., *Energy-Efficient Modular Exponential Techniques*
for Public-Key Cryptography, https://doi.org/10.1007/978-3-030-74524-0_12

Algorithm 1 *High-Radix Montgomery Multiplication*

Input: $X = (x_{k-1}, x_{k-2}, ..., x_1, x_0)_{2^h}$
$Y = (y_{k-1}, y_{k-2}, ..., y_1, y_0)_{2^h}$
$m = (m_{k-1}, m_{k-2}, ..., m_1, m_0)_{2^h}$
$C = -m^{-1} \ mod \ 2^h$
Output: $R = X.Y.2^{-k} \ (\text{mod} \ m) ... R = (r_{k-1}, r_{k-2}, ..., r_1, r_0)_{2^h}$

1: *Initialization* $R = 0$
2: **for** $i = 0$ to $k - 1$ **do**
3:     $t_i = (r_0 + x_i y_0)C \ (\text{mod} \ 2^h)$
4:     $R = (r_i + x_i b + t_i.m)/2^h$
5:     **if** $(R \geq m)$ **then**
6:         $R = R - m$ ▷ Final Subtraction
7:     **end if**
8: **end for**
9: **Return** R

Fig. 12.1 High-Radix Montgomery Multiplication

Then, the Montgomery multiplication $C = XY2^{-\sigma} \ (\text{mod} \ m)$ can be executed by repeating the operation $C = (C + x_i.Y)/2^h) \ (\text{mod} \ m)$ for η number of times.

The sequence of steps described by Akashi satoh et al. (2003) to compute high-radix Montgomery multiplication is discussed in the Algorithm 1 shown in Fig. 12.1.

The ME realization on the dual-core processor requires some modifications in the Montgomery multiplication method. The modification is made to enhance the utilization and to fulfill the requirements of the dual-core processor. The hardware realization is done for various high-radix parameters in the domain: $[2^2: 2^{32}]$. The comparative study of this dual-core processor with already present techniques, over the parameters like throughput, the number of clock cycles, the power consumed and required hardware space is also done. This dual-core processor architecture is implemented over Verilog and synthesized using Xilinx-14.6 ISE for usage in FPGA, and the same has been synthesized using Cadence for ASIC. The results analyzed here are base on FPGA. The results discussed are substantiate promising improvement in throughput for various cryptographic transformations.

12.3   Right-to-Left Modular Exponentiation for Dual-Core Processor

The ME is involved in encryption and decryption steps of the RSA. The only changes are the input parameters. The conventional right-to-left binary exponentiation algorithm is enhanced and customized in such a way, that it can be easily and efficiently implemented over a dual-core processor. The Algorithm 2 shown in Fig. 12.2 gives the step-by-step procedure for the same. The modification of high-radix Montgomery multiplication has been also discussed, for fulfilling the requirement of this enhanced Right-to-left modular exponentiation algorithm.

Algorithm 2 Enhanced Right-to-Left Modular Exponential Algorithm

Input: Base g, Exponent E, modulus m, and the Proposed Constant PC
Output: $R = g^E \pmod{m}$

1: $S_q = MHRM(g, PC, m)$
2: $R = MHRM(1, PC, m)$
3: **for** $i = 0$ to $k - 1$ **do**
4:     **if** $(e_i \neq 0)$ **then**
5:         $R = MHRM(R, S_q, m)$
6:     **end if**
7:     $R = MHRM(S_q, S_q, m)$
8: **end for**
9: $R = MHRM(R, 1, m)$
10: **Return** R

Fig. 12.2 Enhanced Right-to-Left Modular Exponentiation Algorithm

12.3.1 The Enhanced Right-to-Left Binary Exponentiation

In order to compute the modular multiplication using Algorithm 2, there is a requirement to modify high-radix Montgomery multiplication thus, the method is termed as *Modified High-Radix Montgomery Multiplication (MHRM)*. Whenever module MHRM is called, an additional factor $T^{-1} \pmod{N}$ is multiplied to the partial result $P.Q$ moduled with m $(MHRM(P, Q, m) = P.Q.2^{-n} \pmod{m}$, where T^{-1} is the inverse of $T = 2^h$ moduled with m. The removal of this additional factor is not feasible by external means. Therefore pre-processing and post-processing steps are required.

In the pre-processing step, the information g is processed with a new proposed constant $PC = (2^k)^h \pmod{m}$, by calling module MHRM having input parameters: g, PC, and m as stated in the step-1 of the Algorithm 2 shown in Fig. 12.2. The procedure starts with initializing the result as $R = MHRM(1, PC, m)$. Inside the loop, for each bit of the exponent E, the squaring of the temporary variable S_q is done. Whereas, if this bit is a non-zero bit then only the multiplication operation is performed and result R is updated using S_q. This process is repeated for each bit of exponent i.e., k-times. Where the size of the exponent's binary string is k.

For the post-processing step, the partial result is updated by calling the MHRM module with input parameters: Z, 1, and m. This post-processing step gives the final result $g^E \pmod{m}$.

Observation of Algorithm 2, tells us that the square operation and multiplication operation is independent. Therefore, the parallel processing of these two operations in a dual-core processor is possible. This dual-core implementation will save $k_1 \times n$ number of clock cycles, for evaluating the modular exponentiation. Where k_1 represents the count of non-zero bits present in the exponent and n represents the required number of clock cycles for single modular multiplication.

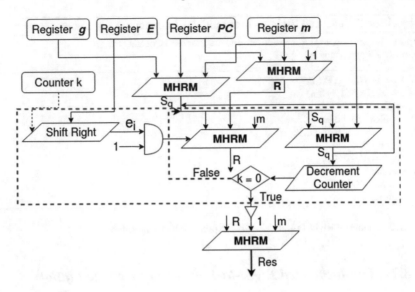

Fig. 12.3 Architecture of right-to-left modular exponentiation algorithm

Figure 12.3 illustrated the hardware design for the enhanced right-to-left ME algorithm. First, the four registers are used for storing the input parameters i.e., base g, exponent E, modulus m and the proposed constant PC. For iteration purposes, the counter is initialized with k (size of Exponent E). Simultaneously, the MHRM module is called for $S_q = MHRM(g, PC, m)$ and $R = MHRM(1, PC, R)$. This is done in the initialization stage of the algorithm. It is the responsibility of the shift register to provide LSB of the exponent E for each iteration, then based on the value of LSB i.e., (e_i) whether it is zero or not the result R is computed. If $(e_1 \neq 0)$ then the value of result R is updated by calling MHRM having input parameters: (R, S_q, m). Simultaneously, the square module is also executed and the value of S_q is calculated by calling MHRM having the parameters: (S_q, S_q, m). After this, the counter value is decremented by 1, this process is repeated until the counter value is greater than zero. Then by performing a post-processing step, the final result for ME is computed by calling MHRM having parameters: $(R, 1, m)$. This post-processing step is performed to eliminate the additional factor multiplied with the result. The three hardware components encircled by the dotted line can execute simultaneously. Therefore, saves the $k_1(n + 3)$ number of clock cycles, which in turn increases throughput. Where k_1 denotes the count of non-zero bits present in the binary string of exponent E and $n + 3$ is the required number of clock cycles for processing the MHRM module.

Algorithm 3 Modified High-Radix Montgomery Multiplication Algorithm

---

Input: X, Y, the modulus m, and m'
Output: $R = XY\sigma^{-1} \pmod{m}$, where $\sigma = 2^{hs}$

1: *InitializationR* $= (r_{s-1}, r_{s-2}, \ldots, r_1, r_0)_{2^h}$;
2: $Z = MHRM(1, PC, m)$;
3: **for** $i = 0$ to $s - 1$ **do**
4:     $U = (r_0 + x_0.y_i).m' \pmod{2^h}$;
5:     $R = (R + X.y_i + U.m) \div 2^h$;
6: **end for**
7: **if** $(R \geq M)$ **then**
8:     $R = R - m$
9: **end if**
10: **Return** Z

Fig. 12.4 Modified High-Radix Montgomery Multiplication Algorithm

12.3.2 Modified High-Radix Montgomery Multiplication (MHRM)

This section discusses the implementation of the MHRM module. The high radix implementation helps in achieving higher throughput, as the clock frequency is increased and the required number of clock cycles are reduced. The relation between throughput and clock frequency is directly proportional whereas the throughput is inversely proportional to the required number of clock cycles.

For mathematical representation consider the modulus $m = (m_{s-1}, m_{s-2}, \ldots, m_1, m_0)_{2^h}$, where 2^h is the high-radix. The multiplier $X = (x_{s-1}, x_{s-2}, \ldots, x_1, x_0)_{2^h}$ and multiplicands $Y = (y_{s-1}, y_{s-2}, \ldots, y_1, y_0)_{2^h}$ such that $0 \leq X, Y < m$. Let $m' = -m^{-1} \pmod{2^h}$, where m^{-1} is the modulo inverse of m with respect to the modulus 2^h. Using this assumption, the evaluation procedure of the Montgomery product $X.Y.\sigma^{-1} \pmod{m}$, where $\sigma = 2^{hs}$ of two numbers X and Y having modulus m is illustrated in Algorithm 3 shown in Fig. 12.4.

Initially the result R is initialized with value 0 then for each bit of multiplier Y, the partial result is updated as $R = (R + X.y_i((r_0 + x_0.y_i).m' \pmod{2^h}).m)/2^h$. This partial result is updated for s number of times and at last, the result is again checked with modulus m. If R has a value greater than or equal to modulus m, then the final result is obtained by subtracting the result R by m. After the required subtraction, the result R has the final value as $XY\sigma^{-1} \pmod{m}$, where $\sigma = 2^{hs}$.

Figure 12.5 gives the architecture for the MHRM module. First, the five registers are used for storing the input parameters k, X, Y, m and m'. For iteration purpose, the counter is initialized with k (number of digits in the m). In the initial state, only the result R is initialized with zero. The implementation of this MHRM module requires few hardware components like multiplier component, adder component, complementing component and shift register. A temporary register T is used for storing intermediate value where T is calculated by multiplying m' to the summation

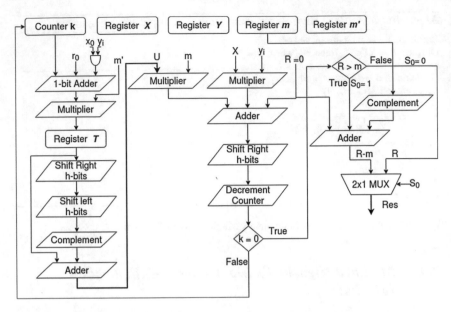

Fig. 12.5 Architecture Diagram MHRM

of r_0 and product of x_0, y_i. Then parameter U is obtained by performing modulus (mod 2^h) operation over T i.e., T (mod 2^h). Which is implemented using formula $U = T - ((T >> b) << b)$. In order to compute R, two multipliers and one adder are used. One multiplier is for calculating the product $X.y_i$ and another multiplier is used for calculating the product $U.m$. Then, three input adder is used for adding the output of this two multipliers with R. Now, this partial result is given as input to the shifter. Using this input the shift register performs the $h - bit$ shifting in order to divide the R by 2^h. After this, the counter is decremented by 1 and this process is repeated until the counter value is greater than zero. The partial result is again checked with modulus m using the comparator component, and if R has a value greater than or equal to modulus m, then the final result is obtained by subtracting the result R by m. Final result is selected using 2×1 multiplexer i.e., either R or $m - R$. After the required subtraction, the result R has the final value as $XY\sigma^{-1}$ (mod m), where $\sigma = 2^{hs}$.

12.4 Performance Analysis and Comparison

These parameters are used for comparing and analyzing the performance of architectures discussed in this chapter

1. Throughput
2. Power consumption

3. Required number of clock-cycles
4. Frequency
5. Required hardware space.

12.4.1 Modified High-Radix Montgomery Multiplication

The discussed MHRM module is used for enhancing the performance of MM. For high-radix representation, the modulus m having binary string size k is partitioned into s words of $w - bits$. While iterating for the square and multiply operation the complete word of $w - bit$ is scanned instead of scanning $1 - bit$ at a time. This results in reducing the required number of clock cycles and increase throughput. For representation of modulus m in $w - bit$ words:

$m = \sum_{i=0}^{w-1} m_i (2^s)^i = (m_{s-1}, m_{s-2}, t_{s-3}, \ldots, m_1, m_0)_{2^w}$

The radix and required number of clock cycles are inversely proportional to each other i.e., by implementing the higher radix, reduction in the required number of clock cycles can be achieved. The formula for estimating the required number of clock cycles for Montgomery modular multiplication, where size of modulus is k and the radix 2^w is given in the Eq. 12.1:

$$\frac{k}{w}(7s) + 2 \tag{12.1}$$

The modulus size k, word size w and number of words s is related with formula $k = w.s$. For different values of radices (ranging from 2^4 to 2^{32}), the required number of clock-cycles are calculated and listed in the Table 12.1 and in Table 12.2 using the Eq. 12.1. The size of the modulus k is considered $1024 - bit$, and $2048 - bit$.

For evaluating ME, the MHRM module is synthesized for different values of radices ranging from 2^2 to 2^{32}. The calculated value of parameters: frequency, power, area and throughput for the MHRM module is listed in the Table 12.3 and in Table 12.4. This computation is done for the 1024-bit key(exponent). By observing the Table 12.3, we can say that the highest frequency is attained when the radix value is set to 2^8.

Table 12.1 Required clock-cycles for ME using MHRM for 1024 bit modulus

Radix	Required clock-cycles for modulus
2^{32}	231424
2^{16}	460800
2^8	919552
2^4	1837056

Table 12.2 Required clock-cycles For ME using MHRM for 2048 bit modulus

Radix	Required clock-cycles
2^{32}	460800
2^{16}	919552
2^{8}	1837056
2^{4}	3672064

Table 12.3 Throughput and power analysis of DCRSAP using MHRM

Radix	Throughput (kbps)	Power (μW)
2^{32}	1982.76	67.88
2^{16}	1145.83	52.32
2^{8}	796.52	41.03
2^{4}	231.29	35.23

Table 12.4 Area and frequency analysis of DCRSAP using MHRM

Radix	Area (μm^2)	Frequency (MHz)
2^{32}	7976185	438.86
2^{16}	4990460	528.00
2^{8}	3135515	732.45
2^{4}	2047845	424.90

12.4.2 Right-to-Left Binary Exponentiation

In order to attain higher throughput, dual-core implementation of the Right-to-Left ME is desirable. The two prime operations of Right-to-left ME is square and multiply operations. Both of them can be executed simultaneously using the dual-core processor. With the help of this dual-core implementation of ME, $k_1 \times (7s + 2)$ numbers of clock-cycles are saved. k_1 is the number of non-zero bits present in the exponent E and $7s + 2$ is the reduction in the number of clock cycles required for performing single modular multiplication. Where s is the number of digits in the modulus. As we know that the required number of clock-cycles are inversely proportional to throughput, therefore this MHRM module is capable of attaining higher throughput. The Tables 12.3 and 12.4 listed the power consumption, area, maximum frequency, and the throughput of the discussed Left-to-Right ME for DCRSAP.

From the Table 12.3 it is clear that increasing the radix results in more power consumption. Whereas, the Table 12.5 shows the performance of the modular exponential technique discussed in this chapter. The tabulation is done for various radices. For radix 2^{16} best value of '*ME time $\times$ power*' is obtained, which is a parameter for analyzing the performance. Similarly, for radix 2^8, this technique obtains the best

Table 12.5 Performance of 1024-bit enhanced R-L ME algorithm

Radix	Delay time (ns)	ME time (ms)	ME time × Power ($\mu m^2 \mu W$)
2^{32}	3.11	01.96	133.0448
2^{16}	2.88	02.58	131.8464
2^8	2.43	04.05	166.1715
2^4	2.02	09.32	328.3436

Table 12.6 Performance of other designs for 1024-bit exponent

ME design	Area	Delay (ns)	Power (μW)	Throughput (bps)
ME42 (McIvor et al. 2004)	852899	2.19	70.6	354.23 k
MME42_C2 (Kuang et al. 2013)	714676	2.21	40.3	433.04 k

value of parameter '*ME time × Area*'. With additional cost of these two parameters ('*ME time × power*' and '*ME time × Area*'), the radix 2^{32} obtains the highest throughput among all the tabulated radices.

The performance of the existing algorithms MME42_C2 (Kuang et al. 2013) and ME42 (McIvor et al. 2004) are given in the Table 12.6, for $512 - bit$ and $1024 - bit$ exponents. In comparison with MME42_C2 (Kuang et al. 2013), as they are claimed to be one of the current energy efficient technology. With the cost of 2.2% additional power consumption, the MHRM technique using radix value 2^8 can achive 83.93% higher throughput. Whereas, the more higher radice i.e., 2^{16} and 2^{32} consume 30.7% and 69.57% more power respectively in order to achieve 166.60% and 357.86% higher throughput respectively. This additional power and higher throughput is achieved in comparison to MME42_C2 (Kuang et al. 2013).

In order to reduce the required number of clock-cycles and attaining higher throughput, the dual-core with high-radix multiplication implementation of ME is performed in such a way, that it should not consume additional power. The high radix Montgomery multiplication implementation is also discussed in this chapter. Architecture having the radix value of 2^8 attains higher throughput and consumes very less additional power. Increasing the radix causes an increase in implementation complexity. Because the high-radix implementation requires more number of multipliers to manage and requires more number of processing elements to execute. This increased number of hardware components, results in more power consumption. However, it also helps in attaining higher throughput. For parameter '*ME time × power*' the best performance is obtained by implementation having radix 2^{16}, whereas for parameter '*ME time × Area*' best performing implementation is using radix 2^8. Organizations having less or no constraint of the area and power consumption and want more throughput can go for the implementation of the high-radix architecture.

References

Galindo D, Martỳn S, Morillo P, Villar JL (2003) A practical public key cryptosystem from paillier and rabin schemes. In: Public key cryptography-PKC 2003. Springer, pp 279–291

Kuang SR, Wang JP, Chang KC, Hsu HW (2013) Energy-efficient high-throughput montgomery modular multipliers for rsa cryptosystems. IEEE Trans Very Large Scale Integr (VLSI) Syst 21(11):1999–2009

Kuang SR, Wu KY, Lu RY (2016) Low-cost high-performance vlsi architecture for montgomery modular multiplication. IEEE Trans Very Large Scale Integr (VLSI) Syst 24(2):434–443

McIvor C, McLoone M, McCanny JV (2004) Modified montgomery modular multiplication and rsa exponentiation techniques. IEE Proc-Comput Digital Tech 151(6):402–408

Miyamoto A, Homma N, Aoki T, Satoh A (2011) Systematic design of rsa processors based on high-radix montgomery multipliers. IEEE Trans Very Large Scale Integr (VLSI) Syst 19(7):1136–1146

Rivest RL, Shamir A, Adleman L (1983) A method for obtaining digital signatures and public-key cryptosystems. Commun ACM 26(1):96–99

Satoh A, Takano K (2003) A scalable dual-field elliptic curve cryptographic processor. IEEE Trans Comput 52(4):449–460

Shieh MD, Chen JH, Lin WC, Wu HH (2009) A new algorithm for high-speed modular multiplication design. IEEE Trans Circuits Syst I: Regular Pap 56(9)

Vollala S, Ramasubramanian N (2017) Energy efficient modular exponentiation for public-key cryptography based on bit forwarding techniques. Inf Process Lett 119:25–38

Vollala S, Varadhan V, Geetha K, Ramasubramanian N (2017) Design of rsa processor for concurrent cryptographic transformations. Microelectron J 63:112–122

Vollala S, Geetha K, Ramasubramanian N (2016) Efficient modular exponential algorithms compatible with hardware implementation of public-key cryptography. Sec Commun Netw 9(16):3105–3115

Vollala S, Ramasubramanian N, Begum BS, Joshi AD (2019) Dual-core implementation of right-to-left modular exponentiation. In: Recent findings in intelligent computing techniques. Springer, pp 43–53

William S (2006) Cryptography and network security: 4/E. Pearson Education India

Yao G, Fan J, Cheung R, Verbauwhede I (2014) Novel rns parameter selection for fast modular multiplication

Index

© Springer Nature Singapore Pte Ltd. 2021
S. Vollala et al., *Energy-Efficient Modular Exponential Techniques
for Public-Key Cryptography*, https://doi.org/10.1007/978-3-030-74524-0

Printed in the United States
by Baker & Taylor Publisher Services